CLANS AND CHIEFS

IAN GRIMBLE

Birlinn

Published in 2000 by
Birlinn Limited
8 Canongate Venture
5 New Street
Edinburgh
EH8 8BH

© The Estate of Ian Grimble

First published in 1980 by
Blond & Briggs

ISBN 1 84158 046 5

British Library Cataloguing-in-Publication Data
A catalogue record for this book is available from the British Library

Printed and bound in Finland by WS Bookwell

Contents

Introduction

In the year 1822 a remarkable event occurred. George IV paid a visit to Scotland, the first sovereign to venture north of the Border since Charles II's ill-starred adventure there in 1651. But there was something even odder about the King's visit to Edinburgh than its rarity. He appeared there in an outlandish costume, tailored specially for the occasion, as the chief of a confederation of tribal chiefs. By this time the British Empire contained many remote territories in which lived tribes of primitive people who wore bizarre clothes, amongst their other curious habits. But the survival of tribes in the mother country itself was not considered to be a matter for celebration, and the spectacle of the sovereign, cavorting among them as their Headman, caused considerable consternation.

Most people knew in a general way that Scotland still contained distinct tribes, and their chiefs were becoming an increasingly familiar sight in the fashionable world of London. Harriet Wilson, the Regency courtesan, used to meet one of them whom she called Clanranald MacDonald in her memoirs, a young man who spent prodigiously, so that some people may have imagined his poverty-stricken Hebridean islands were a Klondike of the sea. More romantic still, there was a real live chieftainess, married to a fabulously rich English Marquess, but subscribing herself *Sutherland* as a Countess in her own right and chief of that clan. She used to keep tall servants on duty outside her London palace, dressed in full tribal costume. But it was one thing for them to be paraded in London by their civilised chiefs, quite another for the King to sail away to the tribal reserves and as it were live in a wigwam wearing the fancy dress of the aboriginals.

The fact that Edinburgh was made the stage for these charades was, in the eyes of some, the most offensive aspect of all. Its classical architecture was to earn it the title of the Athens of the North: its intellectual achievements had already bought it that distinction. To many people it did not appear a suitable place to transform into a tribal resort, especially since the last occasion when the clans had appeared there in strength was during the rebellion of 1745, when they had captured the city in the name of Bonnie Prince Charlie. The citizens of Edinburgh had not enjoyed the experience when the aboriginals had swept into their capital out of their mountain fastnesses, speaking their unintelligible language and wearing their wild costume. After their defeat the wearing of this dress had been banned by statute, and although the proscription had been lifted in 1782, that scarcely excused the sovereign for adopting it.

The Earl of Aberdeen expostulated that no king had worn such a dress since the days of actual barbarism, though he did not indicate what date he had in mind. It was all very well for people in London to be impressed by the Chieftainess of Sutherland and her romantic-looking retinue: she had been reared in polite Edinburgh, and had never set eyes on her tribal territories before she was seventeen years old. MacDonald was a paper tiger too, totally assimilated into the English fashionable world. But Edinburgh had been menaced for centuries by the real savages whom they represented: the royal antics there cannot have been easy for her citizens to stomach.

Except for the citizen who was so largely responsible for them, Sir Walter Scott. He was born, educated, and practised his legal profession in Edinburgh. He had also written poems and novels that had swept Europe and created a vogue for his native land such as it had never enjoyed before. Scott had learned little about the people of the Highlands and Hebrides, and had not attempted to understand their language. But he visited some of the chiefs in their castles and toured a great deal of their territories, and his artist's eye quickly perceived that these provided the most distinctively Scottish and romantic properties for his writings. Novel after novel contained the noble savages of his country, and the nation that George IV knew was Scott-land as the Wizard of the North had depicted it.

Naturally it was the Scottish capital in which the King must hold his court and so, to meet his expectations, it was necessary to transform it into the tartan-bedecked habitat of chiefs and their clansmen, in which the Chief of Chiefs would appear in all the splendour of Highland dress. George was sixty years old by this time and he weighed twenty stone, but the man who had once been dressed by Beau Brummell had not lost enthusiasm for fancy costumes, and nobody could dissuade him from adopting this one. The citizens of Edinburgh just had to put up with it: actually they had to put up with a great deal more.

Scott's own son-in-law, Lockhart, was among those who grumbled: 'It appeared to be very generally thought, when the programmes were first issued, that kilts and bagpipes were to occupy a great deal too much space. With all respect for the generous qualities which the Highland clans have very often exhibited, it was difficult to forget that they had always constituted a small, and almost unimportant part of the Scottish population.' Was Lockhart really right in saying that? Another declared more forcefully, 'Sir Walter Scott has ridiculously made us appear to be a nation of Highlanders, and the bagpipe and the tartan are the order of the day.'

The Highlands had not reared the Adam brothers, whose architecture was to become the wonder not merely of Edinburgh, but of Europe. It was classical architecture, though, not distinctively Scottish: anyway, you could see it in the south of England. The barefoot shepherd's son Thomas Telford, who had become the outstanding civil engineer of Europe, had been born in the Border country, not in a Highland glen. Scott called his aqueduct, which linked the Mersey and the Severn rivers, the most impressive work of art he had ever set eyes on. But it stood in England, and although Telford also built his novel iron bridges in Scotland, they could not be considered as peculiarly Scottish either.

It was not people like these whom Scott wished to assemble in Edinburgh to greet the monarch. He wrote to the Macleod Chief in the isle of Skye, 'do come and bring half-a-dozen or half-a-score of Clansmen, so as to look like an Island Chief as you are.' Indeed, his family had reigned there in this capacity a good deal longer than the house of Hanover had occupied the British throne, or any preceding dynasty for that matter. He was the 24th Chief of Macleod and took his name from Liotr, son of Olaf the Black, King of Man and the Northern Isles; who himself belonged to the dynasty of Godred, King of Dublin, Man and the Hebrides. King Godred was one of those defeated at Stamford Bridge by King Harold in 1066, before Harold hurried to meet another invasion at Hastings. Where was the house of Hanover when all that was going on? Wherever it was then, it was now sitting on the most powerful throne in the world, and the artist in Scott told him that the right people to attend Georve IV's court were the descendants of Godred Crovan and Olaf the Black.

Also some of their clansmen. The word clan is ан anglicised form of the Gaelic for children, and it has become a synonym for tribe throughout the world. It contains within it the implication that every member of a clan descends from the tribal father from which it derives its name; and it is not unlikely that every MacLeod does descend from Liotr. The senior Son of Liotr, the living embodiment of the tribal father, was the representative of the heroic ancestor and his clansmen or children respected him as such.

But Sir Walter Scott expressed a similar respect for the Duke of Buccleuch, the senior bearer (in the peerage) of a name that is simply descriptive, like Inglis for English or Wallace for Welsh. He called the Duke 'my beloved Chief' as though he were the living representative of some heroic ancestral Scott. Yet he must have known that the heroism of the ancestor in this case was that of Charles II in bed, since the Dukes of Buccleuch descend in the direct male line from that monarch's teen-age liaison with Lucy Walter and the illegitimate son she bore him. The heterogeneous collection of people who had become known as Scotts in the Border country and elsewhere could not possibly be supposed to descend from Charles II, or from any other common tribal ancestor. There certainly were tribes who had lived since time immemorial in the Border hills: the administrative records of Edinburgh contain many references to them. But there was no more a genuine Scott Clan than the Duke of Buccleuch was an authentic tribal chief. Sir Walter was hoaxing George IV when he slipped his bogus clan in among the genuine ones, and sought to give the King an impression that the entire country was organised on tribal lines.

As the pantomime got under way some comic scenes took place that were not in the script. George Crabbe, the parson-poet, had been invited from England to attend, and he visited the Edinburgh home of the Scottish bard, dressed respectfully in full canonicals. He found it occupied by Gaelic members of the cast speaking in their native language, who mistook Crabbe for a foreign prelate, while he apologised to them in French for his ignorance of their tongue. He need not have felt ashamed; Scott and all the other citizens of Edinburgh shared his ignorance. Crabbe had long ago written those realistic poems of village life from which the story of Peter Grimes is taken, in which he had declared: 'I paint the cot as truth will paint it, and the bards will not.' By this time the Gaelic word bard had also passed into the English language. Crabbe had no idea how aptly his stricture applied to Scott: it had been directed at Oliver Goldsmith's sentimental picture in *The Deserted Village*.

In the Highlands there were deserted villages in plenty too, as their inhabitants were evicted from cottage and croft while Scott was organising his pageant in Edinburgh. His son-in-law Lockhart put his finger on the anomaly when he contrasted the orgy of kilt and bagpipe in the capital with the present fate of the tribes in their remote glens. 'When one reflected how miserably their numbers had of late years been reduced in consequence of the selfish and hard-hearted policy of their land-lords, it almost seemed as if there was a cruel mockery in giving so much prominence to their pretentions.'

Nothing is more remarkable than the stoicism of the burgesses of Edinburgh as the clouds of tartan enveloped their city. George IV had visited Ireland in the previous year, and after his return from Edinburgh he confided to his surgeon: 'The Scotch were a worldly respectable people, but the Irish are all heart.' In this comment the astute monarch reveals that he had caught occasional glimpses of the plain, sober people beyond the riot of plaid and bonnet, kilt and eagles' feathers, the worldly and respectable Lowland Scots. For he could not possibly have intended these epithets for the marshalled clans and their chiefs.

The discreet fathers of the city played their inconspicuous part in the first royal *levée* to be held in Holyroodhouse since Prince Charles had resided there during the Forty-Five, surrounded by his victorious Highlanders. George IV's court there was arrayed in full Highland dress — even the Lord Mayor of London, a Wapping biscuit manufacturer, appeared in the outfit — and there were similar apparitions at a Caledonian hunt ball. But the ultimate enormity occurred at a banquet given for the sovereign by those to whom the capital really belonged, in the Parliament house. Instead of toasting the Lord Provost and fathers of the city, George IV lifted his glass and said, 'I shall simply give you the Chieftains and Clans of Scotland.' They were in the very building in which the Clan Gregor had been outlawed by statute and its very name proscribed. Now the MacGregor Chief rose to respond with a toast to 'the Chief of Chiefs, the King.'

Scott's novel *Rob Roy*, adapted as a play, was performed in the royal presence, and here King George was able to reflect on the part of Baillie Nicol Jarvie, that worthy and respectable representative of the kind of people to whom Edinburgh really belonged. But he saved his reflections for the private ear of his surgeon. To Sir Walter Scott he expressed himself like this after he had left Scotland: 'The King wishes to make you his channel of conveying to the Highland Chiefs and their followers, who have given to the varied scene which we have witnessed so peculiar and romantic a character, his particular thanks for their attendance, and his warm approbation of their uniform deportment.' The deportment of the burgesses was forgotten for the moment:

it had been neither peculiar nor romantic. Yet when George considered the matter later he found apt words for their heroic restraint, calling it worldly and respectable.

The tribal organisation of society in Scotland, already in its death-throes in 1822, disintegrated rapidly thereafter. The attention that Scott focussed on it in his writings and in that pageant for the King's visit has been condemned as an un-historical and tinselly romanticism. The cult of the kilt and the clan in modern times has been described as nothing more than a commercial racket. Yet a Council of Scottish Chiefs continues to convene undaunted: clan societies flourish all over the world, impervious to such scoldings. The survival of a Scottish tribal spirit remains a fact, and it has extended from the ancient tribal lands to embrace the whole country.

The question is whether such an extraordinary phenomenon could possibly have been engineered by the pen of Walter Scott, the enterprise of canny clothiers or the wiles of money-hungry chiefs. If it could, then why have the expertise of modern advertising and sales promotion not succeeded in creating similar enterprises elsewhere? The pioneer enterprise of the Edinburgh festival was seized upon fast enough in other countries.

Cynicism often blinds people to what lies at the heart of the matter, and so it is in this case. For the clannish pride of the Scots rests upon a real achievement in one of the most difficult and important tasks of life, that of having transformed a misfortune into a privilege.

CHAPTER ONE

Celtic Tribal Origins

The Gaelic peoples of Scotland spoke a language that has by far the oldest literature in Europe after those of Greece and Rome. It is the most archaic surviving form of the family of Celtic languages to which Welsh also belongs, and those who spoke any of these were defined by their tongue as Celtic peoples.

Not only have they preserved very early records of themselves: they also created such a stir as to ensure that Greek and Latin pens were kept busy describing their peculiarities. George IV was not the first to find them romantic and peculiar. The Celtic peoples were Indo-Aryan folk who were migrating westwards into Europe from perhaps as early as 1500 B.C. That is the time of the Vedic writings of India which tell of Mitra son of God by a virgin birth, the time when the magnificent tombs of Mycenae in Greece were being built by the Perseid dynasty. Later, when King Agamemnon set out from there to besiege Troy, Celtic peoples were already settled in what are now Germany and France.

By 700 B.C., when the power of the warlords of Mycenae was only a distant memory and Hesiod was recording peasant life in Greece, the Celtic tribes had established a powerful centre at Saltzburg in Austria, based upon its salt deposits. But neither here nor elsewhere did they establish a city, the practice from which the term civilisation is derived. One of the most distinctive characteristics of these people has been their distaste for a settled, urban life. To the very end, the tribal societies of the Highlands did not easily form a nucleus: crofting townships consisted of houses scattered over a wide area amongst their own crops and pastures.

Cities enabled craftsmen to practise their skills, freed from the time-consuming labour of food production, and during the next two centuries an extremely important new craft was developed as iron took the place of bronze. The Celtic migration was beginning to penetrate Britain by 700 B.C., where the new colonists introduced iron-working and doubtless found it a powerful argument in their dealings with the older inhabitants. On the Continent they were exploiting the new techniques without the benefits of urban organisation. They armed themselves so effectively that in the year 386 B.C. they were able to sack Rome, and in 297 B.C. they looted the shrine of Delphi in Greece.

But lacking cities, they failed to develop any administrative system that might gradually have undermined the tribal basis of their society. The Persians, for instance, were to invent the banking system. The very words bank, cheque and note are consequently Persian. This was just one of the essential weapons of human progress that the Celtic peoples did not learn to use, as they continued to barter salt and slaves and gold arm-bands. Now, as on so many occasions in the future, they were to be defeated by people using an organisation such as they failed to achieve.

Their own was based on tribal hierarchies, the most simple and primitive known to man, a mere enlargement of the family unit. Their restless, mobile, warlike life-style was based on their mastery of the horse, whose trappings are amongst the most impressive of their grave-goods. They harnessed their horses to four-wheeled wagons, and also to two-wheeled chariots that were to become the typical Celtic weapon of war. It was the aristocracy, of course, who enjoyed these amenities: the kings and the order of nobles and priests who occupied the strata below them. Beneath these lived the freemen, whether craftsmen or farmers. To the bottom category belonged those who were not allowed to carry weapons, who owned neither land nor goods, and who included actual slaves. These might be men who had been captured in battle or women and children rounded up in a raid. In the first century B.C. a Greek writer mentioned that the Celts would sell a slave for a jar of wine or a servant for a drink. Such property was too easily acquired to have a higher value. Evidently the Celts who colonised Britain followed the same practice, since slave chains have been found here with iron hoops that were used to fasten their victims by the neck in batches.

Their weakness in political organisation was counterbalanced by an extraordinary cultural unity, which has left the hallmark of the Celtic presence across the breadth of Europe, and even preserved the evidence of eastern origins in a variety of ways. The cohesive influence of shared beliefs played a dominant part amongst the Celtic peoples, as in other societies, and in view of the unique nature of these beliefs at a later period it is worth noticing what beliefs the pagan Celts had not carried with them from the east.

There the Aryan peoples had been the first in human record to evolve the concept of a sole Creator of the entire universe to whom they gave the name Ahura Mazda, which means the Light of Wisdom. It survives in the West today on electric light bulbs. The Celts included no such divine being in their beliefs, neither did they worship the son of Ahura Mazda, the mediator between God and mankind, Mitra, whose name means Contract. In this they differed from the Greeks, whose earliest warlords of Mycenae conceived of a God called Zeus, which means a Lighting-up, the source of enlightenment, comparable to Ahura Mazda; and who accepted from the east Apollo son of God, bringer of healing. If Apollo does not appear to be Mitra under another name, he is a good deal more nearly so than any Celtic divinity.

But the Achaean Greeks combined their beliefs with those of the Argolid peoples whom they conquered when they settled at Mycenae, who followed the more primitive cults of fertility goddesses. Everywhere the goddesses reigned before the gods, and so it was in Greece until Zeus married the reigning earth goddess Hera and gave rise to the pantheon of gods and goddesses of Mount Olympus.

The Celtic peoples possessed a comparable pantheon, and for centuries to come they enacted in their lives and in their religious practices the rivalry between male and female power. One of the most striking differences between Celt and Greek is that the Celtic females, divine and human, held their own so much more successfully. Today Queen Mab is diminished to a little fairy queen. The redoubtable Maebh of Connacht, with whom Irish kings had to mate as the symbol of their sovereignty, was a very different order of being.

The Queen Maebh of the pagan Irish epic *Táin Bó Cuálgne* was defeated in the end by the superman Cú Chulainn. It is possible that both were historical persons, living at the time of the Roman conquest of Britain, though the Romans made no reference to them since they did not attempt to conquer Ireland. They did, however, encounter another Maebh in Britain, the formidable Boudicca of the Iceni tribe, who led a revolt against them. She was 'huge of frame and terrifying of aspect,' they reported; 'a great mass of red hair fell to her knees.' The size of these Celtic women was often remarked upon. Another Roman writer observed: 'a whole band of foreigners will be unable to cope with one of them in a fight if he calls in his wife, stronger than he by far and with flashing eyes; least of all when she swells her neck and gnashes her teeth, and poising her huge white arms, begins to rain blows mingled with kicks like shots discharged by the twisted cords of a catapult.' And a Greek said the same when he reported that they 'not only equal their husbands in stature, but they rival them in strength as well.'

The Greeks had their legendary Phaedra and Electra, but contemporary Greek ladies were never described in such terms. The earliest Celtic writings depict their womenfolk more or less exactly as foreigners did, and they attributed similar propensities to their goddesses. Prominent among these was Macha, who was both a fertility and a war goddess. Although she took many forms, including those of bird, eel and heifer, she was above all the divine mare, worshipped by a society based on the partnership between man and horse. The place that commemorates her in Ireland, the pagan sacred site of Emain Macha, is a monument to the female divinity associated since the remotest antiquity with the still-flourishing cult of the horse.

Many of these gods and goddesses were regarded as divine ancestors, like those of the Greeks and Romans, and some of them may have been real ancestors, deified for some special skill or invention that they introduced, or for some achievement believed to be supernatural. Just as there must have been an original Prometheus, bringer of the gift of fire, so the Celts may have been unconsciously commemorating the horse-breeder of a remote matriarchal society in worshipping Macha.

The effect of belief in a divine physical ancestry was to blur the distinction between divine and human beings. The Celtic gods and goddesses mated with each other and with mortals just as the Greek and Roman ones did. But they were also subject to injury and death on occasion, which brought them far closer to their human worshippers.

Whereas Herakles was wholly exceptional in achieving an afterlife with the immortal gods of Mount Olympus through toil and suffering, the Celts seem to have taken a far more cheerful view of what would happen to them when they died. Life would simply continue, they believed, in much the same pattern of feasting and warfare in another world not much different from this one and not sharply divided from it. This helped to give them their careless attitude to death: it was less terrible than a crippling injury, since they would emerge from it unscathed, able to return to their old haunts at will, invested with supernatural powers.

The behaviour of the Celtic male appears to have been governed partly by this belief, partly by the challenge of mating with such dominant women, living reminders that their goddesses were at least the equals of their gods. The Greek writer Strabo tells us that men who did not keep themselves in training were actually fined, and he has left a description of the attention they paid to their appearance, which rivalled that of the Greeks themselves. 'Their hair is not only naturally blond, but they also use artificial means to increase this natural quality of colour. For they continually wash their hair with lime-wash and draw it back from the forehead to the crown and to the nape of the neck, with the result that their appearance resembles that of satyrs or of pans.' Like the Greek youth, they shaved their beards, but unlike them, they wore long moustaches.

Most remarkably like the Greeks, they flaunted their appearance on athletic occasions stark naked, and of course the most athletic of occasions was a battle, which was the supreme sport in the eyes of the Celtic aristocracy. The outstanding athletes operated outside the tribal framework, in a military company known to classical writers as the Gaesatae. The Greek historian Polybius described them at the Battle of Telamon in the year 225 B.C. Here they stood in front of the Celtic army, festooned with gold jewellery, wearing their bizarre hair-style, which did nothing to diminish the impact of their total exposure, emphasised by a sword belt round the waist. 'Very terrifying were the appearance and the gestures of the naked warriors in front, all in the prime of life and finely built men, and all in the leading companies richly adorned with gold torques and armlets. The sight of them indeed dismayed the Romans, but at the same time the prospect of winning such spoils made them twice as keen to fight.'

The famous sculpture of a dying Gaul, exactly as Polybius described the Gaesatae, has immortalised this cult of male athleticism, while Gaelic legend in the British Isles relates how their organisation and ideals were brought here to enjoy a new lease of life in the deeds of Finn Mac Cumhaill and the other Ossianic heroes. But these appear to have clothed themselves decently, partly (no doubt) as a protection against the climate; chiefly because, although they were still pagan, their deeds were first recorded in writing by Christians, who have everywhere and always adopted an attitude to nakedness that both the Greeks and the Celts of pagan times would have found equally ridiculous. Like the missionaries of another sphere, these chroniclers may have, as it were, slipped their ancestors into mother hubbards as an act of piety.

On horseback the Celts wore clothing, unlike the Greeks who are depicted in their sculpture naked except for the cloaks flowing in the wind from their shoulders. The nature of Celtic riding dress is particularly interesting. Even before the year 500 B.C. they were depicted wearing tight trousers resembling modern trews, at a time when all the other Mediterranean peoples wore some form of toga. They were still dressed in trews on horseback in the year A.D. 136, by which time they had been serving long and with distinction in the Roman army. 'They have hose, not loose like those in fashion among the Parthians and Armenians, but fitting closely to the limbs,' Arrian noticed. The Parthians were by this time the rulers of the Persian empire.

The Celtic hair-style inevitably suffered once a defensive head-dress was adopted, but male exhibitionism appears to have remained undeterred. Arrian also remarked: 'those of them who are conspicuous for rank or for skill in horsemanship ride into the lists armed with helmets made of iron or brass covered with gilding to attract the particular attention of the spectators.'

The warlike habits of these people likewise suffered no diminution with the passage of time. Even the mere provocation of a drunken insult was hardly necessary to start a fight, since warfare was one of their merry pastimes, and if they lacked the stimulus of a foreign enemy they were perfectly content to battle among themselves. But in fighting, as in their other activities, they failed to develop an effective organisation, as Strabo noticed. 'The whole race which is now called Celtic or Gallic is madly fond of war, high spirited and quick to battle, but otherwise straightforward and not of evil character. And so when they are stirred up they assemble in their bands for battle, quite openly and without forethought; so that they are easily handled by those who desire to outwit them.' When Caesar set out to conquer them in Gaul, he found them fatally weakened by internal dissension, and a little later Tacitus, chronicling the conquests of Agricola in Britain, was able to write: 'fortune can give no greater boon than discord among our foes.' Those words echo down the centuries of Gaelic history.

So do descriptions of the way they fought, left by classical authors. Those naked Gaesatae who made such a handsome and intimidating appearance at the Battle of Telamon in 225 B.C. 'rushed wildly on the enemy and sacrificed their lives while others, retreating step by step on the ranks of their comrades, threw them into disorder by their display of faint-heartedness.'

Brave and impetuous in attack, they became demoralised quickly by failure and often suffered defeat through their own indiscipline. Telamon marked the turn of this unruly Celtic tide. From the very gates of Rome it was to recede until the Celts found their ultimate refuge on the western rim of Europe.

But during those centuries they stamped such a vivid portrait of themselves upon the face of this continent that we can still see in it the authentic ancestor of many a clan and chief nearly two thousand years later. There are few people in Europe who have preserved such a continuity, and Sir Walter Scott did not err when he suggested that Scotland possessed nothing so curious as this to show George IV — even if Edinburgh was hardly the most tactful place in which to display it.

The boar emblem of the Campbells, for instance, illustrates the tenacity of traditions reaching back into pagan times. Just as the goddess Macha was incarnated in the form of a mare, so the boar personified the divine spirit of courage, strength and sexual prowess. Effigies of this beast have been found in many parts of Europe, superb examples of Celtic religious art. One stone carving of a god in Gaul has a boar carved up its torso, while other figures of boars were cast in bronze, the bristles along their spines depicted in the manner in which warriors arranged their hair with lime-wash. So those Gaesatae were evidently transforming themselves symbolically into boars: and this they did also by hunting and ritually eating the animal. The cult is commemorated by the name of the Orkney Islands, which means the Boar Islands, in which Celtic people settled long before the Vikings first set eyes on them. A comparable male god was called Moccus, meaning Pig, and this tutelary deity in animal form is commemorated by the isle of Muck in the Hebrides.

As soon as the Gaesatae of classical record reappear in Gaelic legend as the Ossianic heroes, so does the boar. It is told that handsome Diarmaid eloped with the wife of Finn (or Fingal in modern terminology), who took his revenge by asking Diarmaid to kill the supernatural boar that was terrorising the country. When Diarmaid performed this without mishap, Finn asked him to measure the dead animal, which Diarmaid did by walking down its bristles in his bare feet. (So at least his feet were bare.) Finn asked him to measure it again in case he had made an error, and as Diarmaid walked back up the bristles one of them entered his heel, the only vulnerable part of his body, and he bled to death.

Here we have the Homeric story of Helen, Paris and Achilles, brought to Ireland with the Gaesatae and the boar god; from where they were taken to Scotland to explain the origins of Clan Diarmaid, whose descendants are now known as Campbells though in Gaelic they were also known as the Children of Diarmaid of the Boar. Not surprisingly, Gaelic is the first language into which the story of the fall of Troy was translated out of Greek or Latin.

One of the strangest examples of the longevity of Celtic belief and custom is the cult of the human head. It is typical of the paradoxical behaviour of these combative yet sensitive people that they venerated the human head as the repository of wisdom and virtue, and yet debased this concept by the practice of head-hunting. A Greek described how 'they embalm in cedar oil the heads of the most distinguished enemies, and preserve them carefully in a chest, and display them with pride to strangers, saying that for this head one of their ancestors, or his father, or the man himself refused the offer of a large sum of money.' They believed the qualities of the man whose skull they possessed entered into them, just as they supposed that they acquired the strength of the boar they killed and ate. It looks as though they only avoided ritual cannibalism by a narrow margin.

Head-hunting provided yet another motive for warfare. Livy once described the grisly sight of trophies being brought home. 'The consuls got no report of the disaster until some Gallic horsemen came in sight with heads hanging at their horses' breasts, or fixed on their lances.' These violent, yet deeply religious and artistic people also made the human head one of the main themes of their art, and depicted it in a manner uniquely their own. The heads of the Apostles carved on the wooden coffin of St Cuthbert (preserved in Durham Cathedral, though it came from Lindisfarne) reveal a continuity of style that was already at least a thousand years old when the pious craftsmen of the Celtic monastic foundation at Lindisfarne plied their tools.

In the Scottish Highlands the cult of the human head took an extremely refined form. It was believed that those who drank the pure water of life from the skull of an ancestor might obtain the wisdom invested in the one, and the gift of healing associated with the other. The *Tobar nan Ceann* — Well of the Heads — became one of the sacred sites throughout the lands of the Gael. In some cases these were rededicated after the Christian conversion, so that Tobermory in Mull is named the Virgin Mary's Well. But after the second conversion, to Calvinism, the reformers sometimes adopted a less tolerant attitude. In Sutherland, for instance, the very word for a well of pure water, *tobar*, was degraded into meaning a well of tainted water, and people of Clan Mackay were thus made to forget where the sacred wells could be found. The Gaelic word *fuaran* was substituted, which simply means a spring.

But beside Loch Oich in the Great Glen stands an actual Well of the Heads, defiantly marked by an effigy of heads such as the Celts had erected throughout Europe two thousand years earlier. It commemorates the scene of the Keppoch murders that occurred in 1663, though it is impossible to say what dim ancestral memory led those who caught the seven culprits and executed them to bring their heads to this well, to purge them of their evil by washing them here.

We may believe that it was a meaningful ritual in the eyes of those who performed it, although an ignorant observer might have scoffed at it as an unseemly charade: just as we may do in the case of occurrences in Edinburgh in 1822, which have aroused so much derision. Certainly the pre-Christian belief enshrined in a Well of the Heads survived into the twentieth century, even in Calvinist Lewis, where someone dug up an ancestral skull in the graveyard, filled it with water from a healing well, and gave it to a sick patient to drink after the doctor had failed to cure him. The patient recovered. His case is recorded in a university journal, but to identify him here might cause scandal to the living.

It can be seen that the Celtic peoples were as capable of spiritual insights, and of gross superstition, as people have been in every age. Since people can generally perceive only what they already understand, Julius Caesar noticed only the second of these: 'the whole Gallic people is exceedingly given to religious superstition.' Caesar himself permitted Cleopatra to invest him as the incarnation of the sun god Ammon, and returned the compliment by erecting a statue to her in Rome as the incarnation of Venus, whom he claimed as his own ancestress.

It was easy enough for the Celtic pantheon of gods and goddesses to be integrated with those of pagan Rome in the wake of conquest, and this practice was carried to Britain when opportunity permitted. Sulis, Celtic goddess of the waters of Bath, became Minerva: a sacred well on Hadrian's Wall was rededicated to Coventina.

But unlike the efficient, prosaic Romans, the Celts were a deeply imaginative people, living with one foot in another world, and their religion was not simply a department of politics but the very basis of their lives; and in all they made of wood or metal or stone, they gave expression to the flamboyance, the freedom and the religious optimism of those lives. The importance of religion in Celtic society is reflected in the high position of its priests in the social hierarchy and in the scope of their responsibilities. 'The Druids,' wrote Caesar (describing the Celts in Europe), 'are concerned with the worship of the gods, look after public and private sacrifice, and expound religious matters. A large number of young men flock to them for training, and hold them in high honour.' But their influence did not end there, 'for they have the right to decide nearly all public and private disputes, and they also pass judgment and decide rewards and penalties in criminal and murder cases, and in disputes regarding legacies and boundaries.'

As for the laws they administered, these have been preserved in ancient Gaelic, the earliest by far of any European code outside Greece and Rome, and extraordinarily complete in its details. They were designed expressly for a society based on the clan structure, and they provided for education, fosterage, ownership of property and punishment of crime. So old were they by the time they crossed to the British Isles from Europe that they still bore traces of their Indo-Aryan origins. For instance they provided, as in Hindu law, that a creditor might fast before the door of his debtor until he received his due, between the hours of sunrise and sunset. If the defendant in the case failed to do the same, he became liable to double the amount of his debt as a penalty.

This enormous corpus of laws was preserved intact over an immense period of time without being written down. In the same way a rich folklore was preserved by oral tradition alone from remote antiquity. This feat of memory-training was another of the distinctive Celtic arts that has been practised for thousands of years and remains alive today. There was nothing to prevent them from adopting the art of writing from the Greeks or Romans, but they evidently preferred to continue cultivating their own — one that is gravely undermined by literacy. The Filid, or Seers, were the caste responsible for retaining, transmitting and expounding the Celtic corpus of knowledge, and this learned order came next in importance to the Druids.

The presence of these two castes, the men of religion and learning, in the highest rank of the Celtic aristocracy below that of the sacred kings helps to explain how people who were in many ways so barbarous came so near to creating a civilisation without cities. They were so eccentric as to despise the aid of writing, to collect human heads as the repositories of wisdom, and to train their minds to retain their learning with a fidelity that still astonishes. The man of learning, *ollamh* in Gaelic, held one of the most honoured places in Celtic society from the beginning of Irish record: and evidently for a great deal longer than that since this word is almost identical to the Persian *aalem*.

Gradually the whole structure crumbled before the might of Rome. The skills of metal-smith, wood-carver and stonemason that had reached such heights of exuberance to satisfy the Celtic passion for display were debased into producing the shoddy, standardised work required by new masters. The thread of oral tradition was snapped. The dying Gael was made a theme for romantic sculpture.

But by the time this occurred, the Celtic peoples had been consolidating their hold on the British Isles for about 700 years. Roman arms pursued them there, but there were two regions that they never colonised — Ireland and northern Scotland. This was where the Celts were able to preserve their language, their arts and traditions, their flamboyant and combative life-style. And they did.

Those who settled the eastern mainland of Scotland and in Orkney and Shetland became so thoroughly intermingled with the aboriginal population that their Celtic tongue was adulterated by the speech of these people. Later, the Romans were to identify this mixed stock containing the descendants of the earliest Celtic colonists as Picts, a term that it is convenient to use now, although strictly speaking the first Celtic immigrants qualify for it no more than the Lord Mayor of London from Wapping did to wear the kilt.

Unfortunately not a single complete sentence of the Pictish language survives, though many place names commemorate their presence. Of these several, such as Dunkeld and the mountain called Shiehallion, are not Celtic at all but belong to the language of the earlier inhabitants. Both contain the root from which Caledonia derives, and it is startling that the other ancient name for Scotland, Alba, is also pre-Celtic.

It was these proto-Picts who erected the first military structures in the land, dramatic evidence of the strife that followed their arrival. They consist of timber-laced forts whose stonework sometimes fused in the heat when they caught fire, so that they are known today as vitrified forts. Their builders became known to the Romans as formidable in war, and although Agricola marched an army to defeat them at Mons Graupius in the Grampians, the victory was not consolidated and the Picts remained beyond the boundaries of the empire.

The Pictish leader in that battle was named Calgacus, which

means Sword-Bearer, the earliest personal name recorded in Scottish history, and Tacitus placed in his mouth an incitement to battle that has become famous, with its anti-Roman taunt, 'where they make a desolation, they call it peace.' Actually Tacitus was not present at the battle, and he would not have understood the speech of Calgacus even if he had been. But he did not err in attributing such eloquence to a Celtic warlord who spent his time in cattle and slave raiding.

The Irish epic *The Cattle Raid of Cooley* (*Táin Bó Cuálgne*) belongs to the same period, and in it Cú Chulainn is invested with the gift of eloquence before his skill as a plunderer is mentioned. Needless to say, the first gift to be noticed is the one the classical authors had remarked upon in the appearance of the Gaesatae. 'Now Cú Chulainn possessed many and varied gifts: the gift of beauty, the gift of form, the gift of build, the gift of swimming, the gift of horsemanship . . . the gift of battle, the gift of fighting, the gift of conflict; the gift of sight, the gift of speech, the gift of counsel . . . the gift of laying waste, the gift of plundering in a strange border.'

The strange borders were apt to be conveniently near at hand. When the Celtic rulers of Orkney, the Boar Islands, sent a deputation to the Emperor Claudius in Rome in the year A.D. 43, requesting that they might enjoy the *Pax Romana* as a client kingdom, it seems likely that they were seeking protection — perhaps against the very mainland Picts who fought at Mons Graupius. At all events, the step they took shows a sophisticated knowledge of diplomatic procedures quite on a par with the eloquence attributed to Calgacus.

At the same time, the forts they built suggest a degree of internal strife such as had contributed to the downfall of the Celts in Europe. And the most epoch-making collision was the one that eventually gave Scotland her name, her Gaelic culture, her clans and chiefs.

Its origins are obscure. The builders of timbered forts spread westwards as well as north, and crossed the narrow channel to northern Ireland. Here they encountered people very different from the aboriginals who had not learnt to fashion iron weapons. Other Celtic tribes had been migrating in strength from the Continent to Ireland, where it proved that they had found a safe asylum from the power of Rome. They became known as Scots at about the same time as the fort-builders of the northern British mainland were first described as Picts. What may have begun as sporting raids on one another by these two groups of Celtic peoples (such is the theme of the *Táin* epic) escalated into a conflict down the centuries that reached its climax on Scottish soil — Scottish henceforth, because it was the Scots who won.

Or was it entirely? When Fergus son of Erc crossed the sea from Dalriada in northern Ireland to found his little kingdom of the same name in Argyll, he and his kindreds brought with them the Gaelic language, laws and social organisation of the Scots of Ireland. These were different from those of the Picts: their very language had become sufficiently changed for St Columba to require an interpreter when he wished to converse with Picts.

Yet the traditions of those Gaelic-speaking settlers in Argyll told them that they descended from the militant fort-builders who had been spreading in all directions during the past thousand years. Their legends may have been incorrect, but the attitude of the truly Scottish O'Neills of Ireland appears to confirm their accuracy. Even allowing for the infighting endemic throughout the Celtic history, the unremitting hostility of the O'Neills to the tribes of Dalriada, until these actually emigrated *en masse* to Argyll, would be far easier to explain if they were bent on evicting a Pictish cuckoo from their nest. This would not imply that the kindreds of Dalriada were of wholly separate stock. On the contrary, it is certain that they were closely intermarried with the true Scottish Gaels of Ireland; and they could scarcely have become so wholly Gaelic in culture if this had not been so. But it does seem very probable that when the forbears of the clans and chiefs settled in Argyll, it was a mixed stock of cuckoos that moved into Pictish nests.

There was another sort of Celtic folk who contributed their own bones of contention, and who later made their own distinctive contribution to the clans of Scotland. These had migrated to Britain after a change in the language had occurred on the Continent. Many of them had been involved in the final rearguard resistance to Roman conquest, and England was the main area of settlement, though they had spread as far north as the narrow neck of Scotland formed by the Forth and Clyde. The Romans called them Britons and named the whole island after them. It was these Celtic people who fell under Roman rule in Britain; and the term that Germanic-speaking people later used to describe such Romanised Britons was 'Welsh'. Since English belongs to the Germanic family of languages, the descendants of the Romanised Britons are still known as Welsh today, although now they are in no sense Romanised.

But they were at the time when the Picts and Scots were

living in a state of somewhat disorderly freedom beyond the Roman frontier, and although they remained Celtic in language, their lives were deeply affected by Roman administration and also by imperial religious policy. Naturally it was the high-ranking men of religion, the Druids, who played the dominant role in resisting the Romans. They incited their tribes to a high pitch of religious fervour, so that Pliny observed: 'at the present day Britain is still fascinated by magic, and performs rites as though it was she who had imparted the cult to the Persians.'

This remark reveals the depths of Roman ignorance in religious matters. The Persians had by this time observed the religion of Ahura Mazda since before the existence of Rome, a religion so superior to any Roman beliefs that it easily supplanted them, to become the official creed of the empire. It was given the name of Mitra, son of God, and Mithraism was brought to Britain, where remains of Mithraic temples are found as far north as the frontier of Hadrian's Wall.

The Romans set out to destroy the centres of Celtic belief in Britain, not because they had learnt the religious intolerance of a later age, but because these were the focal points of native resistance. The storming of the Druid sanctuary on the isle of Anglesey in the year A.D. 61 was related in all its horror by Tacitus. 'On the shore stood the opposing army with its dense array of armed warriors, while between the ranks dashed women in black attire like the Furies, with hair dishevelled, waving brands.' Those Celtic ladies were at it again.

'All around the Druids, lifting up their hands to heaven and pouring forth dreadful imprecations, scared our soldiers by the unfamiliar sight, so that, as if their limbs were paralysed, they stood motionless and exposed to wounds. Then, urged by their general's appeal and mutual encouragements not to quail before a troop of frenzied women, the Romans bore the standard onwards, smote down all resistance, and wrapped the foe in the flame of their own brands. A force was set over the conquered and the sacred groves, devoted to inhuman superstitions, were destroyed.' Superstitions, then as now, are what other people believe in, though we do not.

The episode reveals yet again the dominant role of Celtic women, and not merely top women like Boudicca of the Iceni or Maebh of Connacht. It also shows the importance of those sacred assembly places, such as Emain Macha in Ireland, and the power the Druids exercised in them. From the holocaust on Anglesey many of these no doubt fled to the safety of Ireland and Scotland.

But the native British who remained were gradually drawn into an altogether different way of life, based on garrison towns connected by roads, the arteries of a commerce employing a coinage. On the northern frontier the natives actually became an integral part of this system, after the Romans had abandoned the wall they built between the Forth and the Clyde, and retired to the safety of Hadrian's Wall south of the Cheviots. In the area between, the southern Scotland of today, lived Romanised Britons, the original Wallace or Welsh, who were consequently left exposed to the unconquered Picts and Scots.

These possessed a choice between joining the enemies of Rome, or seeking safety in the *Pax Romana*, and it is little wonder that most of them chose the same course as the leaders of Orkney did. It was made particularly attractive for them when Rome adopted a new policy of recruitment, enlisting local natives to man the frontier garrisons. Gradually the Welsh tribes collected in cantonments where the families of enlisted men lived, continuing to use their own language and practise their own religion; which availed them not at all when the Picts and Scots swept down upon the northern frontier.

Each of the three Celtic groups could assume as a rule that the other two would hardly do anything so uncharacteristic as to combine against them. But in the year 367 the Scots and Picts actually succeeded in forming an alliance to attack Roman Britain, and when they did so it was naturally the Welsh manning the frontier who suffered the consequences. Before the invasion was repulsed, their settlements had suffered dreadfully: and it was not defeated easily, because so many of the Welsh soldiers in Roman pay deserted to the Celtic cause. These became fugitives beyond the frontier after the restoration of peace, adding to the disorders caused in the Highlands by roving bands who operated outside the tribal network. It is thought that this was when the tales of the Ossianic heroes flowered.

At about this time the man who made the Latin version of the Bible known as the Vulgate, St Jerome, witnessed the behaviour of raiders on the coast of Gaul who presumably came either from Ireland or from western Scotland to assault the empire from the sea. The most extraordinary part of his testimony is that these people ate human flesh. This might have been understandable if they had so far degenerated in their beliefs as to combine the cult of the boar with that of the human head, supposing that they could acquire the merits of the one as they did of the other, by ritual eating. But this is not the impression that Jerome gives:

he suggests merely that they found the meat succulent, as indeed it is.

This is one side of the coin, and it is a sufficiently distressing one; the other is very different. So it has always been, since the beginning of recorded comment. The Celts had always been given to extremes, and their extravagance, attested long before this, was to remain apparent into modern times. And since the very term *Celt* is nothing more than an ethnic one, the longevity of their habits must be connected with their ways of thought and the culture that engendered them, not attributed to any genetic peculiarities.

Above all, the seriousness of their religious habits must help to account for the Celtic paradox: it is the impress of their spiritual life that the other side of the coin contains. The Romanised Britons, the Welsh, were naturally the first who heard the Christian message. It had been established as the official religion of the empire exactly thirty years before the devastating invasion of the northern frontier, in the year 337; but it was not until the following century that the first native Bishop, St Ninian, extended his pastoral activities beyond his own British folk in an attempt to convert the Picts. He does not seem to have had much success, although later dedications to the Saint are found as far north as Shetland. St Patrick, who was growing up during the lifetime of Ninian, later referred to them as 'the most unworthy, most evil and apostate Picts.' Their apostacy no doubt helps to explain Patrick's use of the other pejorative adjectives.

St Patrick is the first person born and brought up in what is now Scotland whose own writings survive. The Romans had recently abandoned Britain to its own devices, leaving behind the Christian Church to continue the use of their Latin language, in the hands of the Romanised Britons. Patrick was exactly one of these, able to record in simple Latin that 'I had for my father Calpornius a deacon, the son of Potitus a presbyter, who belonged to the village of Bannavam Taberniae, for near it he had a small villa, where I was made a captive. I was then sixteen years old.' He was carried off to Ireland, where he was to spend his life preaching the Christian faith. To do this, he stated, he had to exchange his mother tongue, Welsh, for Gaelic.

But the direct links with Europe that the Scots of Ireland had evidently preserved from the time of their first migrations had already brought them the new religious message in a form different from Ninian's, who had been trained 'regularitur' in

Rome. Ultimately the differences resolved themselves into a dispute over such comparatively trivial matters as the date of Easter and the proper kind of hair-style for monks. In fact the differences were as profound as those that distinguished Sufism from Islam after the coming of the Prophet, and in much the same way, and for similar reasons.

For Ireland evidently enjoyed direct access by sea to the ancient philosophies of the Aryan world beyond the Semitic Holy Land of divine revelations, and was not wholly dependent on Welsh missionaries relaying the Christian dogma of Rome. These were busy stamping out the religion of Mithras, son of God by a virgin birth, with its communion meal and its ethical precepts so similar to those of Christ, and so very much older. The Irish Scots had perhaps never heard of Mithras, yet paradoxically it was they who now interpreted Christianity in a manner clearly atuned to the ancient metaphysics of the east, and in doing so they made the Celtic Church the lamp of Dark-Age Europe.

It also provided the men who took the place of the pagan Druids in the tribal organisation, and a new direction for the old religious fervour. The Celtic Church was not based on the organisation of parish and diocese like that of Rome, but on monasteries. These were built into the tribal structure, in fact, since a monastery was maintained by a particular clan, its leaders drawn from the tribe's aristocracy just as the order of Druids had been. People who had believed that their gods and goddesses consorted with them on earth had no difficulty in accepting that Christ had done the same. St Columba, a prince of the royal house of O'Neill, prayed to 'my Druid, Son of God.'

In these monasteries was established the eremitical tradition that had been planted long before in the Egyptian desert. It became associated with the Apostle John there, and in Scotland, where the high cross of St John on Iona commemorates the Celtic Church's particular devotion to him. But in fact the monastic idea does not stem from Palestine; neither does the emphasis on achieving a state of being, rather than doing, have its roots in any of the Semitic religions; nor the practice of meditation as a means of realising our true being. All derive from the Aryan east, where King Asoka had sent missions to Egypt after his ascent to the Indian throne in 270 B.C. Buddhist teaching and practice had already interested Persian philosophers, by then in the tolerant Aryan world. No doubt the interest was mutual, for had not Mitra been known to the Indians since at least 1500 B.C., a thousand years before the ministry of the Persian Zarathustra? Suffice to say, the Celtic Church reveals characteristics that belong more recognisably to the Aryan than to the Semitic traditions.

To cite a single illustration of this, it employed the imagery of Light as it might have been used by Zarathustra himself, as any teacher might do who conceived of God as Ahura Mazda, Wisdom's Light: the Jehovah of the Book of Job would hardly inspire such a concept.

The deserts in which Celtic monks withdrew from the world to prepare themselves by meditation and prayer for their missionary activities were frequently in the wastes of ocean that surrounded their shores. The best preserved Celtic monastery is perched dizzily on the precipice of Skellig Michael off the coast of County Kerry; though this priceless treasure, untended by any custodian, is being destroyed rapidly by tourists. There is another in a more advanced state of delapidation on Eileach Naoimh among the Garvelloch Islands in the Hebrides, but it is more immune from destructive visitors.

The man who played the leading part in planting Celtic monasticism in Scotland was the Irish prince remembered as St Columba. As the great-grandson of a sovereign he was himself eligible for the High Kingship — such was the rule of succession — and in his earlier years he displayed the high-handed, domineering characteristics of the O'Neills. But he also exemplified the traditional love of learning: and these two traits led him into the conflict that resulted in the first recorded judgment on copyright in the British Isles.

Columba found the time, all his life, to copy manuscripts. A Gaelic poem attributed to him contains the lines, 'I send my little dripping pen unceasingly over an assemblage of books of great beauty, to enrich the possessions of men of art, so that my hand is weary with writing.' Once he copied without permission a Psalter that was the property of his teacher St Finbarr, and refused to surrender it when the High King of Ireland ordered him to do so. Instead he took up arms against the King in defiance of the royal judgment: 'to every cow her calf, to every book its offspring.' He won the battle but soon afterwards left his country for Scotland, in the year 563 and the forty-second year of his life.

By this time the Irish Gaels, having at last adopted the art of writing with their conversion to Christianity, were already laying the foundations of their unique literary achievements both in Latin and in their own language. Columba's contemporary,

Columbanus of Leinster, alone founded with his disciples over a hundred monasteries as far afield as France, Switzerland and Italy. By the ninth century this Church had produced John Scotus Eriugena (John the Irish Scot), the most profound philosopher of the age, and one whose wisdom can be seen clearly to have come from the east, although he lived in the far west. It is apparent enough now: it took the Papacy until 1225 to perceive this and to condemn his great work on the division of nature to be burned as heretical.

Such was the wonderful new Celtic tradition that Columba brought to the little kingdom of Scots recently planted in Dalriada, just as it was blossoming into summer flower. He found their affairs in rather a precarious state, in a land in which they were heavily outnumbered by the neighbouring Britons and Picts. Tacitus had recorded five hundred years earlier that the Pictish army of Calgacus numbered 30,000, and even if this was an exaggeration, it suggests a far larger population than one containing 1,500 households, which was all Dalriada contained even a century after Columba's time. The three British kingdoms of Strathclyde, Gododdin and Rheged to the south-west, which had evolved in the latter days of the Roman presence, were probably far more populous as well.

When Columba came to Scotland, his cousin the King of Dalriada had recently been defeated and killed by the Pictish King Brude. In his imperious way, Columba embarked on what probably resembled more nearly a state visit than a religious mission to the Pictish King at Inverness. Brude granted permission for Cormac to carry the Christian message to his client kingdom of Orkney, and for other missionaries to attempt the conversion of his own people. It was almost certainly Brude, not the King of Dalriada, who gave Columba the isle of Iona for the foundation of his new monastery.

Today Iona may appear to resemble those other remote retreats in the ocean deserts to which monks retired to meditate in solitude. In fact it had been chosen with a strategist's eye for its position among the waterways of Pictland, equally accessible to the Great Glen that led to the northern capital at Inverness, to the centres of Dunollie and Dunadd in Dalriada, and to the Columban foundation of Derry in northern Ireland. On Iona, Columba consecrated Aidan as King of Scots, the earliest ordination on record in Scotland, and with the Saint's backing King Aidan became the most powerful sovereign of Dalriada until the succession of Kenneth Mac Alpin.

Although conflict continued between Picts, Scots and Britons throughout Aidan's long reign, an altogether novel amity began to unite them in the field of religion. Iona and Columba have overshadowed other foundations and their saints in human memory, but monasteries as far-flung as Deerness in Orkney, Applecross in Wester Ross and Lismore in the Firth of Lorne once flourished under saints drawn from all three Celtic societies — Maolrubha and Moluag, Kessog, Comgall and Donnan and many more who were to be commemorated among the clans of Scotland.

Just as the Celtic peoples of an earlier age had preserved a remarkable cultural unity despite their conflicts, so they did now under the inspiration of their new beliefs. Their distinctive arts that had withered on the Continent flowered again in new forms which yet preserved an unbroken continuity with the remote past. Of these, Pictish sculpture is perhaps the most remarkable of all: their picture galleries in stone were unique in Dark-Age Europe and they combine originality with a use of styles of distant and remote provenance. But in the fields of sculpture, as of Gospel illumination, the three Celtic societies also stimulated and influenced one another, so that an inspiration that can still be called Celtic is clearly recognisable.

But in the all-important field of language it was Gaelic that triumphed over both Pictish and Welsh. The Picts failed entirely to preserve their tongue: there is no evidence that they even tried.

The case of the Britons is different. By the time St Columba came to Scotland the Angles, forbears of the English, were establishing themselves in Northumbria and menacing the British kingdoms to the north and west of them. Scotland's earliest poem, the long Welsh epic of the *Gododdin*, laments one of the decisive English victories. King Aidan of Dalriada met his end in battle against the English of Northumbria. By the seventh century Edinburgh had become what it has remained ever since, a northern bastion of English speech and literature: that is what made it such an odd venue for a parade of Scottish clans and Gaelic speech on George IV's visit.

Gradually Welsh gave way to a form of northern English now called the Scots tongue throughout the Lowlands, and although British tribal societies continued to live amongst the recesses of the Border hills, they lost their oral traditions with their language. By far the earliest reference to their resistance leader, Arthur, occurs in the *Gododdin* epic, and he is still commemorated by Arthur's Seat, the hill overlooking the Scottish capital. But the legends of Arthur were carried away to where Welsh was still spoken, until he was rehoused as a king in Cornwall. One thing that is certain about Arthur is that he was not a king.

Similarly the Welsh prophet Merlin, who lived in Strathclyde in the reign of King Ridderch when Columba lived on Iona, was transported as far afield as Brittany, where his predictions (or those fathered upon him) were being used to promote the career of Joan of Arc a thousand years later. Of course this precisely resembles what was happening further north, where the legends of the Ossianic heroes were transplanted into Pictish territories. Oral tradition always gives a local habitation to its stories, and generally puts them in modern dress, so that the Arthur of the Middle Ages naturally became a medieval king.

By contrast to the Britons and the Picts, the Scots had moved into the light of their own Gaelic written records by the seventh century, and these preserved oral traditions, including their laws and their epics, from pagan times. So it is only in their society that we can examine the early clan structure and its remote tribal origins in any detail.

The Gaelic society of Scotland was based on three kindreds, of which the most numerous belonged to the kin of Gabrán, with its 560 houses that could place 800 fighting men in the field. Its territory lay on the mainland, with a stronghold at Dunaverty on the Mull of Kintyre and another that was probably built near Tarbert on Loch Fyne. The other two kindreds were those of Lorne and Angus, which could each muster 500 men, although the kin of Angus contained 430 houses, that of Lorne only 420. The tribe of Angus had Islay as its base, later to become the seat of the Lordship of the Isles. That of Lorne occupied the region of north Argyll which still preserves its name, while all three kindreds possessed other islands south of the Pictish sphere of influence. Dunollie near Oban and Dunadd in the moss of Crinan were the strongholds of the kindred of Lorne, and of these it was the rock of Dunadd that was to become the effective capital of Dalriada and the best preserved of its monuments today. On its summit may still be seen the footprint carved into flat rock, on which a king placed his foot at his inauguration.

As in Ireland, there was a King of Kings, *Ard Righ* meaning High King. For the basis of a kinship group was descent from a common great-grandfather, and the head of a particular kin who was later to become known as the Clan Chief was in those days given the Gaelic title for king. Anyone was eligible for the office who was the son, grandson or great-grandson of a king, hence

St Columba's special status as the great-grandson of a High King of Ireland. But the other requirement was that the candidate must be without blemish, for the office had been since pagan times a sacred one, as it was to remain throughout Christendom. Another strange relic of the remote Indo-Aryan past was the continuing belief that the truth has a magic of its own, and can destroy those who flout it. A king was deposed during this period for being untruthful, just as a Highland chief of a later age was to be deposed for his blemishes.

While nothing like this sort of information is available for the much more numerous society of Pictland, it does seem certain that the succession to the Pictish kingship had evolved differently. The Picts had been the earliest Celtic people by far to settle in this land, and they had intermarried with the aboriginal stock to the extent that their language had been affected by it. It seems likely that the pre-Celtic inhabitants practised matriarchy as so many other early societies did, and this would have enabled the proto-Picts to obtain property by marriage as easily as by the sword. But in adopting a matriarchal system of royal succession they were exposing themselves to the risk of a similar take-over, and this was precisely what occurred when Kenneth Mac Alpin of Dalriada obtained the Pictish throne, as much by matrilinear descent as by conquest.

This was one of the two events that gave a new direction to the development of a clan society in Scotland. The other was the Norse invasion which began shortly before it, and continued for long after.

CHAPTER TWO

Evolution of the Clans

The Celtic peoples had entered Scotland from the south, to be followed by the Romans centuries later, and by Angles many hundreds of years later still. Both the Romans and the Angles had tried to penetrate beyond the narrow neck of Scotland formed by the Forth and Clyde rivers, but although they had achieved brief successes there they had won no lasting foothold. In the islands and among the mountains and eastern valleys north of that narrow waist an immemorial way of life had been able to evolve with relatively little outside interference.

Adventurous spirits had sailed in their tiny craft to discover the storm-swept Faroe Islands and Iceland beyond. They found both uninhabited, perfect retreats in which monks could reflect on the stupendous works of God, undisturbed by man. Nobody supposed that any danger threatened this society from the direction of the curdled sea: it could only menace them by land from the south. There was no known ship that could make a long journey across the wide northern oceans carrying a sufficiently large party of armed men.

Then they began to arrive, literally out of the blue, shortly before the year 800. By this time Iona possessed a library containing much of the erudition of the western world, besides its own chronicle. The beautiful illuminated Gospels now known as the Book of Kells were almost certainly nearing completion in the island's monastery. In St Maolrubha's foundation on the Applecross peninsula to the north there were probably other native chronicles unfolding. But the raiders were illiterate as well as pagan, and no books have been found amongst the loot they carried away from the monasteries they sacked, only the precious metals and jewels from their covers. The Scottish chronicles of this age vanished in the holocaust, though not before they had been consulted by Irish annalists whose records were more fortunate. The uncompleted Book of Kells was moved to the safety of the Columban monastery in Ireland from which it now derives its name.

The Viking raiders were a branch of the Germanic peoples,

like the Angles who had previously assaulted Scotland from the south. The invention of the keel around the year 600 enabled them to make the long journey from the Norwegian fjords, and it is thought that a rise in population there was a principal impulse, sending them in search of further food supplies. Undefended monasteries filled with priceless works of piety and art were naturally their easiest targets, and these suffered terribly: and since a monastery was maintained by a clan in many instances, the centre of its wealth, its devotion and its learned men, much of this tribal society had its heart torn out before its limbs were scratched.

The monastery's external links were frequently severed also, as the delicate fabric of civilisation in a savage world was torn to shreds. This was the age of the great Celtic scholars, Dicuil the geographer and Dungal who wrote a learned work on the eclipse of the sun, as well as the greatest luminary of all, John Scotus. Such men began to abandon ravaged or threatened monasteries, to receive a welcome at the court of Charlemagne; a brain drain that was remarked upon at the time: 'almost the whole people, despising the dangers of the sea, migrate with their crowd of philosophers to our shores.'

The Viking raids soon led to extensive Norse settlement, and in the Northern Isles the ancient Celtic tribal structure was obliterated for ever, leaving them Scandinavian to this day. In Shetland two relics survive which suggest the elegance and the conservatism of the aristocratic society that perished there. One is a collection of finely decorated silver objects, including the only silver spoon to have been found in Europe from this age. They were hidden in the church on St Ninian's isle, though they were not necessarily Church property. The other is the collection of inscriptions carved on stone monuments, using a form of writing called ogam, which had been devised in Ireland in the fourth century. The key to this alphabet is preserved in a Gaelic hand-book of learning that was used by the Filid, but in Shetland it was used to carve inscriptions in a pre-Celtic language, and they have never been deciphered.

The Norsemen also settled densely in the Long Island of the Outer Hebrides, where Gaelic had probably been heard little before their arrival, although today it is a bastion of Gaelic culture. Here, as in the mainland areas that the Norsemen occupied, a Celtic language and tribal structure returned in later centuries, and the descendants of the Vikings became integrated in it.

On the whole, it was the fjord folk from Norway who assaulted the northern Celtic realms, but in 839 a Danish host invaded Pictland and wiped out much of its royal house and aristocracy in an overwhelming defeat. At this time the King of Dalriada was Kenneth Mac Alpin, who was menaced by the Norsemen sailing down the seaways of the Hebrides. Iona lay in ruins, but many of its precious relics had been saved, and these were now divided between those that were sent to Ireland for safety, and others which King Kenneth brought to sanctify a new religious centre at Dunkeld, far from the threatened coast. From the central Highlands Kenneth set out to consolidate as much as he could of the remaining Celtic territories, setting himself up as the first king of both the Scots and the Picts. There is little doubt that the Pictish laws of matrilinear succession helped him to secure recognition among the demoralised Picts.

The gradual fusion of peoples whose earliest encounters had been so unfriendly must have been assisted by the gradual conversion of the Norse pagans to Christianity. In this the Celtic Church had an exceptional record, in that it showed characteristics of pacifism and tolerance deeply embedded in Indo-Aryan beliefs; not nearly so noticeably in the history of the three Semitic religions, Judaism, Christianity and Islam. The story of the Celtic Church contains no persecution.

When, by contrast, Olaf Trygvasson, the first Norwegian king to be converted, brought the Christian message to his country, he used the threat of torture and death as his principal form of persuasion. Visiting Orkney in 995, he said briefly to Sigurd the Earl, 'it is my wish that you should be baptised, and all those under you. Otherwise you will die here at once, and I shall carry fire and sword through the islands.' But whereas Norway was still a devoutly pagan country at this time, the Norsemen who had settled in the Boar Islands were living amongst a Christian population whom they had conquered, and probably a very high proportion of them had already been converted by gentler means. At any rate, King Olaf had no need to carry out his threat.

This episode illustrates a novel feature of the situation. Scotland was now the crucible between Ireland and Scandinavia, enriched by the vitality of the one and the ancient civilisation of the other, as the stimulating surge of commerce and conflict swept round the coast of the embattled kingdom of the Picts and Scots. By the time Olaf Trygvasson paid his threatening visit, the earldom of Orkney had emerged as a major power in its strategic position on the busy waterways. The Scandinavians were builders of towns and trading ports to an extent that the Celtic peoples had never been. They established a kingdom of Dublin, and the ruling houses there, in Orkney and in Scotland became intermarried.

Tough Norse rulers sometimes found themselves intimidated by Celtic women of the kind that had impressed Greeks and Romans so much over a thousand years earlier, the breed of Boudicca and Maebh of Connacht. When Earl Sigurd of Orkney, whom Olaf Trygvasson had threatened, debated whether to cross the Pentland Firth and attack King Findlaec of Moray, his mother scoffed: 'I would have reared you in my wool-basket if I had known you expected to live for ever. It is fate that governs a man's life, not his comings and goings, and it is better to die with honour than live in shame.'

This redoubtable lady was the daughter of an Irish king. Once, when the Norsemen carried off an Irish princess together with a number of other damsels whom they planned optimistically to add to the comforts of home, she not only committed suicide herself, but persuaded all her attendant maidens to do the same. So many embellishments became attached to the story (by 1070 Adam of Bremen had inflated the number of martyred virgins to 11,000) that in the end many people concluded it was entirely apocryphal. But if the Norsemen did make up the story, it could only be because it encapsulated their experience of the Celtic female. By the twelfth century the princess was venerated by the converted Norsemen as one of their most powerful saints, and a visiting Dane wrote: 'Bergen is the leading town in the country, adorned with a royal castle and renowned for the reliquaries of the holy virgins. For there rests Saint Sunniva, her entire body enshrined in the cathedral.'

In the southlands of the Norse earldom of Orkney that have become known as Sutherland there was a particularly formidable Pictish matriarch called Frakok who conducted a resistance movement against the invaders until they finally burned her to death in her stronghold in the region of Kildonan. Another trenchant woman of this age was Gormlada, the wife of the High King of Ireland, Brian Boru, until she left him to plot his ruin with implacable hatred. Gormlada was also the mother of Sigtrygg, the Norse King of Dublin, and when she was inciting him and Earl Sigurd of Orkney to unite in an attack on Brian Boru, she offered her hand in marriage to Sigurd as an unsavoury bait. It could hardly have been this that lured him to the Battle of Clontarf in 1014, but come he did, and both he and Brian Boru met their deaths on that fatal field. How delighted Gormlada must have been, Brian Boru slain and herself still free to marry whom she would. Whether or not Maebh of Connacht was an historical person, Gormlada certainly was, and her career helps to make credible the story of Maebh a thousand years earlier.

But despite the inexhaustible fascination of Celtic women down the ages, it is necessary now to turn to their menfolk. Those of pagan Europe had attracted comment by wearing tight trousers at a time when other Mediterranean males favoured the tunic. After the Romans had introduced the tunic and toga into Britain, however, the unconquered aristocracy of Ireland were so eccentric as to adopt the Roman fashion in a modified form. This dress was brought to Dalriada in Scotland as the *leine*, a Gaelic term for a light-coloured shirt, generally of linen which reached almost to the knee, and consequently resembled the Roman *tunica*. In Ireland it was decorated with marks of rank, for the king wore seven stripes on his, one of them purple: and such was the respect for learning that the *ollamh* or man of learning wore six, excluding only the royal purple. There is no evidence that these marks of distinction were also used in Scotland, but the toga was to reappear here in the form of the plaid.

The Norsemen by contrast had arrived from the cold north in their longships wearing shaggy woollen cloaks and trousers that either covered the whole leg or reached to the knee with gartered stockings below. Underneath they were dressed in shirts, and in underpants that sometimes reached to their ankles. In Ireland and Scotland they did not change to the Gaelic fashion copied from the Romans, so that when King Magnus of Norway did so as late as about 1100, his bizarre conduct earned him the title of Magnus Barelegs.

Magnus was killed during his invasion of Ireland in 1109, to earn his place in Ossianic legend. The warrior bands who operated outside the tribal framework had become immortal heroes of tale and poem. They were supposed to have perished before the coming of St Patrick to Ireland, leaving only the aged Ossian, son of Finn, to question the Saint about his new religion. The conversations between the two men, in which Ossian extolled the old pagan virtues of his people, were to survive in Gaelic ballads to modern times, which makes them unique in European balladry for the antiquity as well as the seriousness of their themes. But after the Norse invasions the Ossianic heroes were brought to life again, to engage in combat with Magnus Barelegs and to defeat him.

By this time the consequences of the Battle of Clontarf in

Ireland a hundred years earlier had become fully apparent. The death of the High King Brian Boru in the hour of victory had been followed by a power vacuum in which no Gaelic leader came so near to uniting his country. The fatal inability of the Celtic people to combine in an organised manner, noticed long before by classical authors, was about to leave them a prey to new, nearer and even more ruthless conquerors. In consequence, the Gaelic society of Scotland became less and less effectively underpinned by the parent nation that had engendered it.

Meanwhile the rich northern earldom of Orkney entered into the plenitude of its power. Earl Sigurd possessed an Irish mother: he married a daughter of Malcolm II, King of the Picts and Scots. So his son, who was to become known as Earl Thorfinn the Mighty, was the product of two generations of Celtic mothers, with a claim to the High Kingship in both Ireland and Scotland.

He stood at an apex of the new society called in Gaelic the Foreigner-Gaels, a vigorous cross-breed in which it had often been an invading Norse male who met his match in a Celtic consort. This helps to explain why the Gaelic language prevailed over such a large area of Scotland conquered by the Vikings, even those such as the isle of Lewis in which Gaelic had not been planted before the Norse conquest. It was the tongue that children of mixed stock learned from their mothers while their fathers were sea-roving. This did not occur in Shetland and Orkney, perhaps because the settlers there brought their women-folk from Scandinavia with them in far larger numbers.

But Thorfinn the Mighty himself spent several of his formative years at the Gaelic court of his grandfather Malcolm II: for King Malcolm reigned for twenty years after Thorfinn's father, Earl Sigurd, had perished on the field of Clontarf. So Thorfinn was able to become acquainted with his uncle, Findlaec of Moray, with whom Earl Sigurd had bickered, and with Findlaec's son, Macbeth, whose mother was Malcolm II's sister. One of the great Norse rulers of the age can be pictured consorting amicably with his Gaelic relatives; and so he did throughout a long lifetime, with one notable exception. And the story of all these individuals is of more than sensational interest because it marked a fundamental turning-point in Scottish history, and led directly to the development of the clan organisation that has lasted into modern times.

That extremely tough King, Malcolm II, had murdered his predecessor, and went on to kill off as many rival claimants of the Scottish royal house as he could. He desired to secure the crown exclusively for his own descendants, despite the ancient Celtic rule of succession known as tanistry. This was designed to ensure that the crown always passed to an experienced adult, who might be a brother or a cousin, descendants of different branches of the royal house taking their turn later. It evidently did not always succeed well in practice, and Malcolm II had a good case for changing the rules, though his methods are less defensible.

The complication was that he possessed no sons, so that if he were to succeed in his intentions the crown must pass through one of his daughters to a grandson. His senior grandson was Thorfinn of Orkney, but he possessed another called Duncan by his younger daughter, who had married Crinan, Abbot of Dunkeld. By this time some of the Celtic monasteries which had not been destroyed by the Vikings had grown into centres of great power and wealth, whose abbots did not necessarily practise celibacy. The Abbot of Dunkeld — where the relics of St Columba were preserved — was evidently a fit match for a High King's daughter. But his son Duncan was still junior to Thorfinn by any rule of succession that might be devised.

The details of what occurred after Malcolm II's death are worth recalling, not simply because Shakespeare wrote a play about them which misrepresents every person and event in the story. What gives them importance is that they led to the removal of the organs of Church and State from the lands of the Gael and the Foreigner-Gael, just when these might have superceded the old tribal organisation of society. For centuries afterwards the people of the old Scotland north of the Forth-Clyde waist fell back on a structure based on the simple and well-tried loyalty of their kindreds, as they once again resisted submission to foreign conquest, this time based on a usurped authority.

The High King Malcolm II did not belong to the senior branch of the royal house, which became the principal target in his attempt to secure the crown for his own descendants. By the time he died in 1034 only a female member of it remained alive, named Gruoch, with her baby son. Her husband had probably been one of Malcolm's victims, but she found safety when King Macbeth of Moray married her, the more surprisingly since he was Malcolm's II's nephew and tanist heir to the High Kingship. By the law of tanistry the son of a king's sister was senior to those of a king's daughter.

When Malcolm II died, Gruoch's son was the senior heir of the Scottish royal house, though it was impossible for him to succeed since he was only a child. But Malcolm had murdered so many of his relatives that the crown was bound to pass through a woman. Macbeth of Moray was the legitimate claimant by the law of tanistry, Thorfinn of Orkney by descent from the previous king, but for some reason that remains mysterious they both permitted the crown to pass to their junior cousin Duncan, son of the Abbot of Dunkeld. Duncan reigned for six years, during which he invaded England where he was defeated. Next he quarrelled with Thorfinn of Orkney.

The Boar Islands came under the sovereignty of Norway, but the possessions of the earldom included the mainland territory of Caithness and the coastal plain beyond that was known as its Sutherland. For this Duncan demanded tribute, and when Thorfinn refused the King brought an army north, which does not appear to have penetrated beyond the Kyle of Sutherland before Thorfinn swept down upon it. The Saga of the Orkney Earls was composed later and it makes the mistake of calling the Scottish King Karl, but it may not err in its other details. Duncan, it relates, 'raised the army from the whole of the south of Scotland, both from the east and from the west, and south as far as Kintyre. The whole army he summoned against Earl Thorfinn, and they met at Tarbetness in the south of the Moray Firth. There was a great battle, and the Scots had by far the larger army. Karl had his standard borne against Thorfinn. There was then a great struggle; and the upshot was that Karl took to flight; but some men say that he was killed.'

They were right; and more contemporary Gaelic sources say he was murdered in a smith's bothy in which he was skulking as he fled south through Macbeth's kingdom of Moray. An Irish annalist reported that he had been slain at an 'immature' age, which reveals how young he had been when he was allowed to inherit the crown.

He left two sons, Malcolm Ceann Mór (Big-Head) and Donald Bán, who must have been mere babies, so that they would have been incapable of succeeding even if they had possessed the right to do so. Among children, Gruoch's son was the incontestable heir. As it was, the old law of succession now prevailed rather than the new, and Macbeth rather than Thorfinn became High King of Scots. He and Gruoch had no children of their own, so that her son Lulach remained the sole heir of the senior branch of the royal family, just within the rules as great-grandson of Kenneth III.

Thorfinn did not contest Macbeth's accession, and the two cousins seem to have remained on friendly terms throughout the seventeen years of Macbeth's reign. These were described by the contemporary annalist as peaceful and prosperous years, so that Macbeth may well have been able to leave his kingdom for a pilgrimage to Rome. He was reported to have scattered money among the poor there; and since Thorfinn definitely visited Rome, it may be that the cousins travelled there together. The genuine piety of the two rulers is not in doubt. Thorfinn built the first cathedral in Orkney, while evidence survives of the grant that Macbeth and his wife made to the Devotees of God at Loch Leven. In naming Gruoch as *Regina Scotorum*, this grant preserves the earliest public act of a Scottish queen in the country's history, and it is rather different from those that Shakespeare invented for the character he called Lady Macbeth.

During these years Malcolm Big-Head, now known as Canmore, was being brought up in England, where Danish power had crumbled in the Saxon lands south of Northumbria after the death of Knud the Great. When Malcolm Canmore was old enough, he was brought north with a Saxon and Northumbrian army as a quisling claimant. At first Macbeth succeeded in repelling this foreign invasion, but finally he was surprised near Scone, where he seems to have been wounded. He made his way north, probably to rally the forces of his own kingdom of Moray, but he never reached there. At Lumphanan on Deeside he was killed in a skirmish.

Gruoch's son was twenty-six years old by this time, married, possessing a son, and unquestionably the legitimate heir. It was only required that he should be without blemish, and evidently he fulfilled this qualification also, because he was inaugurated as the High King Lulach. But eight months later he was killed in Strathbogie, 'treacherously slain' according to the Gaelic annalist. The year was 1058 and it is one of the most significant in Scottish history, for it marks the downfall of Gaelic sovereignty, exercised within the bounds of the ancient kingdom. The body of the last *Ard Righ* was carried to Iona for burial among his ancestors, while his descendants were to be numbered amongst the clansmen who fought their long losing battle for the recovery of his crown.

Canmore was as much a Gael by descent as Lulach had been, but he had not been reared as a Gael and he did not act like one. On his return he did marry Ingebjorg of the Orkney branch of the royal house, and it became possible that their son Duncan might replace the crown and seat of government where these had always belonged. But Canmore made a second marriage with the Saxon

Princess Margaret, sister of the Atheling, or Claimant, to the English throne. It was an empty claim since in the meantime England had been conquered by William of Normandy at the battle of Hastings in 1066.

Consequently the Scottish court became filled with English refugees, patronised by the English Queen, and surrounding the King with the same influence as he had enjoyed since his child-hood. Margaret had spent her own early years in Hungary, and being an extremely pious woman, she set out to plant the Euro-pean organisation of the Roman Church in Scotland in place of the Celtic Church; and being as formidable as she was pious, she succeeded. Just as the finest ornaments of pagan Celtic culture had crumbled in Europe before the might of Rome in the time of Julius Caesar, so did those of Celtic Christianity in the time of Margaret and her sons. Indeed, so well did they succeed that for centuries to come Scotland was resisting the claim that the whole country belonged to the diocese of York. As for the English archdiocese, a monastery was founded at Dunfermline by the Forth as a daughter house of Canterbury, and here, not on Iona of High Kings, Malcolm and Margaret were buried at their deaths.

In life, Malcolm Canmore had the temerity to espouse the cause of his wife's people against William the Conqueror. In 1070 he invaded England and the *Anglo-Saxon Chronicle* recorded that in Scotland 'even to this day there cannot be found a hamlet or even a hut without slaves and handmaids of the English race.' They were amply revenged. Two years later William invaded Scotland, brought Canmore to his knees in the ancient Pictish capital of Abernethy, and compelled him to recognise William as his overlord. So was created the fatal claim of the Kings of England that they were Lords Paramount of Scotland.

Almost as serious, William took Canmore's son and heir, Duncan, as a hostage to be brought up at the English court. Yet another King of Scots was to be reared abroad. Margaret can hardly have regretted this, for she had sons of her own, excluded from the throne by the existence of Duncan — boys with such un-Scottish names as Aethelred and Edgar, Alexander and David.

After a long reign Malcolm Canmore was killed in 1093 during an invasion of England. His wife Margaret died a few weeks later. There was an immediate reaction in Scotland with the slogan 'no more English influence', and in a brief revival of Celtic fortunes the late King's brother Donald Bàn was invested as sovereign. He was the heir by the old law of tanistry, he had not been reared as a child in England, and there is no evidence that he had been associated with Malcolm's court or policies. Certainly he now reversed them, as the *Anglo-Saxon Chronicle* noted: 'the Scots chose as King Donald, Malcolm's brother, and drove out all the English who were with King Malcolm before.'

But the Norman regime in England had not made a vassal of Malcolm and a hostage of his son Duncan in order to see their labours lost. He was brought north with an army and imposed on the Scots, who accepted him only 'on the condition that he should never again introduce English or French into the land.' But he was unable to honour these terms to the satisfaction of his countrymen, who murdered him and replaced Donald Bàn.

With Duncan out of the way, it was the opportunity for his younger half-brother to strike, Margaret's son Edgar. Invoking the aid of the hated Anglo-Normans, he seized his uncle Donald Bàn and blinded him. And so, in the year of 1097, the throne passed to the first of the usurping dynasty of the Margaretsons.

Of course the true royal line consisted of the descendants not of Queen Margaret, but of Queen Gruoch. The tanist line was that of the blinded King Donald Bàn, who left a daughter to continue his claim. If the succession was to be by direct descent henceforth, then it belonged to the line of the murdered King Duncan II, who left a son. By no means whatever could the sons of Margaret establish a legitimate claim to the Scottish throne except by wholesale murder of their relatives, which was consequently the course they adopted during the ensuing centuries.

From this fate the son of Lulach escaped by dying a natural death before Canmore was killed, without having left an heir. He even lived and died King of Moray, probably because the hated regime of Canmore was unable to penetrate so far into Gaeldom. But his death left Lulach's daughter in the same position that her grandmother Queen Gruoch had once occupied as heiress of the senior line. The steps which Canmore took to remedy this are not beyond doubt, but the distinguished genealogist Sir Iain Moncreiffe believes that this is what occurred.

Queen Margaret's eldest son was married to her, and was also invested as the last Abbot of Dunkeld, that rich and prestigious foundation of the Celtic Church. His utterly unsuitable name of Aethelred (especially as the Gaelic language possesses no *th* sound) was changed to Aodh, a most ancient name, favoured by High Kings of Ireland. This name ends in the *gh* sound that does not exist in the English language. Such fundamental differences as these have dictated the transformation of proper names when they have passed from one language to the other. For instance Son of Aodh is generally rendered Mackay in Scotland today, although the Irish Magee approximates more closely to the Gaelic original, when Aodh is placed in the genitive case.

Of course a marriage between Queen Margaret's eldest son and Queen Gruoch's grand daughter was the only possible way to legitimise the triple usurpation. But the greatest mystery in this case is that it was not her eldest son who succeeded but her second son Edgar, followed by his younger brothers. So the blood-royal of Gruoch's line never did hallow their take-over. On the other hand, it was invoked at their inauguration in a most curious manner. In the twelfth century the family of Aodh and Lulach's daughter were invested as Earls of what had been the southern Pictish kingdom of Fife, receiving with it the red lion of Scotland as their heraldic emblem, and the privilege of enthroning the Kings of Scots at Scone on their accession. So Scotland's senior clan had its origins, named either Duff or MacDuff. How it received this name is uncertain, but it is certainly the anglicised form of the name of Queen Gruoch's great-grandfather, a King of Scots who was killed in the year 967.

But before Clan Duff became such a pillar of the new establishment it made strenuous efforts to restore the old one. King Edgar reigned for ten years, then died unmarried: his brother Alexander followed him and died without leaving a legitimate heir in 1124. By this time their youngest brother David had been long domiciled in England, where he was premier baron, probably enjoying revenues which exceeded those of the Scottish crown. In Scotland the royal authority scarcely penetrated the northern world of mountains and islands in which the Celtic backlash gained its momentum.

Geography combined with the misfortunes of history to keep it a fragmented world, lacking any unifying central authority. In the north there was the powerful earldom of Orkney with its mainland territories. In the west King Godred Crovan held together a kingdom of Dublin, Man and the Isles until his death in Islay in 1095. In the eyes of a Norseman the Hebrides were the Southern Isles of Sudereys, which remained united to the Isle of Man for long after as the Bishopric of Sodor and Man; while Orkney remained within the diocese of Trondheim in Norway for centuries to come. The King of Norway claimed sovereignty over both, and it was to assert this paramount authority that Magnus Barelegs invaded Scotland in 1098, three years after

Godred Crovan's death and a year after Edgar became the first Margaretson King of Scots.

Edgar had no option but to recognise the Norwegian King's title to all the islands off western Scotland round which he could sail a ship with its rudder in place. Magnus had his ship dragged across the isthmus (which is Tarbert in Gaelic) of Kintyre, while he sat at the helm, and so added the entire Mull of Kintyre to his possessions. The episode illustrates the powerlessness of the usurping dynasty in the lands beyond the Forth and Clyde.

Here the ancient tribal structure of society developed a new lease of life, with the kingdom of Moray in northern Pictland as its most powerful base. In it King Lulach's grandson Angus was reigning when Margaret's youngest son David came from England in 1124 as the new King of Scots. The Gaelic annals recorded what happened to him six years later. '1130. A battle was fought between the men of Scotland and the men of Moray; and in it four thousand men of Moray fell, including their King Angus, the son of Lulach's daughter.' It was after this that David made such handsome concessions to the true heirs, creating the nephew of Angus Earl of Fife with his unique privileges. He also invested Malcolm, younger brother of King Angus, as Earl of Ross.

But he had closed the breach in Moray only to be faced by another that was opened by one of the Foreigner-Gaels of the west. His name was Somerled, from the Norse for Summer-Sailor, which is rather odd inasmuch as both his father and his grandfather had Gaelic names. Somerled married the daughter of Olaf the Black, King of Man, and granddaughter of Godred Crovan; and for himself he carved out a kingdom that included the islands from Bute in the south to Ardnamurchan in the north, with the mainland territories of Kintyre, Lorne and Argyll between — roughly the extent of the former kingdom of Dalriada. Next, King Somerled seized the Isle of Man from his uncle and finally, having taken a sister of Angus of Moray as his second wife, he espoused the cause of the dispossessed house of Lulach. In 1164 he landed an army on the banks of the Clyde near Renfrew, only to be defeated and killed.

Yet Somerled left powerful clans in the lands he conquered. His eldest son was named Dougall, which is Gaelic for Dark Foreigner, a suggestive epithet for one of Olaf the Black's grandsons. Dougall became King of the Isles, Lord of Argyll and Lorne, and progenitor of Clan MacDougall. From Somerled's second son descended not only the MacDonalds, MacAlisters and MacRuaris in the male line, but several other clans through marriage with heiresses of his house. The fragmentation of Somerled's kingdom into separate tribal lands illustrates well the way in which the clans evolved in the vacuum left by the missing crown.

With Clan Duff reconciled by a golden handshake and Somerled defeated, there were still the descendants of Canmore's eldest son Duncan II to reckon with. These had formidable assets. Their claim was incontestable, it passed exclusively through male heirs, and it would last longer than Lulach's line before it expired with the great-grandsons of a king, since King Duncan had belonged to a later generation. In 1181 the Gaels of the north rose in favour of his grandson Donald at a time when Galloway too was in revolt. It was not until 1187 that he was defeated and killed near Inverness, which merely transferred the claim to Duncan II's great-grandsons.

And now the whirligig of claimants brought in another Foreigner-Gael, for such the descendants of Thorfinn the Mighty must be called. His heir Earl Harald of Orkney would have had a good claim to the crown by descent, but for the rule that none beyond the great-grandsons of a king could inherit it. Harald remedied this by marrying Gormflaith, great-granddaughter of King Lulach, and invading Moray on behalf of her family. His earldom reached far down the Moray Firth: the kingdom of Moray in those days extended as far as Loch Duich in Ross, so that they were adjacent. It took King David's grandson eight years to extinguish that threat.

Then the elder of Duncan II's great-grandsons, who had been reared wholly in the Gaelic environment of Ireland and the Isles as the true king, was invited to the mainland in 1211, where he led a guerrilla campaign for over a year before he was captured. He was hung by the heels after being beheaded. It might have appeared that this could go on for ever, but in fact the end was near.

The catalyst was a powerful northern Gael who moved to the King's support against the next rebellion. This one was led by the younger of Duncan II's great-grandsons, acting in alliance with Lulach's great-grandson. The Celtic dynasts had reached the bottom of the barrel, and in 1215 both of these men were killed by the hereditary Abbot of the monastery of St Maolrubha at Applecross. Its lands were by now of vast extent and its abbots belonged to the ancient family of O'Beolan, whose present representative was known as Farquhar MacTaggart (an anglicised form of the Gaelic for Son of the Priest). Farquhar followed the custom of his pagan ancestors by cutting off the heads of the leaders, which he despatched to the King. His reward was to become the first Celtic magnate of the north to enjoy favours similar to those bestowed on Clan Duff. The earldom of Ross that had been bestowed on Lulach's grandson without buying the submission of his family was now handed to the Abbot of Applecross. In its fertile eastern plain he founded the Abbey of Fearn in 1230, where it is most probable that a worn effigy marks his place of burial. That is the year in which the legitimist cause was at last extinguished in a final uprising.

As if to celebrate this belated triumph, Queen Margaret the founder of the usurping dynasty was now canonised as a saint, while devout clergymen were comfortably endowed to compose a pious record of all that had occurred.

If this provides no other useful information, it certainly serves to underline the text that God's ways are not always as our ways. It carried the story back to the time of King Macbeth, who was depicted as a wicked adventurer: the fact that he had been a member of the royal house whose succession was according to the law of tanistry was entirely suppressed. Queen Gruoch was too embarrassing to mention at all, but her son Lulach was described as an idiot: although no king afflicted with such a blemish could possibly have been invested as High King. Canmore's eldest son Duncan II was dismissed as a bastard, despite William the Conqueror's formal recognition that he was the legitimate heir when he carried Duncan to England as a hostage.

Duncan II's son William had been named after the Conqueror, so that his disinherited line became known as the MacWilliams. In describing how these were wiped out in the final rising of 1230, they were dismissed briefly as 'certain wicked men of the race of MacWilliam.' Thus the chroniclers explained how the descendants of a saint had saved Scotland from the offspring of the lunatic, the bastard, and a varied assortment of evil men.

Meanwhile these descendants had been doing more to cement their power in the north than merely to smite the wicked and reward the faithful as opportunity offered. From the time when David came to Scotland in 1124, they pushed the efficient organisation of the feudal system further and further north by degrees, with its rules of ownership based on obligations of vassal services, its military power fanning out from a network of stone castles. Moray, the centre of disaffection, was largely cleared of its native inhabitants and planted with dependable people from the south.

Where did the evicted people go to? North of the earldom of Ross, west of the Caithness plains, there was a vast, barren land of mountains and inhospitable coast known as Strathnaver — and it is noteworthy that the very name Naver has probably survived from a pre-Celtic language. Here the Norsemen had planted settlements in the best anchorages they could find, such as Tongue and Eriboll which consequently still bear Norse names. The mountainous interior probably contained pockets of ancient inhabitants, some of them refugees from the Norse conquest of two centuries before, still speaking the moribund Pictish tongue. Two centuries later, Strathnaver was so populous with Mackays that they were said to be able to muster four thousand fighting men, while their chiefs were of such standing that they married into the families of O'Beolan and the Lord of the Isles. Assuredly these could not have been the descendants of a few outlandish Norsemen and provincial Picts, calling themselves the Sons of Aodh. It cannot be proved that the Mackays of Strathnaver came from Moray, but they must have come from somewhere, while the royal clan of Moray, after maintaining such a formidable opposition to the southern government, must have gone somewhere.

A few were allowed to stay, and a typically mysterious example of these is the family of Brodie. The name bears a close resemblance to the king-name of the Pictish sovereigns, Brude, and whether or not the Brodies actually belonged to the male line of the dynasty that was superceded by Kenneth Mac Alpin in 843, they were certainly an important Pictish family that had kept its head down since then. They did nothing to aid or abet the dispossessed descendants of Alpin's house in Moray, which is the more understandable if they had inherited an ancient hostility to the Gaelic cause. There must have been many in the former northern Pictish kingdom who had done so, in a society governed by such long-lasting traditional attitudes. Naturally these would be the people left in Moray during the clearance of the 1160s, and the Brodies were amongst them.

In the circumstances it is interesting to observe the behaviour of the Brodies during the next eight hundred years, since it more or less exactly resembles the way they had ensured their survival in earlier times. Continuing to live in the lands of Brodie near Inverness in an unbroken male line, century after century, they never played a part in public events commensurate with their social importance; and when public events erupted on their doorstep they drew up the drawbridge and closed the shutters until the emergency was past. As a result, Ninian Brodie of Brodie lives in Brodie Castle still, near the blasted heath on which Macbeth was said to have met the witches. Few families in Europe can show a longer continuity in one place, and few Scottish chiefships are of more mysterious origin.

In the plantation of Moray the Brodies found themselves surrounded by new neighbours, and amongst the nearest were (and still are) a family from France who became known in Scotland as Comyns or Cummings. Their story is a complete contrast to that of the Brodies. The grandson of one of William the Conqueror's Norman knights came north with King David, who appointed him Chancellor of Scotland. His nephew Richard Cumming married the granddaughter and heiress of Canmore's brother, the blinded King Donald Bàn, and this brought him into the Celtic world of Badenoch and Lochaber. By the thirteenth century the Cummings held the three Celtic earldoms of Menteith, Angus and Buchan by a succession of jackpot marriages, as well as the hereditary office of Constable of Scotland. But they went on to make a royal marriage that brought them within reach of the crown, narrowly missed it, and came to rest beside the Brodies with the consolation prize of a baronetcy.

The emergence of Clan Cumming in the north illustrates the way in which the Norman infiltration went hand in hand with the planting of the feudal system in tribal Scotland. In England there had been a Norman Conquest, in which the old English aristocracy had been virtually wiped out. There was no such conquest in Scotland, and the Anglo-Normans who came in search of grants of land and high offices could only obtain any of the thirteen earldoms by marriage with an heiress. These earldoms had once been Celtic kingdoms belonging to branches of the old royal house, and a Norman who acquired one by marriage saw his children reared by a Celtic mother. So it was in lesser properties, until the Normans who gave foreign names to clans north of the Forth gradually acquired the blood and culture of the people amongst whom they had settled.

For instance, there was one called William de la Haye, who arrived in about 1160 and became Butler of Scotland. That, of course, was a mere stepping-stone to a Celtic heiress, whose son David Hay was able to marry higher still, into the ancient family of Strathearn. So the third generation of Hays in Scotland retained only a quarter measure of Norman blood, while two generations of children had been indoctrinated with the difference between descent from a foot-loose mercenary from Normandy and from the Seed of Alpin. The Chief of Clan Hay still lives in the province in which the first heiress was won over eight hundred years ago.

Sometimes expectant Normans had to wait around in the south for a generation or two before a Celtic heiress became available. For instance the first knight in Scotland bearing the French name La Frézelière appears in the records as early as 1160, but although that was a time of great opportunity during the resettlement of Moray, it was not until a later century that his descendants began to spread their wings in Macbeth's kingdom as the burgeoning Clan Fraser. It took the Sinclairs even longer to reach the far north, although today their name is the commonest in both Orkney and Caithness. Henry of St Clair in Normandy possessed lands in the Lothians as early as 1162, yet it was not until 1379 that Sir Henry Sinclair fell heir to the earldom of Thorfinn the Mighty. That was a prize worth waiting for.

Others won even greater prizes, and some (unlike the Cummings) managed to retain them. The most notable of these were to be the descendants of Walter, whom King David appointed Steward of Scotland, an office from which the royal Clan Stewart takes its name. Closely associated with the Stewarts in their good fortune were the Bruces, who retained the name of their place of origin, Brix in Normandy. The first Robert Bruce came over with the Conqueror, the second accompanied David to Scotland; and it appears paradoxical in retrospect that a succession of Robert Bruces (of all names) provide such a perfect example of the Anglo-Norman adventurers who explored Scotland for lucrative pickings without intermarrying with the locals or developing local attachments.

When King David invaded England in 1138, Bruce expostulated: 'when, I ask you, have you ever found such fidelity in the Scots that you can so rashly renounce the counsel of the English and the aid of the Normans? You are turning your arms against the very men to whose support you owe your kingdom.' Even the 6th Robert Bruce preferred the post of Chief Justice of England to the hazards of the Scottish lottery. But the seventh married the heiress to the Celtic earldom of Carrick, and so his sons were brought up in her castle of Turnberry, and evidently their mother did not rear them in her wool basket. So it was that the 8th Robert Bruce, despite such unpromising antecedents, emerged as the patriot king.

There was one area into which the Anglo-Normans did not penetrate during this period and that was the far west, much of it belonging to the Norwegian crown and all difficult of access.

Some of the clans here traced a Norse ancestry, some a Gaelic one, but each was a blend and behind both lay the Pictish stock and the blood of pre-Celtic people as well. For instance the isle of Skye had belonged to Pictland, not to the Scottish kingdom of Dalriada, so that Columba required an interpreter there. It was conquered by the Norsemen, and Clan MacLeod traced their origins from Liotr, a younger son of Olaf the Black, King of Man and the Northern Isles. But this is later than the Battle of Stamford Bridge, in which Olaf's father King Godred Crovan was among those defeated by Harold of England in 1066. King Godred fled, carrying with him the fabric of Byzantine origin that is still preserved in Dunvegan Castle as the Fairy Flag of the MacLeods. This talisman alone gives them an older pedigree than their descent from Liotr.

In Morvern by contrast, a mainland peninsula that had also been Pictish, the Macleans traced their descent from the Gaelic Gillean, descendant through the Abbots of Lismore from the Kings of Dalriada. Gillean the name-father of the Macleans was not living before the thirteenth century, yet his ancestry can be traced back to the earliest historical High King of Ireland, Niall of the Nine Hostages, who was reigning in the middle of the fifth century.

Other clans of the west sprang directly from the old monastic houses, whose hereditary abbots in some cases had a pedigree as royal as Columba's. One clan is actually called Macnab, Son of the Abbot, by descent from the lay abbots of St Fillan near Loch Earn. The Saint himself was a prince of the house of Dalriada who died in 703 and may well be the progenitor of the Macnabs.

In the case of the Mackinnons, the clan took the actual name of the prince of the house of Alpin called Fingon, who was amongst the founder's kin of Iona, and its members maintained their religious office at intervals to the last. In the fourteenth century Fingon Mackinnon, brother of the Chief, was Abbot of Iona. The last Abbot of Iona was Iain Mackinnon, and the memorial effigy erected there for him after his death in 1500 has survived where so many others have perished. Sometimes a clan with such religious origins preserved a precious relic of the Celtic Church, though many of these vanished at the Reformation. The Macleays, for example, were custodians of the pastoral staff of Moluag, a British saint from Bangor, while others preserved the bells without clappers that Celtic monks used to strike to summon the faithful to prayer.

As for the Gaelic learning which had been divided between

secular *ollamh* and Christian cleric, this engendered one of Scotland's most particular clans. In Ireland the O'Dalys had become established in their bardic functions by the twelfth century, when one of them was described as the principal man of learning in both Ireland and Scotland. One of his great-grandsons became known as *Muireadhach Albanach* (Murach of Scotland) because he settled in the Lennox, where he became the founder of the longest literary dynasty in the land. It was not until the nineteenth century that the well of the MacMhuirichs ran dry. Naturally such people became clients of powerful patrons, and while Murach himself composed an elegy for the Earl of Lennox who died in 1217, his descendants attached themselves to the Lords of the Isles, and to the MacDonalds of Clanranald after the abolition of the Lordship. That is why so many MacMhuirichs were to be found in the Hebrides in modern times, their name corrupted to Currie.

The creation of the Lordship of the Isles, and then its destruction, were two of the most crucial events in the history of the clans of the west. It had its origins in the way the MacDougalls, the senior line of King Somerled, resolved the problem of their double allegiance, to the King of Norway for their island kingdom and to the King of Scots for their mainland lordships. The Scottish King tried to persuade Ewen MacDougall to repudiate his allegiance to Norway, and Ewen had the integrity to refuse, offering instead to resign his Norse fiefs. But this would simply have lost them to Scotland, so the King brought a fleet to the Firth of Lorne in 1249 in an attempt to secure them by force. Ewen preserved his honour by retiring to Lewis, where he could not be made a party to the proceeding, while the King fell ill and died on the isle of Kerrera.

He was succeeded by Alexander III, last of the Margaretson kings in the male line. Still a child at his accession, it was not until 1261 that he sent an embassy to the great King Haakon IV of Norway, seeking to purchase the Scottish isles. Haakon replied by complaining (justly) of the raids that had for so long disturbed the peace of his Hebridean realm. Instead of agreeing to part with it he decided on a show of strength, and prepared a great fleet which reached Orkney in August 1263.

There his subjects dutifully joined him. But the MacDougall Chief declined to serve his Norwegian sovereign against his Scottish one, and when Haakon reminded him of his oath of fealty he surrendered his island possessions into the King's hands. The scene is an extremely impressive one. Ewen was described by a contemporary as 'an energetic and most elegant knight:' Haakon, one of Norway's greatest kings, was now an old man. He dismissed Ewen with generous gifts and Ewen undertook that he would attempt to make peace between the two kings since he could not serve them both. He had behaved with tact and honour on both occasions when one of these kings had tried to launch him against the other, and when the inevitable moment of choice faced him, he followed the same course as Farquhar MacTaggart had done.

The Norse fleet sailed south through the Hebrides, rounded the Mull of Kintyre and lay off Arran while negotiations were opened between the two sovereigns. Alexander conceded Haakon's right to the Hebrides, but claimed the islands in the Clyde — Bute, Arran and the Cumbraes. The talks dragged on while summer passed and the provisions of Haakon's fleet were spent. He had come too late, an old man, the tide of history against him, and now the autumn weather. A succession of gales battered his ships, the armed force that he had landed ashore was set upon by the Scots: he limped away through the stormy Minch with his tattered fleet to die in Orkney in December.

So the 3rd MacDougall Chief, the most prominent Gael of his day, remained in possession of his islands and his mainland provinces as the loyal supporter of the Scottish King. His principal strongholds were the castles of Dunstaffnage and Dunollie on the Firth of Lorne, and although the MacDougalls later lost Dunstaffnage, the present MacDougall Chief still lives in a home beside the ruins of Dunollie on their rock north of Oban. After Ewen had been succeeded by his son Alasdair as 4th Chief, Argyll was erected into a sheriffdom with Alasdair as the first Sheriff to be appointed.

But by this time one of the greatest disasters of Scottish history had occurred. Alexander III's son died in 1284. The King was only forty-two years old, and being a widower he remarried in 1285. It was essential that he should produce another son, since there was no other direct heir apart from his daughter married to the King of Norway, and a baby Margaret to whom this couple had given birth. But on a stormy night in March 1286 Alexander III fell over a cliff as he was riding from Inverkeithing to join his wife, and his body was found lifeless on the shore below. The baby Margaret was brought from Norway to be Queen, and she died on the journey. There was no longer an incontestable heir to the Scottish crown, nor any living person within the degree of great-grandson of a King of Scots. In addition, every serious claimant was a subject of the King of England.

The descendants of Margaret and Canmore had proved on the whole to be able and effective rulers, welding their kingdom out of many disparate elements, overcoming the disability that they were usurpers, gaining the support of the most powerful lobbies in the land or crushing them. In the chaos that followed Alexander III's death the country became fragmented again, and just when the clan organisation of society might have faded away at last, it took on a new lease of life as the central government weakened once more.

CHAPTER THREE

The Legacy of Bruce

The fatality of the situation was the claim of the King of England that he was Lord Paramount of Scotland, a claim based on the submission of Malcolm Canmore to William the Conqueror at Abernethy two hundred years earlier. It was a relationship based on the feudal system, the very organisation that Margaret's sons had used to cement their authority in Scotland. They had brought up Anglo-Normans from the south who did homage to them for their offices and lands, and who in turn made vassals of the native peoples on their estates, creating a nexus of rights and obligations that often cut across the older tribal loyalties. A Bruce had reminded a King of Scots in 1130 that all of them, including the King, owed their positions in Scotland in the last resort to the King of England.

The Roman Church which Margaret and her sons had done so much to establish in Scotland provided another reinforcement for the English claim. Throughout Christendom it was recognised that an independent sovereign was one who had been annointed with holy oil in the manner in which Zadok the priest had annointed Solomon King, and no Scottish monarch had ever undergone this ceremony. At Alexander III's coronation he had sat on the sacred stone at Scone while a shenachie recited to him the fanciful pedigree of his ancestors in Gaelic that he could not understand. The representative of Clan Duff had assisted him to his seat. The Gaels had given Scotland immensely ancient trappings of sacred kingship, but even if the King of England had not claimed a feudal right of overlordship, it is doubtful whether the Kings of Scots would have been recognised at this time as equivalent to any of the ritually consecrated sovereigns of Christendom.

Now that the throne was vacant and all the serious contestants were English subjects, the Scots invited the King of England to arbitrate between them, and Edward I agreed to do so after he had been formally recognised as Lord Paramount. The choice lay between the descendants of David I through his youngest son David, who left only daughters. Of these, John Balliol descended from the eldest daughter so he was chosen as the undoubted heir to the throne. From a younger daughter descended the Bruces.

King John Balliol had not been reared with any expectation of kingship and he knew little about Scotland. It was easy for Edward of England to treat him as a puppet, and he yielded to the temptation: which proved to be the one fatal error in the career of an outstanding sovereign. For the country had been unified by the dynasty of Margaret and Canmore to the extent that its inhabitants would not easily surrender their independence, and endowed with the military machinery of the feudal system that enabled them to defend it. The very weapon that had been imported from England to reduce the Scots to obedience was to be the one that finally tipped the scales in their favour, and saved them from the fate of Ireland.

But it was a long, hard struggle, in which the much-despised King John provided a breathing-space for over three years before he finally rejected the demands of Edward I and was deposed. When a Scottish court judgment was taken on appeal to London and he was ordered to appear and justify it there, he refused. Then he was ordered to bring a Scottish army to fight for Edward in France, and responded by making an alliance with the French King. In March 1296 Edward came north to storm Scotland's principal port of Berwick and massacre its men, women and children. At Dunbar he annihilated the Scottish army: at Brechin he witnessed John Balliol's abdication. So a not ignoble name passed out of Scottish history leaving no clan behind, though Balliol College at Oxford has given it eternal fame. Edward carried away the sacred stone of Scone to London, where it remains encased in the coronation chair in Westminster Abbey. Evidently he had decided to do away with the vassal monarchy of Scotland altogether, and incorporate the country in his empire with the same status as his French provinces enjoyed. Ex-King John was kept in England for a few years, then allowed to retire to his estate of Bailleul in France, where he died in the year before Bannockburn.

But Edward found his real authority in Scotland confined to the English-speaking Lowlands south of the Forth, and to a few strongholds scattered about the land. Resistance came, as it had done in the reigns of Canmore's sons, from the old Scotland north of the Forth, and also from the former British territories of the south-west. Here the inhabitants were designated sometimes in Gaelic as Galbraith (Foreigner Briton), sometimes in English as Wallace (Welsh). The son of a Wallace knight named

William presently joined forces with the son of a knight of Moray named Andrew, and between them they inflicted such damage on the regime of King Edward that they were able to announce to foreign governments: 'the kingdom of Scotland, thanks be to God, has been recovered by war from the power of the English.'

But in referring to the kingdom, they perforce spoke in the name of their ordained King John Balliol, and as rivals for the crown the Bruces took no part in this patriotic uprising. A second time Edward returned to Scotland to stamp it out. Andrew of Moray had died by now, probably of his wounds. William Wallace was finally captured, and taken to London to suffer a horrible death.

By this time there was a clan alignment ranged on the side of the legitimate Balliol line, based on dynastic alliances and uniting the greatest houses of east and west Scotland north of the Forth. John Cumming was married to ex-King John's sister, so that their son John, known as the Red Cumming, stood next to the Balliols in the royal succession. And Alasdair, Chief of the great Clan MacDougall, was married to the elder Cumming's sister. At a time when central government was non-existent, the deposed royal house enjoyed a vast network of tribal support, ranging from Buchan and Badenoch westwards to Argyll, Galloway and the isles. So any Bruce claimant to the Scottish crown had not only Edward of England to reckon with, but the most considerable power in the former kingdom of the Picts and Scots.

The asset of the Bruces by contrast was a man of genius, evidently guided by his Celtic mother into very different habits of thought and action from those of his Bruce forbears. By the time it was obvious that the principle of legitimacy was not going to cure the distresses of Scotland, Bruce took the field. But first he tried to reach an understanding with the only man in Scotland whose claim to the throne was senior to his own, the most powerful native in the land besides — the Red Cumming. The two men had been at each others' throats once before when they arranged a tryst at Dumfries in February 1306. William Wallace had been murdered in London the previous August: he had been given a trial in Westminster Hall, but since he was not among the Scots who had sworn their allegiance to the English King, it was still murder.

Now another murder occurred, equally tragic for Scotland. In circumstances that remain mysterious, Bruce slew Cumming at the very altar of the Franciscan church in which they met. If he had intended beforehand to rid himself of such a dangerous rival, he would scarcely have planned an act of sacrilege in addition, one that led to his excommunication by the Church and that united the most powerful network of clans in Scotland against him.

The die was cast by this dreadful act. A few weeks later Bruce had himself crowned at Scone. The sacred stone was gone, but the sister of the Earl of Fife exercised the ancient office of Clan Duff by placing a circle of gold on King Robert's head. It is a fascinating example of the clannish sense of duty, for her husband was none other than the Cumming Earl of Buchan, Bruce's enemy. It also led to a gruesome example of the English King's savagery. After he had captured the Countess of Buchan, he kept her suspended in a cage from the walls of a castle in full public view.

The most remarkable support that Robert Bruce found came from the Church, whose leaders now stood outside the clan network for the good reason that the clergy of the new order kept vows of celibacy, so that they could not belong to dynasties of Macnabs and MacTaggarts. King Robert's coronation was attended by the Bishops of St Andrews, Glasgow and Moray, besides the Abbot of Scone: and it was the Bishop of Glasgow who had the assurance to absolve King Robert after the Pope had excommunicated him for the sacrilegious murder of the Red Cumming. Whatever the Pope would have done with him for this, Edward I imprisoned him in irons with the Bishop of St Andrews when he caught them. King Robert's brother Nigel he hanged, together with two Celtic Earls, Atholl and Lennox, who had rallied to the Bruce cause. Within the year Edward of England was dead himself, but not before he had sown seeds of Anglophobia in the north that continued to bear poisoned fruit for centuries. He had ordered the term 'Hammer of the Scots' to be inscribed on his tomb and it was a fit epitaph, for he had indeed hammered the disunited Scots into a nation. But before Edward died, he succeeded in catching two more of King Robert's brothers, Thomas and Alexander, whom he executed at Carlisle. That left only the King and one other brother out of all the Countess of Carrick's remarkable sons.

After Edward's death, King Robert had still the Cummings to reckon with. The very next year, he embarked on what became known as the Hership of Buchan, a devastation of the Cumming lands more terrible than any of the punitive actions that the descendants of Canmore had conducted there in the earlier centuries of northern rebellion. Then Bruce turned against the Clan Dougall lands of the west, and with the support of Sir James Douglas and his last remaining brother Edward Bruce he gradually shattered the power of Somerled's descendants. Alasdair the 4th Chief died in 1310, and it was his son John whom King Robert routed in the pass of Brander that runs out of Loch Awe towards the Firth of Lorne.

Alasdair's brother retained the castle of Dunollie where his descendant the present MacDougall Chief lives today. John the 5th Chief died as King of Man, and his line did not recover their position in Scotland until his grandson married a granddaughter of a later King of Scots. The Hebridean kingdom of the MacDougalls was lost to them forever: it passed to the junior line of Somerled which supported Bruce, and expanded into the great Clan Donald.

These punitive expeditions occupied many years, and were made possible by the inertia of Edward II of England and his quarrels with his own subjects. As soon as Bruce had secured his position in Scotland, he turned against the remaining English strongholds there and captured them one after another. This was a particularly remarkable achievement because he did not possess the kinds of siege equipment that were considered indispensable in that age to reduce a fortress of any strength. What people remembered best in the legends of his prowess were his patience and his personal courage. His staying-power in adversity gave rise to the story of Bruce and the spider: his valour inspired all who saw him plunge first into a moat to test its depth before calling on his men to follow him up the scaling ladders. All the sons of the Countess of Carrick died violent deaths except King Robert: that is why the Bruces failed to create a numerous clan although they won a crown. It is a wonder that Robert did not perish like his brothers, considering the risks he took.

The greatest risk of all he took at Bannockburn on Mid-summer's Day in 1314, when Edward II arrived with a huge army to relieve his last stronghold in Scotland, the castle of Stirling. He had brought with him 3,000 of what amounted to the medieval tank, horses of the breed that William the Conqueror had introduced into England, whose descendants are our splendid shire horses. They were capable of carrying the enormous weight of a knight totally encased in armour, and heavy metal plates on their flanks in addition. Scotland possessed no such horses, only the far smaller Scottish breed of about the size of the modern Highland garron. When King Robert defeated the English army at

Bannockburn, it was the first victory in Europe of an infantry force over heavy armoured cavalry, the final triumph of Bruce's patience, courage and tactical skill. His own little mounted company he reserved skilfully to scatter the Welsh archers when they were endangering his hedgehogs of armed men bristling with spears, on which the chivalry of England flung themselves in vain.

Such were the circumstances in which the Clan, by far the oldest tribal organisation in European record, moved into its final span of life. The Red Cumming's only son died on the field of Bannockburn, fighting against his father's murderer. No descendant of King John Balliol's sister was left alive to confront the new dynasty with its senior claim. The Cummings declined into a small clan, although its chief remains the lineal heir of Canmore's brother, the Donaldbane of Shakespeare's play.

Among the Bruce supporters who moved into the Cumming lands of Buchan and Badenoch was Sir Gilbert Hay, whose forbears had become so thoroughly integrated in northern society by residence and marriage. He was granted the Cumming castle of Slains on the coast of Buchan and invested in the hereditary office of High Constable, both of which the Chief of Clan Hay enjoys to this day. Constable means Companion of the Stables, or controller of that essential aid to administration and military activity, the creature whose willingness to co-operate with man may almost be termed the foundation of civilisation — the horse. As for the Marischal, or Keeper of the royal Mares, the Keiths had already enjoyed this hereditary office for long before a Keith played his skilful part on the field of Bannockburn. Henceforth the Keiths flourished as Scotland's Earls Marischal, founding a college at Aberdeen and gradually enlarging their tremendous castle of Dunnottar a few miles to its south. The Keiths are another of the clans that grew in the old Pictish north-east where the Gaelic influence arrived late and receded early.

Among the people who fled when their country was wasted by fire and sword during the Hership of Buchan were a number of small tribes who had been living under the protection of the Cummings, and now required new patrons. Naturally the evidence from such a time of troubles is scarce and consists largely of oral traditions. One of these tells how a man called David Dubh led his people to the relative safety of the Mackintosh fold, and so created the client clan of the Davidsons. It is curious that they should have adopted an English form of the name in an area that had been Gaelic-speaking ever since the Pictish language died out, but they were not the only clan to do this.

They had moved into territory dominated by the confederation known as the Children of the Cat since long before the earliest surviving record. Like the boar and the mare, the cat had been a symbol of superhuman power since pagan times, as in ancient Egypt, and there had been a cat-headed King of Ireland called Cairbre, renowned in early Gaelic poetry. The dominant clan among the Children of the Cat were the Mackintoshes, Sons of the Toshach, an ancient Celtic office of state that might be translated Headman. The original Headman is identified as Gillechattan, which means Cat-Child, and he was related to the newly-arrived Cummings, although he is believed to have descended from Clan Duff. This may easily be believed when the Mackintoshes held such a dominant position in the former kingdom of Moray.

The MacGillivrays were among the ancient tribes that had become a client clan of the Mackintoshes. The Shaws were another. This names derives from *Sidheach*, Gaelic for a wolf, and it is first recorded as a personal name in the Gaelic entries of the Book of Deer during the twelfth century. During the same century a monk of the Celtic Church subscribed that name in Perthshire also. The wolf was another of the significant animals of pagan Celtic mythology: Cormac, King of Ireland was allegedly suckled by wolves, and the species was privileged because they had fostered him. Shaws were recorded in Badenoch before the war of independence, and after the fall of the Cummings the clan is found in the Clan Chattan confederation.

The 6th Mackintosh Chief had raised the men of Badenoch to help Alexander III repel the invasion of Haakon IV of Norway in 1263, which placed him high in royal favour. That was when the MacGillivrays sought security by becoming Children of the Cat. The 6th Mackintosh was equally astute when he supported Robert Bruce despite the Cumming connection, and so earned his family the barony of Moy in which the present Chief still lives today. The Mackintosh umbrella consequently provided the nearest and best shelter for such as the Davidsons when the storm broke over the Cumming lands.

It was a similar story in the MacDougall kingdom of the west. There the process of subjugation does not seem to have been nearly so punitive as the devastation of Buchan, but certain clans suffered severely for their adherence to MacDougall. For instance the MacNaughtons, who took their name from Nechtan, a name favoured by Pictish Kings. In the twelfth century they are to be found as proprietors of Strath Tay, and in the following one Clan Nechtan had added other possessions in Argyll. Alexander III bestowed on Gilchrist their Chief the island in Loch Awe called Fraoch Eilean in 1267, on which the ruins of their castle can still be seen. This ancient and prosperous tribe lost many of their lands by forfeiture, though they restored their fortunes later by giving loyal support to Robert Bruce's son.

Another ancient and unlucky clan were the Macnabs, Sons of the Abbot, who lost the lands of Glendochart that they had presumably occupied since the Celtic Church was dismantled. Like the MacNaughtons, they were discreet enough to support Bruce's son David II when the opportunity presented itself, and so recovered them.

But the misfortune that outshines all the others in the west is that of the MacSweens, because it is the subject of a contemporary Gaelic poem that keeps alive the optimism and bravery of the defeated cause. The poem is also illustrated by what is probably the earliest stone castle built on the Scottish mainland, the stout fortress called Castle Sween that overlooks the waters of the Firth of Lorne in Knapdale. Exactly who built this powerful structure before any King of Scots did the same remains a mystery. The earliest reference to a Sween in Gaelic occurs in 1034: 'Suibne son of Cineadh, King of the Foreigner-Gaels, died.' That was the year of King Duncan's accession to the throne in the time of Thorfinn the Mighty and Macbeth of Moray.

The MacSweens had survived nearly three centuries of turbulent history since then, when they launched their expedition in 1310. King Robert had already laid Buchan waste and daunted MacDougall, so that John MacSween displayed much temerity in accepting a grant from the English King to all the lands his ancestors had enjoyed in Knapdale, provided he could recover them by force. The fleet with which he made his attempt is described exactly as if it belonged to an alliance of Irish Scots and Norsemen in the days before there was such a thing as a Scottish nation. The poem is filled with the spirit of a bygone age.

> Tryst of a fleet against Castle Sween;
> Welcome is the adventure in Ireland;
> Horsemen travelling the billows;
> Brown ships are being prepared for them.

Of quilted hauberks is arrayed
The ship's prow in the form of jewels,
Of warriors with brown-faced girdles:
They are Norsemen and nobles.

They took their womenfolk with them, lying about on cushions
of satin and sendal in their ships, so confident were they of the
outcome. But needless to say the MacSweens were scattered,
and although some remained in Argyll for centuries to come,
others carried the name to the Outer Hebrides, where they are
found today in particularly large numbers in the isle of Scalpay.

In Moray it had been the Children of the Cat who acquired new
dependent clans in the aftermath of Cumming's downfall: in
Argyll it was the Children of the Boar. The Sons of Diarmaid
of the Boar were already known as *Caim Beul* (Crooked Mouth)
by the time Sir Colin Campbell of Loch Awe married the sister
of King Robert. He and his two sons served the Bruce cause
in the teeth of the MacDougall power, and the Campbells were
rewarded accordingly. MacSweens became their vassals,
MacNaughton property fell into their lap. To this day the Chief
of Clan Diarmaid (now the Duke of Argyll) is called *Mac Cailein
Mór*, Great Son of Colin, in tribute to Colin of Loch Awe. There
the chiefs continued to live in their island castle of Innischonaill
and hold their clan gatherings by its shore until they moved their
headquarters to Inveraray by Loch Fyne in a later century.

The stage was set for the great contest of the future, between
Clan Campbell and Clan Donald, both of them raised to eminence
by King Robert as a reward for their support. Of the two, the
Campbells were of the purer stock of Strathclyde and Dalriada,
and they were surrounded by tribes of similar origins. Some,
such as the MacGregors with their motto *Is Rioghal mo Dhream*,
My Blood is Royal, claimed descent from the house of Alpin.
Such clans were known in Gaelic as *Siol Ailpein*, The Seed of
Alpin.

The MacGregors inhabited Glenorchy which runs down to
Loch Awe, and took their name from Gregor of the Golden
Bridles in the reign of King Robert. To the south the Lamonts
lived in Cowal, a district named after King Comgall who died in
537. In 1200 there was a chief in Cowal named Ferchar, yet it
was not he who gave his name to the clan, but his grandson
Ladman, though the Lamonts claimed to be of King Comgall's
kindred.

Others derived their origins, like MacTaggarts and Macnabs,

from the Celtic Church. For instance a Macmillan is the son of a Tonsured Man, and a Macmillan chief acquired lands in Knapdale by marriage with a MacNeill heiress, and so Castle Sween acquired its Macmillan tower. In the Lennox to the west, a clan became identified as derived from the Canon's house, Buchanan, as early as the thirteenth century.

The most powerful and prolific intruders into this world of reshuffled clans were the Stewarts, who obtained the crown by inheritance through King Robert's daughter when his son David II died childless in 1371. The game got off to a good start when the first Stewart sovereign, Robert II, sired at least twenty-one children, legitimate and illegitimate. His son Robert was invested in the MacDuff earldom of Fife and created the Duke of Albany, the first duke in Scotland, and bearing the old name for Scotland in addition. From him descended the Earls of Moray, with their great castle of Doune in Menteith. Other Celtic earldoms were distributed to the first royal Stewart's sons as well, Strathearn to David, Atholl to Walter. His natural son John was appointed Sheriff of Bute, and from him the Marquess of Bute descends. The Steuarts of Cardney originate from another bastard son, while Sir John Stewart of Invermay married a co-heiress of Lorne, and so founded the septs of Grandtully and Appin.

The most prolific dynast among Robert II's legitimate sons was Alexander, whose imposing effigy in black marble may still be seen in Dunkeld Cathedral. Like Robert III and the Duke of Albany, he was the offspring of Robert II's first marriage to Elizabeth Mure, another family that profited exceedingly from the royal connection. Alexander received the former Cumming possessions of Buchan and Badenoch, with the impregnable stronghold of Lochindorb in its loch in the Grampian mountains. Here he earned himself the title of the Wolf of Badenoch by his depredations — in Gaelic of course. In that language the *a* vowel appears three times, and in order to rhyme must be pronounced correctly as in argument. But people ignorant of Gaelic now pronounce Badenoch to rhyme with maiden: just as they pronounce Atholl to rhyme with apple, whereas it too should be pronounced like the first vowel in argument.

When the Bishop of Moray excommunicated the Wolf of Badenoch for his sexual infidelities (the good Bishop evidently considered these more reprehensible than his repressions) Alexander descended upon Elgin Cathedral, the Lantern of the North as it became known, and burned it. The ruins of Elgin Cathedral and Lochindorb Castle remain as memorials to this vigorous Stewart thug.

So does a sizeable portion of the Scottish population, as his descendant General David Stewart of Garth noted in 1822. 'There are now living in the district of Atholl, within its ancient boundary, 1,937 persons of the name of Stewart, descendants of this man in the male line, besides numbers in other parts of the kingdom. The descendants in the female line are considerably more numerous, as few women leave the country, in proportion to the number of men who enter the army and resort to different parts of the world. We have thus upwards of 4,000 persons now living in one district, descended of this individual.' In the population explosion of the next 150 years the number must have been increased enormously.

Descendants may or may not multiply from a single progenitor: from the Bruce King Robert I they did not, from the Stewart King Robert II they did. But in reverse, everyone's ancestors increase at the same rate, doubling from two parents to four grandparents and eight great-grandparents. After that, the size of the increase in ancestors depends on whether people are marrying within or outside their tribal group, because if they are marrying their first or second cousins, their descendants simply acquire the same ancestors many times over. But in any circumstances there is only a slim chance that any Scot does not possess more Stewart blood than the Queen, whose family have generally contracted foreign marriages. It is the seniority of Her Majesty's Stewart blood, not its density, that makes her the present Chief of Clan Stewart.

But although the Stewart royal house later fell into the habit of making dynastic alliances abroad, the first two Stewart sovereigns in a sense went native when they won the crown. Robert II married two Scottish wives; his son Robert III followed his example, and so did an increasing number of the magnates who shared their Anglo-French background. The effect of Bruce's war of independence had been to cut them all off from the international society in which so many of them did homage to two or three kings for properties that they possessed in several countries. Bruce himself had forfeited all his lands south of the Border, and his subjects had been forced to choose whether they wanted to be Scots or Englishmen. The Stewarts, who had also come from France through England, set the admirable example that created Clan Stewart.

For the present they did not extend beyond the Great Glen, where Farquhar MacTaggart had been created Earl of Ross and had become founder of Clan Ross. *Ros* is Gaelic for headland, and must have been applied to the promontory of Easter Ross before it was used to comprehend the mountainous territory to the west as well. It is impossible now to discover why the clan adopted this territorial designation rather than preserving the founder's name as MacFarquhar or MacTaggart — although there are also Highlanders using both names. There were five chiefs who were also Earls of Ross before their great inheritance passed through an heiress to another name, and the chiefship went to the last MacTaggart Earl's brother, Hugh Ross of Balnagown.

In the interval, three subordinate clans appear dimly in the records of this remote area. They were all believed to descend from a Gaelic dynast called Gilleoin who lived in about 1100 and sprang from the ancient kindred of Lorne, and the most signifi- cant of them in future history were the Mackenzies. The clan name is rendered in English, Son of Kenneth, but only because this happens to be the nearest equivalent to the Gaelic *Coinneach*, which actually means a Fair or Bright Person. Who this was can only be surmised; perhaps Gilleoin himself.

The second clan claiming descent from him were named Anrias, which is Andrew in English. But it did not prosper after the sole daughter of their last chief gave their lands by marriage to the 8th Chief of Clan Ross at the end of the fourteenth century. The name MacAndrew is still used in Scotland, though it does not imply descent from this clan, and Gillanders preserves the Gaelic form for a Devotee of the Apostle Andrew, which also has no connection with Clan Anrias.

The other clan in Ross that is supposed to descend from Gilleoin is that of the Mathesons. Their lands lay close to the straits that divide the mainland from Skye, called Kyleakin from the Gaelic for the Narrows of Haakon, because the Norwegian King sailed through them in 1263 on his way to Largs. Cormac Mac Mhathain, the 2nd Matheson Chief, joined the Earl of Ross in support of the King of Scots on that occasion, and was among those who received an extremely severe write-up in *Haakon's Saga* for his behaviour in Skye. There they burned dwelling houses and churches and took 'the little children and laid them on their spear points, and shook their spears until they brought the children down to their hands, and so threw them away, dead.' But the Mathesons profited by their active support of the Scottish King, and avoided the clan rivalries of the war of independence that might so easily have been their undoing.

So did the Mackays of Strathnaver to the north of them, and a number of smaller tribes in the borderlands between them and the Norse plains to the east. It must have been easier for them to stand aside in this remote area beyond the spheres of influence of Cumming, Mackintosh and MacDougall, and they cannot have felt much concern over an issue that was so irrelevant to their daily lives.

A typically mysterious tribe of the far north is the one called Gunn. The Gunns inhabited the mountainous area which contains Morven and the Scarabens. To the south the hills descend to a level plain along the Moray Firth, which provided the Norsemen with their accessible Sutherland. But north of the Helmsdale river the east coast consists of huge cliffs, as intimidating as the hill country behind them. The entire area is rich in prehistoric remains, proto-Pictish defensive structures and later Pictish sculpture of superb workmanship. It was in the hinterland that Frakok was finally burned to death, and it was exactly the sort of refuge that the old inhabitants were likely to have chosen when invaders arrived. This has been the territory of Clan Gunn from the beginning of record to the present.

One theory of their origins is that their name derives from Gunni of the Norse saga, another, that it comes from the Norse *gunnr*, meaning war. It is tempting to fall back on the language and literature of the invading Vikings in search of origins when the Pictish language has disappeared, taking all its traditions with it. But for all we know, the word Gunn might be so old that it belongs to a pre-Celtic language like the name of Strathnaver near by, which has been favoured with an unlikely Gaelic meaning.

What seems most likely is that the Gunns were a Pictish tribe, especially in view of the inveterate hostility that continued for so many centuries between them and the Mackays, who were of Gaelic origin and had almost certainly invaded their neighbourhood in large numbers. Anyway, Picts must be looked for somewhere. They had been a more numerous people than the Gaels, a formidable power in the eyes of the Romans, and modern methods of genocide did not exist in those days. The Gunn territory is exactly where one would expect to find the survivors of so many centuries of misfortune. That incomparable Highland novelist Neil Gunn felt in his bones that his people were Picts: it influenced his work deeply, and it seems very probable that he was right.

The evaporation of the Pictish language without leaving any records has its parallel in the south of Scotland, where the Welsh language also disappeared. It did leave behind Scotland's earliest

poem, the Welsh epic the *Gododdin*, which preserves the evidence
of where the resistance leader Arthur really belongs. Welsh has
also survived elsewhere, a light that casts its distant beams on
the vanished British kingdoms of the north. But these do not
show us what we should like to know about the survival of British
tribes through the period of Anglian conquest from Northumbria.
We may merely assume that they cannot have been wholly
exterminated, and that they are likely to have survived in the
recesses of the Border hills when the more fertile lands were
seized by their conquerors.

A Border tribe comparable to the Gunns of the far north is
the one called Turnbull, not least because its name is equally
equivocal. The Turnbulls inhabited Teviotdale in historical
times, and a sixteenth-century historian wrote that their name
derived from a hero who saved the life of Robert Bruce from a
wounded bull which attacked him in the forest of Callander. 'For
this valiant act the King endowed the aforesaid party with great
possessions, and his lineage to this day is called of the Turnbull.'
Unfortunately for this fanciful story, they had been called by the
same name for a very long time before Bruce was born, the
earliest actual record dating from 1130.

But apart from that, the story itself is clearly the same as
Diarmaid's slaying of the boar, one of the most ancient and far-
flung in Celtic legend, somehow outlasting the death of the Welsh
language in the Border country. And so it may be surmised that
the Turnbulls were members of the older race, surviving the
Anglian conquest followed by the Anglo-Norman intrusion. A
Turnbull was among those whose heraldry (a turned bull's head,
later increased to three of them) appears on the Ragman Roll
of those who gave fealty to the King of England when John Balliol
received the crown. This raises the question whether he was
himself one of those incoming Anglo-Normans; but the legend
and the name are against it. By this time William Wallace's
father was a knight, which was a very Norman thing to be, yet
he was in fact as British as his name implies. A Turnbull too was
a knight when he challenged any one of the English to fight him
in single combat at the Battle of Halidon Hill in 1333.

As to whether any of these Border tribes ought to be called
clans in an area in which Gaelic was never spoken, the Scottish
government used this term for them, although it scarcely ever
employed a Gaelic word in its records.

Gradually all the Border clans were dominated by one which
extended its tentacles from Galloway. Its name was Douglas,

which is Gaelic for Grey-Black, and it appears in historical documents as early as the twelfth century in that great province of the south-west where Gaels had moved in after the fall of the old British kingdoms. Like other clans that had since become paramount, it owed its good fortune to the gratitude of Robert Bruce for its services in the war of independence. Sir William Douglas of Douglasdale, known as William the Hardy, had supported William Wallace until he was carried off to die in the Tower of London. His son the Good Sir James Douglas occupies the third place, after Bruce and Wallace, among the heroes of the freedom movement. He attended King Robert at his death and swore to carry his heart to the Holy Land, but was killed in Spain on his journey.

So the family of the Good Sir James became Earls of Douglas and Lords of Galloway. By the fifteenth century the Douglas Chief had become the greatest magnate in the realm, possessing all the Border lands of Annandale and Lauderdale, Eskdale and Teviotdale, in addition to the huge lordship of Galloway.

There was another southern name that rose to high prominence during this period without any benefit either from Bannockburn or from marriage with the prolific Stewarts. In the year 1379 Henry Sinclair of Rosslyn in the Lothians became heir by marriage and inheritance to the great earldom of Thorfinn the Mighty. It had lost its Sutherland to the Scottish crown but it still included Caithness and the islands, the one held by allegiance to the King of Scots, the other of the Norwegian King. The Sinclairs came from Normandy, and had obtained their lands in Lothian as early as 1162, where Sir Henry resided at the time when he fought for Robert Bruce at Bannockburn. It was his son who married the Orkney heiress.

A few decades later Norway lost her independence to Denmark, so that both Shetland and Orkney passed to the Danish crown. When a King of Scots married a Danish Princess in 1469, these islands were made the pledges for her dowry, and since they were never redeemed, they remained for ever after the property of the Scottish crown. But this did not affect the Sinclair title to Orkney: it merely transferred his allegiance as Earl from the Danish to the Scottish King. However, he had already consented to hold Caithness as a separate Scottish earldom, and he parted with his title to Orkney in exchange for a grant of lands in Fife. Despite this, the name of Sinclair, which arrived so late in the far north, is now the commonest in both Caithness and Orkney, and in lands in which the old Pictish tribal structure had been totally destroyed by the Norsemen with its language and traditions, the Sinclairs were to constitute a clan of sorts in future history. Their Chief is the Earl of Caithness to this day.

In addition to the Celtic peoples, and to the Anglo-Normans who had married into their tribal organisation, there were other immigrant settlers from abroad, such as the ones identified as Flemings. These came from a region of Europe that had developed an outstanding urban and commercial civilisation by the fifteenth century, and naturally it was in the Scottish burghs that they generally put down their roots. But there were remarkable exceptions. For instance a Fleming called Bartolf acquired property in Aberdeenshire in the twelfth century, and his family became known by its name of Leslie. It can be assumed that Bartolf had made a prudent Celtic marriage in order to become a dynast in this way in old Pictland, rather than the father of worthy tradesmen in some burgh.

With equal prudence his descendants avoided involvement with the Cummings and so escaped their downfall. A knighted Leslie was even among those who signed his country's freedom charter in 1320, the Declaration of Arbroath. Before the century was out the Leslies had become members of the royal house by marriage and blood, and moved among the greatest tycoons of the north as inheritors of the earldom of Ross. What makes it such an astonishing success story is that Bartolf's descendants were such outsiders, displaying a modern astuteness in a somewhat primitive and most belligerent age.

Another Fleming became the founding dynast of a clan even farther north, apparently by marrying into the royal house of Moray. His name was Freskin and he too lost the name of Fleming in his tribal environment in favour of a territorial designation. It was the southland of the Orkney earldom that fell into his lap, which was not the entire Sutherland of today (for that now includes the Mackay province of Strathnaver), but the lands along the Moray Firth south of Caithness. This had been confiscated after Earl Harald of Orkney joined the cause of Queen Gruoch's descendants and was defeated. The King of Scots then erected it into a lordship for the house of Freskin, with the responsibility of standing guard on his northern borders. So the Clan Sutherland and its Chiefs had their origin in a region that had been transformed from Pictish to Norse, and then placed under the feudal power of a royal servant of Flemish origin.

In this kaleidoscopic world of rising and declining clans, it was the Lordship of the Isles that played the most dramatic part after the Stewarts had succeeded to the crown. Unlike Orkney and Shetland, the Hebrides had been subject to the King of Scots ever since the defeat of Haakon of Norway in 1263. But they had enjoyed the status of a kingdom in the Norse empire, with almost complete autonomy, and the Chiefs of Clan Donald took a traditional view of their position that was not easy for a King of Scots to correct effectively, especially since his administrative machine contained few if any who could understand the language of the Hebrides, and none with any experience of island government. The Lord of the Isles issued charters as though he were an independent sovereign, and they were written in Gaelic with his signature Mac Donald also spelt in Gaelic.

Fertile and strategically placed Islay was the Chief's eyrie, and as his wings grew, more and more western clans sought their shelter. The MacPhees of the isle of Colonsay became hereditary keepers of their records. Today it is a name of the dispossessed, given to itinerant tin-smiths or tinkers: in 1164 it was that of the Lector of Iona. It appears to derive from *Mac Dhuith Shith*, Son of the Dark Fairy, the luck-bringing dark stranger who must be the first to cross a threshold at Hogmanay. In Colonsay the MacNeills also established themselves, a clan claiming descent from the Irish King Aodh O'Neill, whose reign ended in 1033, the year before the ill-fated Duncan's began in Scotland. But the MacNeills also inhabited Gigha and Barra, and it is there that Kisimul Castle has been restored as the home of the MacNeill Chief.

From the mainland of Morven two Maclean brothers, Lachlan and Hector, crossed the straits to the isle of Mull. By this time Lord John, 1st of the Isles, had made his second marriage to the first Stewart king's daughter Margaret, a union that was to give royal lineage to half the clans of the Hebrides. Their daughter married Lachlan Maclean, whom the Lord of the Isles established as befitted his wife's station at Duart on the promontory of Mull that faces the mainland. There his descendant Lord Maclean of Duart, former Chief Scout of the Commonwealth and 27th Chief of the Clan, lives in a castle that has few rivals in the magnificence of its surroundings.

The chiefship of Lachlan's descendants did not go uncontested by those of his brother Hector, who claimed that he had been the elder, even if he had not made a royal marriage. They settled at Lochbuie, inconveniently close to Duart for relatives who did not agree, and the dispute over the chiefship was still agitating them in the nineteenth century. An episode in the conflict that occurred three centuries earlier was long remembered. The head of the Lochbuie branch, *Iain Òg* (Young John) lost his only son when he was killed in an insurrection. Maclean of Duart thereupon kidnapped the childless rival of Lochbuie and placed him on a small island with only an ugly old crone to look after him. But she gave birth to a son called Stunted Murdoch who was bundled away to Ireland, while his uncle seized his estate. He returned as an adult to recover his inheritance by force, secured his legitimisation in 1538, and begot the heir from which the present head of the Lochbuie branch descends.

A clan of the Outer Hebrides who also claimed descent from Somerled were the Morrisons. These, like the Mathesons and Davidsons, allowed their name to be bowdlerised in English from the Gaelic *Mac Ghille Mhuire*, which means Son of the Virgin Mary's Servant. The Morrisons became hereditary judges in Lewis, perhaps still applying the immensely ancient Celtic Brehon laws. This was the age in which Gaelic finally took over the Long Island that has become its bastion today.

Different clans have dominated that remote little world in their turn — the MacLeods of Lewis, then the Mackenzies of Seaforth. Mathesons crossed the Minch to settle there also, and it was a Matheson who brought a fortune from the east in the twentieth century to purchase Lewis and rebuild its castle at Stornoway. Perhaps the MacAulays of Lewis also came from Ross, where the name of Ullapool commemorates Olaf's palace. As Sons of Olaf, it is suggested that they may descend from Olaf the Black, King of Man as the MacLeods do; but in fact their origins are entirely speculative. They can be compared to the Hebridean MacArthurs, who were to become such famous hereditary pipers. These appear first in the mainland records of the Campbell country of Loch Fyne, and only their name suggests that they may have descended of the British stock of the old Welsh kingdom of Strathclyde.

To what extent was there intermarriage between members of these clans? If the lesser folk followed the example of their chiefs, there must have been a great deal, and a medieval Gaelic poem reflects a pride in mixed ancestry that may have been widely shared.

> I am kin to Clan Dougall,
> A company of kindly conversation.
> Although they are fierce and brave,
> It is not on them that I would depend.

My ancestral country is in Airlie:
I am a great-grandson of Clan Donald.
I descend from Clan Maclean
That has waged many a battle.

MacPhee of Colonsay,
It was no sorrow to have him in my ancestry;
And MacNeill of Barra,
Fair and noble his descent.

The Clan of the Cat and of the Toshach,
Though they are my kin,
Cameron and Clan Gregor,
The men of Breadalbane,

The Stewarts, though they are far-flung,
Scattered over the world of conflict,
It is an old story, sure and fast-travelling,
That my father's grandmother was one of them.

The pride of kinship is distributed impartially, including also the MacSweens and Lamonts and several more. The Mackintoshes are the most distant from the isles to receive mention.

The supreme patriarch in the Hebrides until his death in about 1380 was John of Islay, 1st Lord of the Isles, who earned himself the title 'the Good.' Before he married Robert II's daughter he had taken as his first wife the MacRuari heiress of Garmoran, who descended like him in the male line from King Somerled. It was their son Ranald who gave his name to the MacDonalds of Clanranald in the Hebrides, and he was also the founder of the MacDonells of Glengarry in the Garmoran lands. Ranald was the senior heir, but although he was well-endowed, the Lordship went to his younger brother Donald, the grandson of a king.

Donald, 2nd Lord of the Isles, made a yet more fateful marriage, as it was to prove, to the heiress of Ross. This northern earldom had already passed recently with an heiress from the MacTaggarts to a Leslie, and this had rendered the descendant of Bartolf the Fleming eligible to marry a granddaughter of Robert II. But she proved less fertile than her grandfather, and gave birth only to a nun, so that the earldom fell unexpectedly into the lap of Donald of the Isles, who was married to Leslie's sister. It proved to be a fatal legacy, because Donald had to fight for it, and the conflict started a chain reaction which ended in the forfeiture of the MacDonald Lordship.

The Battle of Harlaw which Donald of the Isles fought in 1411 to assert his title to the lands of the earldom of Ross assumed a larger significance than he could have intended. It bore a disquieting resemblance to those earlier conflicts in which the Gaels had attempted to assert the legitimate rights of Queen Gruoch's descendants, and in much the same area. Certainly the burgesses of Aberdeen armed themselves to oppose him, not because they disputed his rights, but out of fear that his Gaelic clans might sack their city. The confrontation became, in fact, to some extent one between Highlander and Lowlander, Gaelic and English speaker, the old and the new Scotland.

There was no such contrast between the protagonists in the battle. MacDonald found himself opposed at Harlaw by Alexander Stewart, Earl of Mar, who was his first cousin. Mar was the wild son of a lawless father — none other than the Wolf of Badenoch — and was himself described as a 'leader of caterans.' He possessed no authority to fight MacDonald. The Lord of the Isles by contrast was widely known as a most elegant and cultured person, since he had been a frequent visitor to London where another of his first cousins, James I King of Scots, was a prisoner. It was the King's absence that gave his Stewart relatives the opportunity for such unrestricted private enterprise, until he returned to punish them.

As on the fateful field of Culloden three hundred years later, there were Gaelic clans fighting on both sides at Harlaw: such is the convention in tribal societies. Even on MacDonald's march through his own lands he was attacked by the Mackays, who had come all the way from Strathnaver to block his journey. MacDonald brushed them aside, but took care to rectify matters on his return. He gave his sister Elizabeth in marriage to the Mackay Chief, who brought the royal Stewart blood to the remotest corner of the kingdom.

The clan apparatus of Gaelic Scotland can be seen in motion in MacDonald's expedition to Harlaw. In his host were MacLeods of Lewis and Skye, and Macleans of Duart besides his own clansmen and many others from the islands. Mackintosh provided members of the Cat confederation amongst the mainland levies. The MacMhuirich bard composed an incitement to battle in classical metre which has survived.

The battle was such a fierce one, with so many killed in the indecisive engagement, that the field has been known ever since as the Red Harlaw. It marked the turning of the Gaelic tide in the old Scotland, which continued to ebb ever after. What neither Gruoch's descendants nor Somerled had been able to achieve was equally impossible for MacDonald. He returned undefeated from Harlaw, but he was unable to enforce his claim to the lands in that area which belonged to the earldom of Ross.

A touching lament commemorates young John MacLeod, son of the Chief of Dunvegan. It pictures his father and mother, looking over the sea for his returning sail. 'I am displeased with the wind from the south, for it keeps John from land . . . Janet's son, white his sails, did he wish to come over sea, it is not a wind from the south that would delay John, son of William, of swift steeds . . . Son of William who dispenses mead, son of Janet of royal lineage, were I to hear of your coming from the north, my gloom would then vanish.' But John MacLeod lay dead on the Red Harlaw.

Although the tide of Celtic civilisation continued to ebb throughout the fifteenth century, in the lands of the Lordship people perhaps enjoyed the happiest period in their history during these years. The evidence that survives may not suggest this, but that is because it consists largely of the crime records of a distant administration. No society would present a very favourable picture of itself if it were to be judged exclusively by such evidence.

The Beatons, for instance, present us with a quite different picture. They are thought to have come from Ireland to Scotland in the time of Angus of Islay, the grandfather of John the Good, 1st Lord of the Isles, and in Islay they became physicians and shenachies to the chief. Nor was their medicine the kind of mumbo-jumbo that passed for medical science in much of Europe at this time. The man whose canon of medicine was to be the foundation of all European teaching for five centuries was the eleventh-century Persian known in the west as Avicenna; and by the fifteenth century the Beatons possessed his teachings translated into Gaelic long before they appeared in English, considerably before there was even a faculty of medicine in any university of either England or Scotland. Their library also contained the earliest translation of the story of the fall of Troy into any European language. The Beatons carried their learning to Mull, Skye and the Outer Hebrides, comprising another clan comparable to the MacMhuirichs.

This was also the age of the harpists, performers on that delicious little instrument called in Gaelic the *clarsach*. The oldest that has survived in Scotland is known as the Lamont harp, and it can be dated to at least as early as 1464, when it was taken to Lude in Perthshire with a Lamont bride. The Galbraith Clan, whose name (Foreigner-Briton) clarifies their origins, became hereditary harpists in the isle of Gigha, and a composition by one of them during this century illustrates the way in which they would end a song. 'Tomaltach, not mean in his promises, has given me food and wine, a harp as well to reward my song. That hand is the best I have experienced.'

The singer, accompanying himself on the clarsach, gave public performances in the hall of the chief, in which his clansmen could enjoy with him the tales of the Fingalian heroes and of his ancestors. And these songs extolled the wonders of nature as the Celtic monks had done in Gaelic verse hundreds of years earlier; as no other literature in Europe did until centuries later. There is a praise-poem to Malcolm, Chief of Clan Gregor from 1415 until his death in 1440, which expresses delight in 'all that they found of wonders beneath the banks of each swift stream, that is such of Malcolm's abundance as was held by Muirne's son.' When the bard takes us indoors, it is to inform us that 'in the hero's stronghold is concert of harps in hands of minstrels; his household go from games of backgammon to walk in shaded garden.'

The race of women who had played such dominant roles in an earlier age did not keep silent in this one, but made their own distinctive contribution to its arts. For instance the widow of MacNeill of Gigha, who held Castle Sween as Constable for the Lord of the Isles in 1455, composed a most touching, heartfelt lament at his death. 'O rosary that has awakened my tear, dear the finger that used to be laid on you: dear the heart, hospitable and generous, that owned you always until tonight.' There are sixteen of these verses, deepening in their sorrow to: 'my heart is broken within my body, and will be so until my death, left behind him of the dark fresh eyelash, O rosary that has awakened my tear.'

For sheer candour, the most remarkable of these women poets was Isobel Stewart, who became the wife of Colin Campbell, 1st Earl of Argyll. Her husband was born in 1457 and died in his mid-thirties, but it is impossible to say when she gave such startling expression to her feelings. Not even today would many girls leave such a poem around, to fall into the hands of strangers.

Alas for him whose sickness is love,
Whatever the reason I should say it!
Hard it is to be free of it;
Sad is the plight in which I am myself.

That love I have given in secret,
Since it is not in my interests to declare it,
If I do not find quick relief for it
My bloom will be slight and scant.

He to whom I have given love,
Since I cannot tell it openly,
If he should cause me pain
May he have cause to say a hundred times, Alas!

And again, Alas! To mention the names of MacGregor and Campbell is to rekindle memories of a long and bitter clan conflict, and to face the darker aspect of this age. The setting for this tale of discord is the beautiful district of Lorne in which Ben Cruachan rises above Loch Awe with its island castles of the MacNaughtons and Campbells. The most spectacular of these ruins today is Kilchurn, the castle built in about 1440 by the founder of the Breadalbane sept of the Campbells on a low promontory that runs into. the east end of the loch. It dominates the entrances to the valleys that curl into the hills beyond, Glen Lyon, Glenorchy and Glenoe.

In this last, smallest glen, which runs round the flank of Ben Cruachan, there lived the Macintyres. The name means Son of the Carpenter, and for centuries they were hereditary foresters to the Lords of Lorne. But despite the trade name of this clan, which is wholly exceptional, it also contained bards and pipers. Macintyres became hereditary pipers to MacDonald of Clanranald and to the Menzies' Chief. In 1490 the Mackintosh Chief took a Macintyre bard under his protection, and three hundred years later Duncan Bàn Macintyre was to be among the last and greatest exponents of the ancient tradition of Celtic nature poetry, immortalising the beauties of Glenorchy and its surrounding hills.

The little valley called Glenoe, home of the Macintyres, was relatively poor and somewhat inaccessible, so that nobody seems to have coveted it, and the Sons of the Carpenter (whoever he may have been) found safety in dependence on more powerful neighbours, whom they served with their impressive variety of talents.

There was another band of hereditary tradesmen in the

neighbourhood, the arrow-makers. The Gaelic for Son of the Arrow-maker is *Mac an Fhleistear*, but these were known simply as Fletchers, without any suggestion of a clan progenitor. Yet the saying went that it was Fletchers who first raised smoke and boiled water on the braes of Glenorchy, and this was tantamount to calling them an aboriginal, pre-Celtic people. Their occupation is entirely consistent with such a theory, since this region contains the evidence of arrow-making over a thousand years before the arrival of the Scots of Dalriada. It would also help to explain why the Fletchers did not receive a normal clan designation, but only the name of their craft.

It was the Clan of Glenorchy that kept them busiest making arrows. John their Chief had been captured by the English in 1296, the year in which King John Balliol was deposed. In the long run this could only have benefited his clan along with all who had fought against the English; but presently Campbells of Loch Awe swooped in to marry the neighbouring heiress of Glenorchy, and the fatality of this union was that it remained childless. The Campbells thereafter claimed to have become the owners of Glenorchy and the tribe that lived in it, without any blood-relationship.

A man called Gregor, who may have been the nephew of Chief John, set himself up as the leader of his threatened kinsfolk, to hold their lands by the sword, and so they were still doing in the time of the fifteenth-century bards and harpists, to whom they were evidently such generous patrons. To another Chief John of Clan Gregor, who died in 1519, a poet sang: 'Receive and protect me, MacGregor. Greet me well when I come to you. I have tried to make my peace without an advocate, you favourite of poets, you darling of churches.' But at Chief John's death the Campbells set up a rival line of MacGregor Chiefs to serve their interests. The stage was set for the bloody final act.

Though such conflicts as this are the hazards of any tribal system, they were not necessarily more distressing than what was going on in countries without a tribal structure. Nothing so terrible as the carnage of the English Wars of the Roses occurred in Scotland during the fifteenth century. This possibly helps to explain why a comparatively small and poor country enjoyed a richer heritage of poetry and music in two separate languages and traditions, as well as vernacular medical treatises.

Every time the clan system had been placed under strain, by the Viking invasion, by the usurpation of Queen Margaret's sons, by the war of independence, it had proved resilient enough to achieve a new equilibrium. But in the end any attempt to maintain its institutions against the centralising forces of the nation-state were doomed to failure, and this was the challenge that next faced the clans. The families of the first two Stewart kings, Robert II and Robert III, used their privileged position during two weak reigns to infiltrate the clans as a Stewart clan, penetrating their structures in the traditional manner until almost every important clan from the Douglases on the southern Border to the Mackays on the north coast possessed royal Stewart blood.

But then came the first of the six King Jameses, matured by years of English imprisonment, determined to place the entire country under his law and government, clans and all.

CHAPTER FOUR

Stewarts Stir the Pot

'In those days there was no law in Scotland, but he who was stronger oppressed him who was weaker, and the whole kingdom was a den of thieves.' So the *Register of Moray* commented in the days of the Wolf of Badenoch, with Stewart thieves particularly in mind. The Wolf's elder brother Robert III, elderly and incompetent, ordered as his epitaph: 'Here lies the worst of Kings and the most miserable of men.' His most dangerous kinsman was not even the Wolf but another brother, Duke of Albany, believed by many to have murdered the King's elder son. If his younger son were to die also, Albany would become heir to the crown. Robert III planned to send him to France for safety, and he was captured at sea by the English: and so when the most miserable of kings died, Albany obtained the regency — and did nothing to ransom James I from his captivity. It was not until seventeen years later that James was restored to his realm and the Stewart bonanza was brought to an end.

James I was a most cultured man, a good poet and a strong ruler. The Regent Albany was dead, but he had been succeeded by his son Murdoch. James executed Murdoch, his father-in-law the Earl of Lennox, and both of Murdoch's sons within months of his return. In this way he was able to recover for the crown the three ancient earldoms of Lennox, Fife and Menteith. He regained Buchan also when Murdoch's brother died in France, then Mar on the death of the Wolf's son. Finally he simply took Strathearn away from Robert II's great-grandson Malise Graham, though he compensated him with Menteith. It was his own clan whose wings he clipped first, as he set about strengthening the monarchy.

Then with far less justification or principle, he set upon others. In 1428 he summoned fifty Highland chiefs to the castle of Inverness, and when they arrived to greet their sovereign he imprisoned them all and executed three of them. It was the first act in the perfidious treatment by the six King Jameses of their Gaelic subjects, and its consequences were dire. Donald, the MacDonald Chief who had brought his host to Harlaw, was dead now, and his son Alasdair was Lord of the Isles and Earl of Ross. James dismissed him with a caution, but he was so enraged by the King's conduct that he returned to Inverness in the following year and burned the seat of royal authority in which he had suffered his humiliating imprisonment. James retaliated equally fast, bringing an army to Lochaber which routed the Lord of the Isles.

An extraordinary meeting followed between these two cultured and high-spirited cousins, each so jealous of his own authority. On a feast day in August, while the King and Queen were attending mass in the abbey of Holyrood, the Lord of the Isles entered wearing only his tunic, that long linen garment which the Gaels had borrowed from the Romans. In his hands MacDonald carried his naked sword, which he presented to the King, kneeling before the high altar. The Queen then interceded for Alasdair of the Isles: she was a Beaufort, and had probably met him on several occasions during her husband's confinement in London. James granted MacDonald his life in response to her plea. It was the kind of ritual that people fancied in this age, and Alasdair had probably been advised that this would be the most satisfactory way of healing the quarrel without loss of face to anyone.

But James made the mistake of sending his cousin a prisoner to Tantallon Castle, that enormous fortress on the coast of Lothian which still presents such a majestic appearance as a ruin. The royal ineptitude is all the more surprising because he might have remembered what had occurred in his own kingdom when the apex of authority was withdrawn. He could not replace it with his own because he did not possess the apparatus to do so. Neither he nor his officials could even understand the language of the Gaelic west, and the central government had never administered the region beyond mounting occasional punitive expeditions into it.

James I's error was one that the Stewart kings repeated constantly, and the lesson of this one taught them nothing. Alasdair's kinsman Donald Balloch acted differently from the King's Stewart relatives when he had been a prisoner in England. They had left him there without making any attempt to rescue him, while they ran amuck in his kingdom. Donald Ballach by contrast raised a rebellion on his chief's behalf, futile though this was. He was defeated and fled to Ireland, leaving the Gaelic lands tranquil for the remainder of James I's reign; not least when the Lord of the Isles was permitted to return and keep them so.

James made Perth the centre of his administration, and it is strange that this city, placed so strategically astride a navigable stretch of the Tay on the edge of the Highlands, did not become the capital of Scotland. Perth was also the centre of Clan Drummond, although the name is derived from Drymen in the Lennox. The Drummond Chief's title is *An Drumanach Mor*, the Great Man of Drymen. But in 1345 the Drummond Chief married the heiress of Stobhall near Perth, where his successor the present Chief, 17th Earl of Perth, still lives today.

In the interval the Drummonds made other marriages of even greater consequence. Robert Bruce's son David II married the Chief of Stobhall's sister, but the couple had no children. Then the second Stewart king, Robert III, married Annabella Drummond who gave birth to James I. His preference for Perth consequently had a double motive.

When James returned to Scotland he said, 'if God grant me life, though it be but the life of a dog, there shall be no place in my realm where the key shall not keep the castle and the bracken-bush the cow.' In his energetic attempt to make good those words he created new courts of law and reformed the Three Estates of Parliament, and prepared a busy programme of legislation for it. He proved to be the most effective king since Robert Bruce a century earlier, and it was a tragedy for Scotland that he was murdered in his prime by his own Stewart relatives. But he had provoked them, just as he provoked the Highland chiefs.

The author of his downfall was his uncle the Earl of Atholl, brother of Albany and the Wolf of Badenoch, last surviving son of Robert II. He would be heir to the throne if James I's only son were to die, and since Atholl's own son was dead, his grandson Sir Robert Stewart came next in the succession. They were joined by their cousins the Grahams, also descended from Robert II and still smarting from their loss of Strathearn. These were the men who plotted the murder of the King, and their opportunity came on a night in February 1437 when James was staying in the undefended Dominican priory at Perth.

The event was afterwards believed to have been heralded by all kinds of prophecies. Atholl had been promised that he would wear a crown. James had been warned when he was about to cross the Forth on his way to Perth that he would never return. As he sat playing chess in his private chamber with a young courtier who had been called 'The King of Love,' James told him jokingly that they must both beware, because yet another prophecy declared that this year a king would die in Scotland.

Finally the courtiers left and the King prepared for bed, only the Queen and some ladies still in his company. This was when Atholl's grandson admitted the conspirators, Sir Robert Graham and his son, and a few others. A servant of the King, seeing armed men outside his chamber, cried 'Treason!' and was immediately despatched. The bar which secured the door of the room was missing, and it was said that Katherine Douglas, one of the Queen's attendants, thrust her arm through its sockets and held the door until her arm was broken. Meanwhile the King tore up floorboards with tongs from the fire, in an attempt to reach the vault below his room, since there was no other hiding-place. But the murderers broke in too soon and even injured the Queen as she tried to defend her husband. The King fought them with his bare hands until he fell dead with 28 wounds.

Whatever the conspirators had expected to gain, this atrocity brought them nothing but a fate more dreadful still. The Earl of Atholl, about seventy-five years old and the son of a king, was tortured in public for three days in Edinburgh before he was allowed to die. A diadem of red-hot iron was placed on his head in fulfilment of the prophecy that one day he would wear a crown. But the worst torment was to have his body wrapped in cloth after a day's flogging through the streets, and then to have this covering ripped off the following morning, so that he was partially flayed before the beating began again. Sir Robert Graham was subjected to similar treatment, and it was believed to have been the Queen who emulated the savagery of Esther in the Old Testament, in insisting on this revenge.

Her son James II was only six years old, so that she might have enjoyed a long and influential regency if she had not taken the anomalous step of marrying another Stewart and adding three more children to this turbulent and already prolific clan. Her second husband was Sir James Stewart, known as the Black Knight of Lorne, and with him she attempted to take possession of the infant King. They were both arrested, and the Queen gained her husband's freedom only by resigning her own right to the custody of her first-born. But the children of her second marriage did well enough. One became Earl of Atholl, from whom the present Stewart-Murray Duke of Atholl descends; the second secured the earldom of Buchan while the third was elevated to be Bishop of Moray.

Meanwhile, through the behaviour of James II's guardians, he was menaced by his Douglas rather than his Stewart relatives.

Two men, Keepers of the royal castles of Edinburgh and Stirling called Crichton and Livingstone, at first competed for possession of the young King, then spotted the advantage of making common cause. The most powerful magnate in the realm, now that so many Stewart heads had rolled in the dust, was the Chief of the name Douglas. He was something more: he was the only Scot with a double descent from Robert II, through both his marriages, and he now stood next in line for the crown after a solitary Graham who was a prisoner in England.

So the Earl of Douglas was made Guardian of the realm, but he promptly died, leaving two teen-age sons, William the 6th Earl and his brother David. If anything were to happen to James II, these two lads scarcely older than the King would become the puppets of one of the rival gangs. Crichton and Livingstone invited them both to dine with the nine-year-old King in Edinburgh Castle.

It was said that at that feast a black bull's head was placed before the Douglas boys, that ancient symbol of the sacrificial victim. Certainly they were both seized, whether before or after the dinner, and tried in the presence of the King on a charge of treason. The elder had enjoyed his earldom for little over a year and was about sixteen years old: his younger brother David could scarcely have found an opportunity for treason either. His crime was that he would succeed at his brother's death. So despite the tearful entreaties of the little King they were both taken out into the courtyard and executed.

> Edinburgh Castle, town and tower,
> God grant thou sink for sin,
> And that even for the black dinner
> Earl Douglas gat therein.

The English-speaking peoples of southern Scotland were now composing ballads also, and while the themes of the Gaelic ones were often over a thousand years old, the folk of the south depended on more recent events — and were provided with plenty of them.

What made the murders so pointless was that there were other Douglases waiting to step into dead men's shoes, and there is a piquancy in the spectacle of William, the 8th Earl of Douglas, skilfully cracking the Crichton-Livingstone alliance and encouraging the two crooks to ravage each other's lands while he harried both of them. When James II came of age in a country torn by disorder, the Livingstones who had been amassing property and offices during his minority were disgraced. The unscrupulous Crichton was somehow clever enough to retain his place in the royal service despite his past crimes: perhaps his abilities helped to save him at a time when there was not a large pool of trained men available for the public service.

James II proved as able a ruler as his father, but where James I had been bedevilled by his Stewart kindred, it was the Douglases who faced his son with their implacable resentment. He did what he could to reconcile them. He gave the 8th Earl a part of the property forfeited by the Livingstones: he named the Douglas Chief his ambassador in the jubilee year 1450, enabling him to travel as a prince to the courts of England, Burgundy and France. But his efforts were wasted.

The issue was as simple as this. During the fifteenth century the first four King Jameses were attempting to build on the concept of a single nation of Scotland that Robert Bruce had instilled during the war of independence. It was a novel idea at the time, hardly to be found anywhere in Europe as early as this, and it was inconsistent with tribal loyalties, which are regional in their scope. It is indeed an extraordinary paradox that a country which has clung so obstinately to tribalism as to have given its name for a tribe to the world should also have been a pioneer in the history of nationalism. Behind all the narrower motives of ambition, revenge, fear and greed, this was the fundamental issue of the century in Scotland.

The King's own relatives remained tribal in their outlook, Douglases, MacDonalds, even the Stewarts themselves, and they were based on regions that corresponded with the ancient ethnic divisions of the country; Galloway in the British southwest, the Pictish north, the Gaelic territories of the Lordship of the Isles and Ross. This showed clearly when clansmen of the Douglas Chief refused to take an oath of fealty to King James, and he was forced to march into Douglas territory and destroy a number of their strongholds. It became even more apparent when Alasdair of the Isles came to the mainland in support of Douglas and once again sacked Inverness. It marked the beginning of a plan agreed by the two great clans to recognise the claim of the English King that he was Lord Paramount of Scotland, in order to preserve the autonomy of the old British and Gaelic regions of Scotland under his protection.

This has been described as 'unpatriotic,' but that is to view a Celtic society through English eyes, and a medieval society through modern spectacles.

King James made one final attempt to bind to himself the most powerful of the chiefs, the great Earl of Douglas. He invited his cousin to visit him at Stirling Castle, and when the Earl suspiciously demanded a safe-conduct, the King provided it. The two men dined, and then retired to a small room, where James asked Douglas to prove his good faith by cancelling the private treaties he had made with the Lord of the Isles and other magnates. Douglas refused: the King pleaded with him. Finally shouts were heard as the two men lost their tempers, and when the guard rushed in to protect the King, they saw that he had already stabbed Douglas in the throat. They killed him with a pole-axe and threw his body through the window into the garden below, where it was buried.

Like Bruce, James II regretted the atrocity he had committed. As in the case of the Red Cumming's murder, it sowed the seeds of implacable hostility. The dead man's brother, now 9th Earl of Douglas, rode into Stirling with his followers and dragged the royal safe-conduct at his horse's hooves before setting fire to the town. James pursued him with a large enough army to persuade Douglas to issue a public statement of forgiveness for his brother's murder; and the King responded by restoring the confiscated earldom of Wigtown among other favours. There was a deceptive calm as even the Lord of the Isles came into the King's peace with the rest of the allies of Douglas. Only that dedicated secessionist Donald Balloch continued his hard-line attitude from the safety of the isles: but in his actions he revealed what was in the hearts of others.

The showdown occurred in 1455. Alasdair of the Isles was long dead by this time, and his son John, the new Chief of Clan Donald, had been lured to the side of the King by the royal favours that James was always so generous in bestowing. In their final rebellion the Douglases fought alone, opposed even by several of their own clan. They were utterly defeated and two of the Earl's brothers were killed while he fled to the Lord of the Isles in a vain attempt to win his support. When he had failed, he left to offer his allegiance to the English crown, which was now being tossed around in the Wars of the Roses. The entire Douglas properties were forfeited, though some were transferred to another of the King's kinsmen, a Douglas who had helped to destroy the Douglases.

He descended from an illegitimate son of the 1st Earl who had married a daughter of Robert III and received the earldom of

Angus to assist him to maintain her. When the line of what were called the Black Douglases was destroyed, the Red Douglases took their place in the shape of the Earls of Angus. Even such a determined king as James II could not sacrifice the claims of kinship altogether for the authority of the crown.

This authority had been asserted by means of a new weapon, whose introduction probably owed much to the influence of the King's wife. This remarkable Queen came from highly civilised Burgundy, which led Europe not only in its arts, but also in its commercial wealth and its technical expertise. From here Scotland received for the first time a kind of artillery capable of battering down the walls of the strongest castle: a kind of weapon that only the King could afford to maintain. The great gun called Mons Meg, still to be seen in Edinburgh Castle, probably dates from this time, and it may even have been dragged all the way to Castle Threave in Galloway, the strongest of all the Douglas fortresses when King James captured it.

He developed a lively enthusiasm for his new weapon, which was his undoing. In 1460 he was attempting to recover Roxburgh Castle from the English. The loyal Lord of the Isles had brought a Highland force to assist him. While James was inspecting his gunnery, 'mair curious nor became him or the majesty of ane King,' as the sixteenth-century chronicler complained, a gun exploded as it was fired and one of its wedges struck James and killed him. It was a tragedy as disastrous for Scotland as his father's premature death had been. His eldest son was only nine years old.

With admirable fortitude, the Burgundian Queen hurried to Roxburgh with the infant James III and urged the Scottish leaders to continue the siege until Roxburgh Castle, a gigantic structure of which little remains today, was recovered from the English. The boy-King was crowned in the nearby abbey of Kelso, and his mother took over the direction of the state, aided by that outstanding churchman, Bishop Kennedy.

Their difficulty was that Scotland had generally supported the Lancastrian cause in the English civil war, and in the year following James II's death Edward IV won the throne for the Yorkists. At his court was the last of the Black Douglases with his sole surviving brother, and it was natural that Edward should try to use the forfeited Earl as a stick to chastise the Scots for their Lancastrian sympathies. Nor is it surprising that the Lord of the Isles was attracted by the offer which the English King, Lord Paramount of Scotland, made to him. For it proposed that the ancient Gaelic kingdom north of the Forth should be revived, while Douglas was restored to the former British lands of the south-west. In 1462 Douglas, John of the Isles and that veteran Gaelic separatist Donald Balloch put their signatures to this arrangement.

They were condemned as traitors then, and they are castigated as unpatriotic still by scholars who ought to be capable of a more dispassionate view. To describe John of the Isles as a traitor is precisely equivalent to calling a Welshman a traitor who resisted the incorporation of Wales into England. Since the time of Canmore the royal regime in Scotland had been neither more nor less English than that of London, the difference being that there was rather more of England and relatively less of Wales. During much of the four hundred years since Canmore had seized the throne, the inconvenience had not been very great in Gaelic Scotland, since the institutions of the monarchy had hardly penetrated there. But now they were getting perilously close.

On the other hand, during this period the emergency had occurred in which Wallace, Bruce and their associates had fought for the concept of a Scottish nation, their dream enshrined in the immortal words of the Declaration of Arbroath. Since then the King Jameses had been attempting to transform this dream into reality, but it was such an exotic plant, hardly identifiable anywhere at this time, that anyone might have been forgiven for doubting whether it could take root, especially in such a fundamentally tribal society as Scotland still contained. Nor can men be described as traitors because they fell back on traditional solutions in troubled times in their attempt to safeguard all that was most precious to them.

This is not to say that the Lord of the Isles made a wise decision. He was in fact displaying the fatal conservatism which is the Achilles heel of people who venerate their long traditions, so that they are accustomed to look backwards for precedents when they ought to be trying to peer into the future. The step he took was typical of the many that Clan Donald chiefs and those of less important clans were to take for centuries to come, to their irretrievable loss. John of the Isles moved to Inverness to set up his autonomous government there, a privilege that the Highlands were not to enjoy again in any form until the Highlands and Islands Development Board was planted there in the mid-twentieth century. Taking this step in collusion with the English King on the basis of his claim to overlordship in Scotland, rather than trying to negotiate such an arrangement with an adult King of Scots, MacDonald was bound to fail, and the ability of the Queen Mother made it more certain still.

The Black Douglas invaded the south of Scotland with his brother, who was captured and executed, leaving the Earl the last survivor of five brothers. It was now that the Queen Mother made her brilliant decision that the most effective means of undermining the separatist movement in Scotland would be to come to terms with the Yorkist King of England. It was made more difficult for her by Bishop Kennedy's opposition, but she persuaded him in the end, and it proved to be her last great service to the land of her adoption. She died, only thirty years old, in the year before John of the Isles made his submission to young James III in Inverness.

When James was fourteen years old and both Bishop Kennedy and his mother were dead, he was declared of competent age to govern, so that his personal rule began with a vacuum behind the throne and an adolescent occupying it. Into the void moved the Boyds of Kilmarnock, chiefs of a small clan that now attempted the hazardous sport of bettering themselves through the royal connection. Their name is taken from the island of Bute in the Firth of Clyde, which is *Bod* in Gaelic. Since this language possesses a genitive case that alters even proper names, a man of Bute becomes *Boid*, hence the form Boyd. A lord of Bute is on record as early as 1205, and during the ensuing century it is to be found in many parts of the south-west, though whether the Boyds were of Welsh or Gaelic origin is hard to determine. They supported Robert Bruce, and one of them was chaplain to the second Stewart king, Robert III, from whom he must have heard depressing confessions. James II created the first Lord Boyd, though today the Chief holds the title of Lord Kilmarnock.

The Boyds of Kilmarnock seized the fourteen-year-old King, won three years of unrestricted power and then, like the Livingstones during the previous royal minority, lost all they had gained in a counter-coup. Their most ambitious move took them into the bosom of the royal family itself. Lord Boyd married his son to the King's sister Mary, and the bridegroom was created Earl of Arran. He earned the highest praise for his character and abilities, but this could not save him from the consequences when the Boyds fell from power. They were forfeited, one was executed, and Arran fled the country and died before his prime. More unhappily still, his son of royal blood was murdered and his inconsolable widow was forced to marry Lord Hamilton, an elderly widower who founded one of Scotland's nastier noble families and one that stood distressingly close to the throne owing to the disposal of the Boyd heir.

But during their short period of office the Boyds performed a service of lasting benefit to Scotland. They arranged the King's marriage to Margaret of Denmark, a lady of such excellence that James III actually petitioned Rome for her canonisation a year after her death. In addition, the isles of Orkney and Shetland were made the pledges for her dowry, and since they were never redeemed they returned at last to the Scottish crown, nine hundred years after they had been Pictish territory in the time of St Columba. By now they were wholly Norse, and their inhabitants were probably not much pleased by the change of sovereignty.

Happily for Queen Margaret, the third King James proved to be the most cultivated sovereign Scotland had yet possessed, and one of the most enlightened princes of Europe in that age. He was not a poet like his grandfather, but he patronised poets. His greatest love was music, though the most lasting monument to his taste is the great hall at Stirling, recently restored after years of neglect.

James possessed, however, three qualities that endangered his position as a king. In the first place, he was extremely compassionate. On one occasion he was in the company of the Papal Legate and Bishop Elphinstone when a man was being taken to his execution for the crime of murder. The man flung himself on the King's mercy, pleading that he had killed by accident. James turned to the Papal Legate for his advice and he replied: 'let justice be done.' 'Is this the mercy of Italian priests?' James asked the Bishop. 'You used to give me different counsel. Let there be compassion.'

Doubtless the good Bishop Elphinstone, who instructed him when he was young, had helped to plant the leniency in his character, just as his mother from civilised Burgundy must have helped to form his tastes. But neither of these could have suggested to him the wisdom of preferring low-born persons on the grounds of their personal merit. Still less could any youthful instruction have encouraged his distaste for the war-game, one of the principal pastimes of the baronage throughout Europe at this time, not least in Scotland.

Some of the magnates there, seeing upstarts in positions they coveted and opportunities for strife thrown away, began to pay court to the King's two younger brothers, both of whom possessed the manly qualities they preferred. So it happened that in the penultimate round of the contest between Stewart, Douglas and MacDonald, James III was vexed chiefly by his Stewart kin, as his grandfather had been.

In due course James felt compelled to imprison his brothers, and when the younger died in captivity the King was suspected of having murdered him. Considering his lifelong record of leniency, this seems improbable, but the whispers injured his reputation. From prison his other brother the Duke of Albany escaped, and when he made common cause with the King of England and the exiled Black Douglas, it became clear that he aimed at nothing less than the crown. His treason cannot be condoned like that of a Lord of the Isles, attempting to preserve the autonomous institutions of Gaelic Scotland. It was a naked bid for rights that were not his, and it cost his country dear when the English army of invasion captured the country's principal port of Berwick, never to be recovered. A gang of Scottish nobles chose this emergency to murder some of the King's favourites at his army headquarters near Lauder Bridge, and to carry him back a prisoner to Edinburgh.

Pacifically as was his nature, James received Albany and made him Lieutenant of Scotland. Albany in turn negotiated with the English King, who offered to assist the Black Douglas to recover his estates in return for recognition by the Scots as Lord Paramount. Then Edward IV died, and in the turmoil that followed, culminating in the victory of Henry Tudor at Bosworth, Albany and Douglas were left to act on their own. The patient policy of James III succeeded at last when the two raised a rebellion and were defeated. Albany fled to France where he was accidentally killed at a tournament. Douglas was captured, and James sentenced him, characteristically, to spend the remainder of his life a penitent in the abbey of Lindores. If the report of the Black Douglas's reaction is true, the King's concern for his redemption may have proved ineffective. 'A man who can do no better must be a monk,' he was said to have remarked philosophically. So ended the senior line of the good Sir James, Robert Bruce's devoted companion.

And so King James finally succeeded, without the harshness of his predecessors, in taming the last Black Douglas and his own Stewart kinsmen. He had already clipped the wings of the Lord of the Isles when that potentate appeared to be asserting too much independence. He summoned MacDonald to appear before Parliament, and when he failed to come, invaded his mainland territories until John of the Isles submitted to him a second time.

Though James was peace-loving and tolerant, he was not weak. He stripped the island Lordship of its great mainland earldom of Ross, which he annexed to the crown. On the other hand he gave John a formal title to the remainder of his lands, and he also appointed him a Lord of Parliament, so seeking to integrate him in the government of the kingdom as a whole.

Unhappily the Lord of the Isles had trouble-makers amongst his closest relatives, just as the King had. His own son Angus rose in rebellion and tried to seize the Lordship from him, and he was able to enlist the support of several who ought to have placed their armament at the disposal of the Lordship when they were called upon to do so.

Amongst the island clans, this consisted of a certain number of galleys, maintained according to the quota decreed by the Lord of the Isles. For instance, in 1354 John of the Isles permitted MacDougall of Lorne to construct eight vessels, each possessing between twelve and sixteen oars. There were three men to each oar, and this type of naval craft was called a birlinn. The largest galleys might contain as many as twenty-four oars. When Angus fought against his father in 1480, hundreds of these ships met near Tobermory in the Sound of Mull, in a battle so fierce that the sea ran red with blood and the nearby cove is called Bloody Bay to this day. It was an ominous event, echoing yet again the words of Tacitus: 'fortune can give no greater boon than discord among our foes.'

Yet the Lord of the Isles succeeded in reasserting his authority: it was James III who failed in the end, though the rebellion that led to his death had little to do with Stewarts, Douglases or MacDonalds. The Campbell Chief is the most noteworthy amongst the rather sleezy gang of conspirators who took the King's fifteen-year-old son from Stirling Castle to give a colour of legality to their treason. James was not without loyal supporters, but he was no military commander: he did not even sit a horse well. He was worsted in a fight outside Stirling, fell from his horse as he fled the field, and was carried into a miller's house, where he was murdered by some unknown assassin. It was left to his son to complete the destruction of the Lordship of the Isles.

James IV was arguably the most attractive of Stewart sovereigns and ablest of Stewart chiefs. To the qualities he had inherited from the saintly Margaret of Denmark and from his cultured father he added a flair of his own. Where his father had lived fatally remote from his subjects, preferring the limited company of those who shared his own intellectual interests, James IV displayed an openness and charm to all. Where his father had appeared mean, except to people such as musicians and architects, he appeared generous. His gift of communication showed itself in a remarkable mastery of languages, amongst which he had the wisdom to include that of his Gaelic subjects. A Spaniard remarked that one reason why he was so greatly loved was that he was so humane, another legacy from his father. His own greatest legacy to his country was the establishment of a faculty of medicine at his new university of Aberdeen, before either Oxford or Cambridge possessed one, and his foundation of the College of Surgeons in Edinburgh. It is the more tragic that a King so good and so gifted failed to treat the problem of tribal Scotland with more insight.

To some extent he was the victim of a fatal legacy, and the MacDonalds themselves must share the blame for the outcome. The tragedy remains, its consequences still with us to this day.

The most fateful step that James IV took was to hand out vice-regal powers to two families over areas of the north and west in which they had no previous authority. In these regions there had been earlier pioneers into Celtic Scotland from without, Fraser and Menzies, Cumming and Hay and Stewart, who had become integrated in them by marriage and sentiment. Some had obtained ancient Celtic earldoms by marriage or royal grant. Not until the fifteenth century were new earldoms created, comparatively modest affairs carrying a title that may have appeared over-inflated but which really indicated a trusted servant of the crown. Among these was the creation by James II in 1445 of the earldom of Huntly.

The property it defined was the fertile oasis of Strathbogie in the Grampain mountains, strategically placed between the pass that runs south to Aberdeen, and another that winds north through the hills to the plain of Moray. Here Robert Bruce had placed a certain Adam from Gordon near the southern Border in gratitude for his somewhat belated support, and here a Gordon clan had begun to extend its branches. But the senior male line died out in 1402, and another southern aspirant moved in to collect the rewards of marrying a Gordon heiress. His name was Alexander Seton, but his son took his mother's name, and it was he who was created Earl of Huntly and received the old Cumming lordship of Badenoch to augment his possessions. Huntly, needless to say, was among those who had rallied to the support of James III before he was murdered.

So it is understandable that James IV should have looked to

such people as upholders of the royal authority in the north. What he evidently overlooked was that in this distant Celtic world they were apt to be regarded as foreigners on the make, distrusted as such with good reason. He apparently did not consider that it might have been wiser as well as fairer to give almost unlimited authority to a Lord of the Isles than to a Gordon of Huntly. This region had already been plagued by the Stewart Wolf of Badenoch: henceforth it was to be afflicted by the predatory Gordons.

Disorders within the Lordship hastened its downfall. John of the Isles' son Angus was murdered by his own harpist in 1490 in Inverness, which may not appear to have been much of a misfortune considering his conduct. Yet the support he had been given at Bloody Bay shows what popular support he enjoyed, and it was the Dean of Knoydart who composed his Gaelic elegy, saying, 'dear to me was his noble palm, ungrudging of gold or silver, who joyed in feast and hunting.' He left a young son called Donald who would be the last to attempt to save the Lordship from extinction: in the meantime Alasdair of Lochalsh led the militant MacDonalds to the capture of Inverness in the year after the death of Angus.

This was when the Mackenzies of Kintail made their debut on a larger stage, sweeping down to defeat the MacDonalds on behalf of the crown. James IV, who was not yet twenty-one years old, acted with impetuous haste, forfeiting the aged Lord of the Isles whose only fault was that he had been unable to control his clansmen as he might have done with greater support from the central government. Instead of strengthening his powers, the King deprived him of them altogether and removed the apex of that tribal society to live as a pensioner at his court until he died in the abbey of Paisley.

In doing this, James IV unleashed a state of complete anarchy, setting in train all those clan conflicts that are now such a romantic element of Highland history. It cannot have been so attractive at the time, and to this misfortune is probably attributable the loss of the records of the Lordship's administration and of the greater part of the ancient Gaelic literature. As an example of this, only a solitary Gaelic charter survives, sufficient evidence that there must have been hundreds of them. Apart from the collections of the Beatons and MacMhuirichs, only a single anthology of literature remains, the Dean of Lismore's, to hint at the riches of that age which are lost.

For this loss MacDonald must share the blame with the King.

James IV understood Gaelic, and he had a sufficiently enlightened approach to learning to found a faculty of medicine at a Scottish university. He would surely have listened sympathetically if the deposed Lord of the Isles had suggested the creation of a centre of Gaelic studies at any of Scotland's three universities. As it was, no such faculty was established until the twentieth century, by which time much was irretrievably lost. John of the Isles could have found few at the court of James IV apart from the King himself able to speak his native language, and he stands as an early example of the Highland chiefs who gradually left the only European tongue with a literature that dates back to the age of Latin and Greek to degenerate into the speech of an illiterate peasantry.

James IV visited the western Highlands twice in 1493, the year of the forfeiture, and three times during the next couple of years. He appointed his cousin Duncan Stewart of Appin to the post of Chamberlain of the Isles, and it was this man who built Castle Stalker on the Cormorant's Rock in the Firth of Lorne, which has been restored as a residence recently, after remaining for centuries a ruin. There are few more arresting sights than this fortress in the sea, the mountains of Morvern and Mull rising behind it. This may be the very place in which the young King so rashly forfeited John of the Isles.

In the following year he brought a fleet into those waters and planted a garrison at Dunaverty Castle in Kintyre. But John MacDonald sailed in from Islay to capture Dunaverty and hang its newly-appointed Keeper before the very eyes of the King. Then the MacDonalds of Ardnamurchan recaptured the castle for James, and sent John of Islay with his four sons to Edinburgh, where they were all hanged. So the rifts grew, not only between clans, but between the septs of the great Clan Donald. When MacDonald of Lochalsh rose once more, it was the Ardnamurchan MacDonalds who defeated and slew him. It ought to have occurred to the King that he might easily have succeeded in pacifying this society without submitting its clans to masters introduced from without.

But it did not. In 1498 he continued his father's policy by appointing the Earl of Argyll Lieutenant of the Isles and the Earl of Huntly Lieutenant of the North, each of them with sweeping vice-regal powers. He thus farmed out the problem of what to do with the old tribal Scotland, that had puzzled his predecessors for the past four hundred years, to the Campbells and the Gordons. It was not to prove a happy solution. When James IV died on the field of Flodden in 1513 he had only three Highland chiefs with him. The 2nd Earl of Argyll died courageously with his king. Huntly fled the field to complete an act of pillage that he had been plotting for some time.

It was made easier for him by the extreme youth of the new king, James V, crowned when he was less than two years old. If many of the qualities of James IV can be attributed to his admirable Danish mother, some of the characteristics of his son may be explained in the same way. It would have seemed impossible that kings so humane as James IV and his father could have been followed by one so callous. It was remarked with horror that he once ordered a thief to be burned alive, 'which was done, binding him to a stake, and was burnt: which deed was never seen in this realm of before, nor will be hereafter.' The observer proved wrong about that.

The mother of James V was Margaret Tudor, sister of Henry VIII of England, the most vicious, evil Queen in Scottish history. After Flodden she soon remarried to the Red Douglas, Earl of Angus, and although she divorced him almost as soon to marry a Stewart (to the scandal of her brother, of all people), the Douglases closed in on the person of her infant son. Douglases became his Treasurer, his Master of the Wine Cellar, Master of his Larder, of his Household. Instead of giving the youth a training in kingship, they encouraged his dissipations, hoping that when he came of age he would leave the government in their hands while he enjoyed his pleasures.

But when James finally escaped from their clutches, he pursued the Douglases with vindictive hatred. The head of them, Earl of Angus, he besieged in Tantallon Castle until the Red Douglas submitted and withdrew to England. He was more fortunate than his sister Lady Glamis, whom James burned alive on a charge of witchcraft as soon as he found the opportunity. She was young and beautiful and she suffered her ordeal with great courage, which made the public scandal all the greater.

The severity of the King's treatment of the Douglases was matched by the violence of his attitude to the Highlanders. He was barely eighteen years old and little instructed in the complexities of the problem when he issued letters of fire and sword to exterminate the entire Clan Chattan, the Children of the Cat, sparing the lives of priests, women and children, who were to be deported to the shores of Shetland and Norway. Of course such monstrous orders could not be implemented, but they sufficed to create a distrust for Stewart rule which was strengthened by the King's close friendship with the Earl of Huntly, who might expect to be a principal beneficiary from this policy of genocide.

It is curious that James V did not form a similar attachment to his other royal Lieutenant, Campbell of Argyll. Unlike the Gordons, the Campbells were of the aboriginal Celtic stock. The Gordon chiefs never became integrated in the Gaelic world they pillaged so ruthlessly, though many of their clansmen inevitably did over the centuries, as they were settled in lands that their chiefs had seized. James V went so far as to allow the Campbell Lieutenancy to lapse, and to grant a commission in its place to Alexander MacDonald of Islay, who informed him of the Campbell practice of fomenting strife in order to profit by suppressing it. This was what both Lieutenants had been doing ever since their offices had been created, and James would have done better to abolish both.

The success of his policy in the west offered him further instruction, but not sufficient to restrain his impetuous nature when Donald Gorm MacDonald of Sleat in Skye once again raised the banner of the Lordship of the Isles.

The fate of the true heir Donald Dubh, grandson of that court pensioner John of the Isles, had been an exceedingly pitiful one. Years before his father Angus was murdered by his harpist in Inverness, Donald Dubh had been kidnapped by Campbells in Islay and carried off to their castle of Innischonaill in Loch Awe, which they had maintained as their prison since they had moved to Inveraray. There the wretched child spent his entire youth until he was nineteen years old, when a rescue party of MacDonalds from Glencoe succeeded in rescuing him by stealth, rowing across the loch so silently that they took the castle completely by surprise. He then enjoyed three years of freedom before a rising in his favour was suppressed in 1506 and Donald Dubh was taken to spend another thirty-eight years in captivity, this time in Edinburgh Castle. There he lay when Donald Gorm in Skye raised his standard.

He joined forces with Ruaridh MacLeod of Lewis to assault the forfeited earldom of Ross on the mainland opposite. Here stood the great fortress called Eilean Donnan in Loch Duich. Its name derives from the Celtic Saint Donnan, martyred on the island of Eigg, who had perhaps built a cell on this tiny island surrounded by the incomparable panorama of mountains called the Sisters of Kintail. When the Mackenzies were rewarded for their services to the crown by the erection of the barony of Kintail in 1508, the maintenance of this castle became their responsibility, and they placed it in the hands of Clan MacRae, who became known as Mackenzie's Shirt of Mail. It is said to have been Duncan MacRae, Chamberlain of Eilean Donnan, who succeeded in hitting Donald Gorm with an arrow from the battlements. Pulling it out, Donald severed an artery and bled to death.

MacRae subsequently received the estate of Inverinate that his descendant made famous in the following century by the collection of Gaelic literature which he transcribed there. The MacRaes were never more than a small, dependent clan, but to this day they have a well-attested reputation for breeding men of exceptional size and strength; and they have a second claim to literary distinction also. When John MacRae emigrated from Kintail to America in 1774, he composed the only Gaelic poetry of the New World which subsequently returned to his native land to be preserved amongst its traditional songs.

What feelings motivated men who risked their lives for a chief in prison and a forfeited lordship? The remaining heads of that island society enjoyed a far greater degree of independence in the absence of MacDonald, yet they gave their lives in the forlorn hope of securing his return, a display of loyalty in sharp contrast to what the Stewart kings generally experienced from their own nearest relatives. Even the insurrection of Angus against his father John of the Isles must have been based upon an ideal, otherwise he could never have attracted such support, nor earned that encomium after his death from the Dean of Knoydart.

As usual in this society fleeced of its records, it is a surviving Gaelic poem from the heart that echoes down the ages, telling us what emotions moved these desperate men.

> It is no joy without Clan Donald,
> It is no strength to be without them,
> The best race in the round world,
> To them belongs every goodly man.
>
> The noblest race of all created,
> In whom dwelt prowess and terribleness,
> A race to whom tyrants bowed,
> In whom dwelt wisdom and piety.
>
> A race the best for service and shelter,
> A race the best for valour of hand,
> Ill I deem the shortness of her skein
> By whom their thread was spun.

For sorrow and for sadness
I have forsaken wisdom and learning;
On their account I have forsaken all things.
It is no joy without Clan Donald.

There are seventeen verses to this moving expression of grief when the Lordship of John of the Isles was forfeited.

What awareness did James V show of these aspirations and loyalties when he mounted his expedition by sea round his Gaelic dominions after the death of Donald Gorm in Kintail? He set out from the Forth in May 1540 with twelve ships containing artillery and 1,500 men. He was accompanied by his stepfather the Red Douglas, with whom he was now reconciled, and most ominously by the Earl of Huntly, prospecting for new pastures. In the course of his journey the remotest chief was introduced to the habits of treachery with which the Stewarts so often sought to endear themselves to their Highland subjects. Mackay of Strathnaver was ordered to his presence, and instantly taken prisoner. The enormous, remote province of Strathnaver was to prove the ultimate goal of Gordon ambitions, and that encounter the opening scene in a tragedy that ended in the Sutherland clearances three hundred years later.

From Orkney the King sailed to Lewis, where he carried off the MacLeod Chief and his nearest kinsmen. Then he moved on to the castle of Duntulm at Trotternich in Skye, where he arrested Glengarry, Clanranald and other leaders of Clan Donald. So it continued until James reached Dunbarton with his hijacked chiefs, whom he locked up in the castle there. Some were soon released; others such as Clanranald remained in captivity; disorders in the tribal lands increased in the absence of those upon whom their administration depended.

There has been a great deal more dispute than the facts warrant over whether James V was an able and determined ruler, effectively imposing law and order in the farthest corners of his kingdom. His methods were exactly the same in the Border country, where their effect produced more instantly disastrous results, and where his infamy was immortalised in Border ballads.

A new clan had emerged in Liddesdale with the curious name of Armstrong. The earliest reference to this name in Scotland is as late as 1370, and tradition gave it an origin similar to the Turnbull legend. But there was no killing of a boar or bull in this case. The Armstrongs' heroic ancestor was said to have saved

the life of the king by lifting him on to his own horse after the
king had been dismounted in battle — no mean feat in the case of
a man carrying the weight of armour. Both legends have too late
a context, equally obvious in the Armstrong story, since the name
cannot have originated in the rescue of a medieval king in
Scotland when it existed so much earlier south of the Border.
It is far more plausible to conclude that the Armstrongs were
people of the original British stock, living in the debatable land
of the Border hills as the Basques have done in the Pyrenees
between France and Spain. Unlike the Basques, these hill folk
lost their native language if they were Britons, but like them,
they were able to stray unnoticed over the boundary between two
countries, as it is always easier for a pastoral people to do than for
those tied to the fields in which their crops are planted.

By the time of James V they had expanded from Liddesdale
into Annandale and Eskdale. There they operated from two
well-sited peel towers, Hollows Tower and Gilnockie, beside the
River Esk, and Johnnie Armstrong their Chief was reputed to
possess three thousand armed men to his name.

It is true that Armstrong of Gilnockie was a reaver who operated
a protection racket, levied blackmail, and endangered the peace
with England by his cattle raids across the Border. His neighbours might well have felt gratitude to a king who removed such
a menace from amongst them. But they did not, and we know this
because they expressed their feelings so emphatically in the
ballads they sang. This traditional literature, like that of the
Gaels, is virtually the only source that remains of the real feelings
of ordinary people, and it is bound to be genuine because they
would not have repeated by word of mouth from generation to
generation anything that did not express their real opinions.
Scotland is fortunate to possess such an exceptional mine of
traditions in two languages, and the Border ballads are especially
eloquent in their delineation of that handsome, melancholy, cruel
young man, James V.

On the subject of the King's habitual perfidy, this is confirmed
by the account of Lindsay of Pitscottie who described James's
expedition to Liddesdale at the time when he was pursuing the
Douglases and ordering the extermination of the Mackintosh
confederation. The teen-age monarch arrived in Liddesdale
ostensibly to hunt and invited Armstrong to join him, who did so
with as little fear of treachery as Mackay of Strathnaver, at the
other end of the kingdom. In like manner, he was arrested with
his companions.

'So when he entered in before the King,' Lindsay tells us, 'he came very reverently with his foresaid number very richly apparelled, trusting that in respect he had come to the King's grace willingly and voluntarily, not being taken or apprehended by the King, he should obtain the more favour.' How wrong he was. When he saw that the King meant to execute him and his companions, and that no plea could touch that stony heart, he said: 'I am but a fool to seek grace of a graceless face. But had I known, Sir, I should have lived upon the Borders in despite of King Harry and you both: for I know King Harry would down weigh my best horse with gold to know that I was condemned to die this day.' The words of Johnnie Armstrong in the ballad are no less trenchant:

> To seek hot water beneath cold ice
> Surely it is a great folie.
> I have askèd grace at a graceless face
> And there is none for my men and me.

No Scotsman would have passed such a judgement on James V's father or grandfather.

Nemesis overtook James V when he agreed to meet his uncle Harry at York, and the English King, who had never travelled so far north in his life, dragged his ailing bulk all the way there to await his arrival. But being treacherous himself, James feared treachery; he was afraid he might be kidnapped as he had kidnapped so many others. Instead of honouring his engagement, he sent an excuse.

Henry VIII, by this time fairly psychopathic through the ravages of syphilis, invaded Scotland in a fury. The English army, not half the number of men that Johnnie Armstrong was said to have been able to muster, moved up the River Esk, not far from the towers of Gilnockie and Hollows in which he had once held sway. There was an army of King James there to meet it, but so little loyalty did he inspire that it scarcely put up a fight, and the number of Scots who surrendered was equal to all the English soldiers present.

James V lay ill in the palace of Falkland: the nature of his disease remains a mystery. He died in despair, leaving a girl one week old to succeed as Mary, Queen of Scots, and his country in a predicament such as it had not experienced since King John Balliol was kicked off the throne by the Hammer of the Scots.

The grand design of the Stewart monarchy had been to

establish one body of law, effective throughout the country, a single administration reaching to the farthest corners of the kingdom. What had been achieved by the time James V died was this. The source of legal titles to property throughout a large area, the Lordship of the Isles, had been abolished, and nothing effective put in its place. Charters had been seized, cancelled or duplicated, chiefs responsible for maintaining justice had been carried off, while Campbells and Gordons used delegated regal authority to exploit the chaos for their own ends. The shambles could hardly have been more complete at the time when the Scottish crown passed to a baby girl who was brought up as a French princess, married first to a French king, and trained to an almost exclusive obsession with her dynastic claim to the English throne.

It was in these circumstances that so many people in Scotland, at a time when all Europe was moving out of the medieval into the modern age, fell back in self-defence on the frail redoubts of their clan loyalties and prepared to fight for the narrow limits of their own tribal lands.

Yet there was one demonstration of remarkable unity in pursuit of a loftier aim. A few months after the King's death the Chief of Clan Donald, that lifelong captive Donald Dubh, escaped from Edinburgh Castle and the people of the Hebrides rose in his favour spontaneously. Clanranald, MacLeod of Lewis, MacLeod of Dunvegan, Maclean of Duart, Maclaine of Lochbuie, MacNeill of Barra, the MacDonalds of Ardnamurchan, people who had not always been in amity with one another — all displayed the loyalty King James might have won for himself if he had understood the meaning of the word. They gave it to a chief few of them had ever seen: they were to give it later to a Stewart prince they had never set eyes on. When Donald Dubh fled to Ireland and died there, he was given a state funeral, all that could be offered him in compensation for the misery of his life.

CHAPTER FIVE

Children of the Mist

The most famous of the dispossessed clans are the MacGregors. They claimed descent from the royal house of Alpin and were proprietors of Glenorchy when Iain, son of Malcolm of Glenorchy, died in 1292. The heiress was Mariota who married Iain Campbell, and whether or not these had a child who died in infancy, the Campbells thereafter claimed the superiority of Glenorchy. Had an heir survived, he or she would have been expected to adopt the maternal name as Chief of the tribe of Glenorchy.

So it is today. The sole surviving daughter of the 19th Lord Saltoun has inherited the Chiefship of Clan Fraser, and preserves and transmits this name together with the peerage title. The late Countess of Cromartie transmitted the Chiefship of Clan Mackenzie with her surname and its earldom to the present Earl. The Countess of Sutherland, Chief of that name will likewise pass on her name, chiefship and earldom to her son, irrespective of his father's designation. In the case of Clan Hay the late Chief, Countess of Erroll, was married to the Chief of the ancient name of Moncreiffe, derived from the sacred hill called *Monadh Craoibhe* in Gaelic. Consequently their elder son has succeeded as 24th Earl and Chief of the Hays of Erroll, while his brother is heir presumptive to the Chiefship of Moncreiffe.

But in the case of the royal tribe of Glenorchy the Campbell marriage produced no surviving heir, so that it was faced with the prospect of feudal vassalage to the Campbells without the leavening of kinship. Consequently a grandson of Malcolm of Glenorchy, who might in earlier times have been considered the tanist, led his people in an attempt to defend their homeland by the sword. His name was Gregor, and he became their Chief and name-father of the clan, to be followed by his son John the One-Eyed, who lived until 1390. These were the turbulent years before James I returned from his captivity with the avowed aim of restoring order in his realm. There is no sorrier example of his failure and that of his descendants than the fate of Clan Gregor.

Yet it appears that during much of the fifteenth century the MacGregors sustained relatively little harm. In the course of it, for instance, there lived in Glen Lyon John MacGregor, son of a vicar and father of the Notary Public, Dougall MacGregor. Dougall's son was Sir James MacGregor, Dean of Lismore by the year 1511 and compiler of the collection of Gaelic poetry that bears his name. Apart from the ancient literature it preserves from earlier ages, it contains poems which do not give an impression of continual strife, nor of inveterate hatred between Campbells and MacGregors. In one instance a Campbell Chief if praised for his literary taste. Another commemorates the Campbell Chief who became Chancellor of Scotland and rode to his death on the field of Flodden in 1513, encouraged by the words: 'Thou, Archibald, who would refuse no man, thou art the Lugh [an ancient Celtic hero] of this latter time; thou, Earl of Argyll, be thou a champion triumphant. Send the summons east and west for the Gael from the field of Leinster; drive the Saxons westwards over the high sea, that Alba may suffer no division.'

However uncertain the poet's geography, he is expressing the same desire for unity as the Stewart kings tried to promote, and a Campbell leader was perfectly acceptable to him. The most savage stricture in the Book is addressed to Allan of Clanranald, who died in about 1505: 'it was thou who stirred up evil in the Isles, thou didst impoverish her tribute and her sanctuary; thy behaviour hath ever been a coward's.' A MacGregor anthology as impartial as this, covering the whole of the fifteenth century, suggests that the feud with the Campbells might have been resolved quite happily if the Campbells had not been invested with powers that proved an irresistible temptation to them.

It has been noticed that the Chief of Clan Diarmaid was among those who hounded James III to his death in 1488. No sooner was this accomplished than an Act of Parliament empowered Sir Duncan Campbell of Glenorchy and Ewen Campbell of Strachur amongst others to enforce law and order in the country. In 1492 Campbell of Glenorchy obtained the office of baillie of the crown lands of Glen Lyon and Glandochart and by 1502 this had enabled him to obtain a charter to Glen Lyon. This empowered him by due process of law to exterminate MacGregors over a wide area, using those who had no option but to become his vassals as hired assassins. When these prospered, he enjoyed the benefit, when they did not, the MacGregors were blamed.

By this time the leadership of Clan Gregor had passed to the branch that lived in Glenstrae, since they still possessed a legal title to their lands here as tenants of the Earl of Argyll, while those who survived in Glenorchy were now in the position of illegal squatters. But in 1519 the Campbells found a quisling to put forward as the MacGregor Chief. His only credentials, apart from his willingness to betray his clan, were that he had married Colin Campbell of Glenorchy's daughter after he had raped her. The Campbell's own record of these times, the *Black Book of Taymouth*, confesses that he 'was not righteous heir to the MacGregor.' It was therefore necessary to murder the true heirs, and they did not succeed in doing this until over thirty years later when Colin of Glenorchy caught Duncan, the Tutor of Glenstrae with two of his sons by treachery and beheaded all of them. His son-in-law the bogus Chief succeeded in murdering the third of the Tutor's sons: but this still left a grandson of the Glenstrae branch as legitimate heir enjoying the protection of the Earl of Argyll as his vassal — for what that was worth.

James IV might have halted all these enormities when he came of age; and he was already fifteen years old when he became King. Yet he took the opposite course of investing the Campbell Chief with vice-regal powers. It was from this time that the tragedy of the MacGregors began to assume its darkest colours; from the time of James V who promoted the solutions of kidnapping and genocide; of Mary, Queen of Scots, the disorders of whose reign were greatest in the remotest corners of her kingdom; of her son James VI, the most pathologically anti-Gaelic of all the Stewart kings.

By this time the Campbells had managed to steer a statute through Parliament, forfeiting the MacGregor Chiefship of the title it still held as a vassal of Mac Cailein Mór in Glenstrae. Alasdair MacGregor of Glenstrae begged Argyll to take him to the King to plead his distressing case, and the Campbell Chief agreed to aid him, only to inveigle him to Edinburgh where he was given a mock trial and then hanged with seven of his followers.

Generally the Campbells did their paperwork with such skill that none of their actions appeared other than devotion to the public service as laid down by statute, or enforcement of their legal rights attested by charters of ownership. But on this occasion the wretched Alasdair of Glenstrae managed to leave behind his own account of what had been going on, and it reveals all. 'I, Alasdair MacGregor of Glenstrae, confess here before God that I have been persuaded, moved and enticed, as I am now presently accused and troubled for. Also, if I had used counsel or command of the man that has enticed me, I would have done and committed sundry high murders more. For truly, since I was

first His Majesty's man, I could never be at any ease by my Lord
Argyll's falsity and inventions, for he caused Maclean and Clan
Cameron commit hership and slaughter in my room of Rannoch,
the which caused my poor men thereafter to beg and steal; also
thereafter he moved my brother and some of my friends to commit both hership and slaughter upon the Laird of Luss; also he
persuaded myself with message to war against the Laird of
Buchanan which I did refuse, for the which I was continually
threatened that he would be my unfriend . . .'

Is this devastating recital to be believed? It is not easy to sort
out the dirty work to which the MacGregors were driven by the
blackmail of their Campbell persecutors from the brigandage that
had become their own way of life. One thing is certain: it is just
as creditworthy and a good deal more credible than any of the
official evidence planted by the Campbells in Privy Council
records and the statute book.

It marks the end of the road which the MacGregors reached in
1603 and it raises the question, did Argyll set the MacGregors
against the Colquhouns of Luss, or did the MacGregors attack
the Colquhouns on their own initiative? The Colquhouns were
another offspring of the Celtic Church, hereditary guardians of
the crozier of St Kessog, who had lived in Glen Luss and on an
island in Loch Lomond that is still called the Monk's Isle. He
enjoys greater fame today from the Kessock Ferry which runs
from Inverness to the Black Isle.

Maelduin of Luss had been custodian of the crozier when he
was Dean of the Lennox in 1220, but his descendants did not
receive their present name until about 1368 when his possessions
passed with an heiress to Sir Robert Colquhoun of Colquhoun,
Chief of a clan that had supported Bruce in the war of independence and prospered accordingly. The Colquhouns never
wavered in their support of the Stewart kings either, a wise
precaution on the part of a clan living so close to the Campbells.
The trust they inspired led to the appointment of a Colquhoun
as Governor of Dunbarton Castle, that unassailable fortress
which had once been the capital of the British kingdom of
Strathclyde. Their discretion has maintained them in Luss to
this day, and the daughter of the 32nd Chief of Colquhoun is the
present Duchess of Argyll.

But they had their vicissitudes. For instance, the 16th Chief
conceived a liking for the wife of the Macfarlane Chief and was
caught by him while satisfying his emotions. Colquhoun fled in
these most embarrassing and distressing of circumstances, and

took refuge in one of his castles, where the Macfarlanes tried to smoke him out. Rather mysteriously he was killed by an arrow, and there were those who believed that his younger brother fired it, with one eye on the chiefship. At any rate he was executed for this crime in Edinburgh. Macfarlane gained access to Colquhoun's corpse, from which he cut the genital organs, and gave his wife a fit of the vapours by serving them to her for dinner.

A different kind of misfortune befell the 17th Chief when the MacGregors invaded Luss in 1603 and killed many of the Colquhouns who resisted them. Off went their womenfolk to the King, bearing the blood-stained shirts of their dead and (it was said) many more that had been dipped in sheep's blood. James VI, who could not stand the sight of blood, sent them home with authority to pursue Clan Gregor with fire and sword. That was when Alasdair of Glenstrae returned to Luss with four hundred of his clansmen, incited, so he claimed, by Argyll. Could he possibly have known that he was now opposing himself directly to royal authority? There followed the battle and massacre of Glenfruin which resulted in his execution and the proscription of the MacGregors.

MacGregor could not have expected his submission to be properly investigated. James VI was so prejudiced against his Gaelic subjects that he gave orders for their wholesale extermination as his grandfather had done. Anyway, he travelled to London in 1603 to occupy the throne of Queen Elizabeth, leaving the very men in control in Edinburgh who had the greatest interest in suppressing MacGregor's story. The steps all these people took in the aftermath of Glenfruin appear perfectly hysterical. The Privy Council fired the first salvo by abolishing the name of MacGregor and ordering the adoption of other surnames on pain of death. All who had been at Glenfruin were forbidden to carry any weapon in future other than a knife without a point for eating their food. The Campbells were left to deal with the true Chief of the proscribed clan as they pleased: they ran him to earth and murdered him in 1604. The Privy Council then added an order that nobody who had previously been a MacGregor could assemble in a group of more than four persons.

These rules were enshrined in an Act of Parliament in 1607, which added a prohibition on children taking the names of their former MacGregor parents, lest this should help to bring a new clan into existence. But it was the statute of 1633 that contained the ultimate enormities. No clergyman was to baptise any male child of the MacGregors and it was no longer a punishable crime to kill a member of this clan. Bloodhounds were used to assist in exterminating them, and they were hunted like vermin. The policy of the Stewart kings towards their tribal subjects had reached its apotheosis.

Yet paradoxically it was precisely these people, traditional and conservative to the last, who supported the Stewart dynasty when its other subjects grew weary of their misrule, and the outlawed MacGregors were among the first to do so when the English-speaking peoples of the realm rebelled against Charles I. Of course they had an ulterior motive as well as nothing to lose, for Campbell of Argyll was among the King's opponents. So it was a rare occasion for rejoicing among the Children of the Mist when Charles II was restored to his throne in 1660, the Campbell Chief was executed in Edinburgh, and the disgusting statute of 1633 repealed, 'considering that those who were formerly designed by the name of MacGregor had, during the troubles, carried themselves with such loyalty and affection to His Majesty as might justly wipe off all memory of their former miscarriages.'

By this time few if any of the culprits of Glenfruin could still have been alive. The living were being graciously forgiven the faults of the dead.

But the recovery of the MacGregors depended on the eclipse of Campbell power, which lasted only so long as the Stewarts retained their throne. In 1688 the last King James was expelled from it by William of Orange, supported by the exiled Campbell Chief, who lost no time in replacing the punitive legislation against the MacGregors on the statute book in its entirety. There it remained until 1775, and if this achieved nothing else that was worthwhile, at least it helped to provide Scotland with another of the country's folk-heroes, Rob Roy.

It is a commonplace that people can be brutalised by ill-treatment and the official records suggest that the MacGregors had been rendered thoroughly savage. But just as the fifteenth-century evidence shows how remarkably cultured and civilised many of them remained under stress, so do their achievements during the period after the proscription was reimposed. Rob Roy was certainly a rogue, though an engaging one; so were his sons. But during this time his own family produced a dynasty of learned men (such is the Celtic fashion) almost without parallel in Europe during the same age.

These had selected the name of Gregory, of whom James was the inventor of the reflecting telescope, his nephew David Professor of Astronomy at Oxford, while the inventor's own son became Professor of Medicine at Aberdeen. His name was James, and he was followed by his son James in the same Chair at the university; until this James died in 1755 and was followed there by his brother John. Nor were these the only academic dynasts in the family. Another James Gregory, who was Professor of Mathematics in Edinburgh in the reign of Charles II, was still represented in this Chair by his great-grandson, while his great-great-grandson became Professor of Chemistry in Aberdeen in 1839. The publications of most of these men earned them an international reputation at a time when the Scottish universities achieved their highest European fame.

Such were the relatives of Rob Roy, whose letters written in English, his second language, reveal that he too was a cultivated man. His appearance and behaviour gave a different impression. Red-haired as his byname implies, his tree-trunk legs (of which more could be seen than today's form of kilt reveals) were also covered by a thick coat of red hair. He was not unusually tall, but his arms were so long that he could tie the garters of his hose, two inches below the knee, without bending down.

Rob Roy was a younger son of Gregor the Chief, his mother the sister of Robert Campbell of Glen Lyon, who allowed himself to be used as a tool by the administration that planned the massacre of Glencoe. Unable to use his proper clan name, Rob Roy called himself Robert Campbell. In 1693 when his father died he became Tutor (or guardian) to his nephew the adolescent Chief of the Clan, who used the name James Graham. The responsibility had fallen to him at an extremely sensitive time, between the restoration of the penal laws and the first Jacobite uprising of 1715. If Rob Roy proved unscrupulous and tortuous, there was more than his Campbell ancestry to account for it.

His sport was to play off against each other the three surrounding Dukes, Murray of Atholl, Campbell of Argyll and Graham of Montrose, those victorious tycoons of the revolution. He had been brought up on a farm in Balquhidder on the Atholl estates, adopted the clan name of Argyll, and tutored a Chief called Graham. He cannot be blamed if he felt not the slightest loyalty to any of the three. Sometimes he double-crossed one or more of these potentates, sometimes they tried to get the better of him: and it is a measure of his cunning that he generally made them pay through the nose for their efforts.

As a freebooter he made enough money to buy the wadset of a property in the old MacGregor country east of Ben Lomond, whose western face looks down on the lovely Colquhoun lands of

Luss beyond Loch Lomond. A wadset was a title acquired by paying a lump sum that amounted to a loan. It could be bought in by repaying the loan, but in the meantime the profits of the estate constituted the interest on it.

In this property Rob Roy lived with his wife Helen, also a MacGregor and one of the stern old Celtic breed; and the Duke of Montrose advanced money to him that enabled him to extend his enterprises as a cattle dealer. But in 1711 he absconded with money placed in his hands by other cattle traders. Montrose lured him back with a promise of protection that he promptly dishonoured. Convicted of fraud in Edinburgh, Rob Roy had to go into hiding to avoid arrest and feared to return to his home. Montrose thereupon evicted his wife and young children in the depths of winter, and this is when Helen MacGregor is believed to have composed her famous pibroch known as the MacGregor Lament.

Rob Roy wrote to the Duke of Atholl, explaining that he had offered Montrose, his principal creditor, payment in full but that Montrose had rejected his overture out of a wish to ruin him. Rob Roy then placed himself under the protection of John Campbell, 1st Earl of Breadalbane, who had played such an unsavoury part in the Glencoe massacre without showing his hand in it, and who lived in Kilchurn Castle by Loch Awe. Rob promised that the lands of Montrose would supply him with his cattle in future, and that he would make the Duke regret the day he had quarrelled with him. That was a promise Rob Roy kept. To assist his enterprises he captured and held the fort of Inversnaid, and that was where he was when the Jacobite standard was raised in the Highlands in 1715.

Off went Rob Roy to rally his clansmen who had settled in the surroundings of Aberdeen under assumed names, and it is a measure of his magnetism that he managed to raise a force of two hundred men although he was not the Chief, and the descendants of the proscribed clan might have been forgiven if they had begged him to go away and leave them alone. Amongst those who welcomed him hospitably was his cousin James Gregory, the Professor of Medicine at Aberdeen University, and it nearly cost him dear. For Rob Roy expressed his gratitude by offering to take the Professor's son back with him to the Highlands to foster, an honour that it would have been difficult to reject without grave offence. Dr Gregory thanked him profusely, but suggested that the child should be left at home for a little longer since he was so young. Rob Roy was invited to return for him in the following year: and as soon as his back was turned, the Professor sent him to more law-abiding relatives, well out of harm's way.

Rob Roy's part in the 1715 rebellion is typically equivocal. The Campbell in him evidently made him determined that who-ever won, he would not lose. He went about drinking ostentatious toasts to the Pretender, but did not bring his force to the Battle of Sheriffmuir where the Jacobites were defeated. The Grahams tried to seize him while he was in the hostelry at Crianlarich, but he felled each intruder who tried to pass through the door, and so escaped. Then he moved east into Fife, where he attacked some Hanoverians on his own initiative. Behind his back his home in Breadalbane was burned down, and to revenge this he seized Graham of Killearn as he was collecting the rents, set him free, but kept the money.

The Duke of Montrose captured him, but he escaped. Then the Duke of Atholl offered to take him prisoner, inveigled him to Blair Castle, disarmed him, and placed him in a dungeon at Logierait. Again Rob Roy escaped, and now he harried the lands of Montrose without mercy for years. Very probably he was being abetted by the Duke of Argyll, following the traditional Campbell practice of using MacGregors to do their dirty work. Rob Roy irritated Montrose especially by writing challenges to him in which he offered to settle their differences by single combat.

The part of Mac Cailein Mór is particularly difficult to interpret in the events of 1722. Whether he had no further use for Rob Roy and wanted to dispose of him, or whether he genuinely desired to reconcile his neighbours to one another, he arranged a settlement between Rob Roy and Montrose, after which Rob made a formal submission to the government's Commander in the Highlands, General Wade.

What casts the greatest suspicion on Argyll is that Rob Roy explained his behaviour during the 1715 uprising by stating that he had been engaged in obtaining intelligence which he passed to the Duke. His eccentric actions during the rebellion certainly appear more comprehensible if he was in fact a government agent. But whether his story was true or not, Rob Roy was not the kind of man who would have put his head in the lion's mouth unless he had been assured by Argyll that he would back the story.

He paid the penalty for trusting Mac Cailein Mór when he was carried off to Newgate, just as Alasdair the Chief had been carried to Edinburgh to be hanged after he had trusted an earlier Campbell Chief who undertook to intercede for him, nearly two centuries earlier. In 1727 Rob Roy was taken to Gravesend, handcuffed to Lord Ogilvie, to be transported to Barbados. But such a career could not end on this banal note. A pardon, such as would not be credited in a work of fiction, reached his ship before it sails were unfurled. Rob returned to Balquhidder, to end his life where he had begun it, a convert to the Catholic faith, and there are few confessionals at which it could have been more entertaining to eavesdrop than his.

He left five sons, who followed their father in illustrating the dangers to society of proscribing a clan. Robert the eldest shot Maclaren of Invernenty and absconded before he could be brought to justice. His brothers James and Ronald were put on trial for the murder but escaped from prison before the verdict of not proven was brought in. Like their father they were all good at escaping, though most of them were caught in the end. Robert presently joined the 42nd Regiment, while James espoused the cause of the Young Pretender in the 1745 uprising, and escaped the consequences a second time. Then James, Duncan and Robert were arrested on a charge that they had abducted a young widow with an enticing fortune, in order that she should marry Robert. Evidently she was not attracted by him, which is not surprising considering the description of him as tall, thin, pale-coloured, squint-eyed, pock-marked, ill-kneed, and knock-kneed. It is a surprising description of a son of Rob Roy, perhaps the result of hardship in extreme youth.

Nor was Robert dexterous as a lover. He raped the girl with such brutality that she died, for which he was hanged. Duncan was pronounced not guilty, his brother James, guilty, but with extenuating circumstances. James escaped to France, where he died in utter destitution, while Robert's corpse lies beside those of his parents in the graveyard of Balquhidder.

So the outlawed clan displayed the extremes of behaviour to which people can be driven by misfortune, and if the Gregorys appear wise to have cut themselves off entirely from the tribal society in which they could see no future, Rob Roy proved more wily in his own way. All those famous books that the Gregorys published, all the honour and acclaim they received throughout Europe have not brought them one tenth of the fame that their disreputable kinsman enjoys to this day. He remained in the tribal lands to defend a lost cause, using all the dirty tricks that had been employed for centuries against his clan, and his courage and ingenuity have placed him among the immortals.

There is another MacGregor, an equally hilarious product of his clan's history, who would certainly have been as well known as Rob Roy if Walter Scott had cared to write his story. But since they were contemporaries and Scott's neighbours in Edinburgh were among his principal victims, he could expect no such favours from the Wizard of the North.

He was able to use the name MacGregor because he was born after the raising of the proscription in 1775, but his grandfather had been compelled to use the pseudonym of Gregor Drummond. However, he had become more generally known as Gregor the Beautiful. The Gaelic epithet is generally translated as Handsome, presumably because the other is thought to convey an impression of effeminacy. There was certainly nothing effeminate about Gregor the Beautiful, but the same might be said of Cú Chulainn who was described in the same way in the *Táin* epic, and a term that had probably been used to describe masculine grace since the days of the Gaesatae need not now be dropped out of squeamishness.

Gregor was a soldier in the Black Watch when George II asked in 1743 to be shown a sample of Highland troops. Gregor and another were chosen to visit St James's Palace, where the King watched from a window as they gave a demonstration of the use of the broadsword and Lochaber axe in the courtyard below. They were then taken into the palace to be presented to His Majesty, who gave each a golden guinea — a considerable gift in those days, and still by no means to be despised. As the two soldiers left, they handed their guineas as a tip to the flunkeys at the door.

Years later, when Gregor was a Captain and Adjutant of the Westminster Regiment of Militia, he was among the petitioners for the restoration of the name of Clan Gregor, evidence that he had not lost his tribal loyalty and pride. Also, when he retired he did not remain abroad as so many expatriate Scots have been inclined to do, but settled as Laird of Inverardine in the former clan lands of Breadalbane. Such was the family heritage of Gregor MacGregor his grandson, who likewise joined the Black Watch.

But when he was barely twenty years old a representative of the cause of independence against Spanish rule in South America arrived in Britain in search of support. Gregor MacGregor sold his patrimony and sailed away to Caracas, where Simón Bolívar had first raised the standard of revolt. He arrived in 1811 and in the following year lost all he possessed in the great earthquake there, but like Rob Roy he displayed a talent for recouping his losses in a large variety of ways.

He found that he was not the only Highlander there. Colonel Campbell was in command of a corps of riflemen and there was Mr Mackintosh the saddler, and many other names that had strayed out of Scotland. But none of them won such lustre as the former gaolbird name of MacGregor. In a tropical climate such as he had never experienced before, in a country utterly unfamiliar to him, amongst races whose languages he could not have understood, Gregor won victory after victory. He displayed outstanding personal courage, an innate flair for strategy and tactics. It was as though all the skills that had enabled Clan Gregor to survive during so many centuries of persecution had been poured into his lap.

Miranda his General was captured and carried off to Spain, where he was chained and collared to a prison wall until mercifully he died four years later. But Gregor became first a General of Cavalry, then a General of Brigade. In five years of warfare he had risen to the rank of General of Division. Simón Bolívar came personally to invest him with his new Order of Liberators, and Gregor married his beautiful niece Donna Josepha.

It was now that General MacGregor, at the height of his fame, moved beyond the frontiers of Venezuela to carry the war against Spain into the Caribbean. Already he had fought with infantry and fought with cavalry. He had brought his men safely through tropical jungles, leading them for hundreds of miles amongst enemies in overwhelming numbers. He had created a legend that he was invincible, and now he took it to the sea. He captured the port on the isthmus of Panama that had once fallen to Sir Francis Drake; he surprised one of the old treasure ports; with only two small boats and 150 men he seized one of the most important and well-defended fortresses on the Spanish Main. Then he sailed north to what is now the east coast of Nicaragua, and landed.

The five hundred miles of the Mosquito Coast were a most unhealthy region that had been used in the seventeenth century as a pirates' hide-out of the Spanish Main. Its wretched natives had offered Britain the sovereignty of this area in the hope of winning protection from buccaneers, and perhaps other benefits, and so for a while it became a British colony. But life there proved so insupportable for Europeans that in 1788 the administration was withdrawn and the colonists left, some for the nearest colony of British Honduras to the north. That was little over thirty years before General MacGregor landed on the Mosquito Coast, yet there was already no trace of the settlement they had abandoned. But he did find an aged Indian Chief, a descendant of one of those who had attempted to sign away their independence in return for protection. From this man MacGregor obtained a wholesale concession of territory, and with it he sailed away to carry out his greatest coup, a stupendous act of revenge against the society that had humiliated Clan Gregor for four centuries.

Sailing back across the Atlantic, he landed as His Serene Highness Gregor I, Prince of Poyais, accompanied by his charming Princess. By what magic charm did the grandson of Gregor the Beautiful succeed in hoodwinking the court protocol experts, the foreign officials? The year was 1820, in which the mad King George III died and was succeeded by George IV. To this sovereign Prince Gregor presented his letters of credence at the Court of St James where his grandfather had demonstrated the use of the broadsword to George IV's grandfather. He appointed one William Richardson, 'Commander of the Most Illustrious Order of the Green Cross, Major in Our Regiment of Horse Guards, to be Our Chargé d'Affaires in the United Kingdom of Great Britain.' The glittering Court of St James had never seen the illustrious Order of the Green Cross before: but then, neither had a British sovereign ever entered into diplomatic relations with the royal house of Clan Gregor. Soon the Prince would have the presses busy printing Poyais bank-notes on which were inscribed in Gaelic the boast of the Seed of Alpin, *Is Rioghal Mo Dhream*, My Blood is Royal. It was fitting that the parvenu house of Hanover should greet a MacGregor prince as an equal, but how it could have been hoaxed into doing so is still a mystery.

Even the Order of the Green Cross was taken seriously, although there were teams of experts on the orders of chivalry throughout the world, and their scales of precedence. To this day Prince Gregor is referred to as a knight, even in the *Dictionary of National Biography*, even though his Order could have no existence outside his imaginary principality.

With the same speed and tactical skill as he had used in his military campaigns, Gregor moved straight from the position he had captured to the next objective. His chargé d'affaires prepared a brochure on Poyais with remarkable speed to satisfy the curiosity of a somewhat mystified public. Pictures were sold that displayed the wonders of Prince Gregor's capital. It lay on a river, near its mouth on the Caribbean, and it contained bridges and domes and broad streets lined with trees. Down these the monarch would ride on state occasions, surrounded by his knights of the Green Cross, attended by his bodyguard of lancers. The scenes bore a startling resemblance to those of London, although Poyais lay in the tropics and surely some people must have recalled that this region had been abandoned as uninhabitable only a few decades earlier. But evidently Gregor's prospectus was accepted without suspicion by the public at large.

It must have been, because he next succeeded in raising a loan of £200,000, a colossal sum in those days, sponsored by a former Lord of Mayor of London who controlled a bank. It was secured upon the assets of Poyais, as set out in the official hand-book. This explained that the country was rich in gold, which flowed down the rivers as gold flowed down the rivers of Peru, out of the Andes. It also contained silver-mines as in Bolivia, while precious stones were as plentiful as the *conquistadores* had found them three centuries earlier. The mountains yielded timber — redwood, cedar and mahogany — while the plains groaned beneath cattle, crops and all manner of fruit trees. All this amounted to the myth of El Dorado, which ought to have imposed on nobody by the nineteenth century. But Gregor had cast his spell and deprived Court, City and Public of their critical faculties.

So he reached his final target, the capital from which all the misfortunes of Clan Gregor had originated. Prince Gregor favoured Edinburgh with a visit, accompanied by his Princess, and there they had their portraits painted, she wearing both a mantilla and a coronet. The painting of her husband now hangs in the National Portrait Gallery of Scotland.

The gratified citizens entertained not the slightest suspicion of Gregor's intentions as they clamoured to emigrate to Poyais: land in the Principality was sold at four shillings an acre: 70,000 banknotes of the Bank of Poyais were printed in Edinburgh, and people hastened to exchange their Scottish currency for it, so that they would have no money problems when they reached Gregor's realm. In 1822, the year of George IV's visit to Edinburgh, the first ship left the port of Leith for the Mosquito Coast, with fifty of its citizens on board: and others waited their turn to follow. Such was Gregor's efficiency that he had accom-modated another 150 emigrants in a second ship in time for it to catch up with the first by the time they both reached their destination near the mouth of the Black River.

The emigrants stood on deck in their best clothes, straining their eyes for a glimpse of the wonders that awaited them as the ships hoisted their colours and fired signals of their arrival and waited for the port authorities to appear. When nobody came in sight on that empty shore, they supposed they must be slightly off course, so they landed themselves with all their belongings and waited on the shore while a party went in search of the nearest township. But there were no settlements to find: and even before they had finished unloading, a hurricane struck which swept their two ships out to sea. Two hundred citizens of Edinburgh, including women, children and old people found themselves in the predicament so familiar in the past to homeless MacGregors.

In the appalling heat they built themselves a camp of sorts, while some of the able-bodied went off in a useless search for help. The rainy season came, bringing with it malaria and yellow fever. Over two-thirds of those wretched people perished, and other ships were on the way. Clan Gregor had endured sufferings like this: now the citizens of Edinburgh were getting a taste of them; and at least they had someone to rescue them, although they had never lifted a finger to succour the MacGregors in their times of trouble.

News of what had occurred reached British Honduras, five hundred miles to the north. Here the Colonial Agent was a Scotsman called John Young, who immediately sent a ship to rescue the survivors. In Honduras emergency measures were taken to house and nurse them, while the administration flung itself into the task of saving the passengers in seven more ships before they could be landed on the Mosquito Coast. To Britain John Young sent a devastating report, which was widely published.

Prince Gregor treated it with lofty disdain, instructing his chargé d'affaires at the Poyaisan Legation in London to issue a rebuttal that was published in *The Times*. Its only concession, though this was a very considerable one, was to dispense with the royalty of His Serene Highness, while clinging to the Order of the Green Cross and handing Gregor in addition the ancient Scottish title of Chief. This was soon after the Chief of Chiefs in Edinburgh had given such unprecedented prestige to this rank.

On Tuesday last I unmasked to the world the secret enemy of Sir Gregor MacGregor — Mr John Young, the Honduras Agent. He then told me that he had opposed the undertaking of Sir Gregor MacGregor from its commencement, knowing the dreadful climate of Poyais would kill all the European settlers that went out to that country; and this gentleman finished by saying that he ought to know the country and climate well, for he had lived in it 25 years. This, Sir, you will allow me was a strange reason for Mr Young, who is a robust Scotsman, to give as the badness of the climate of Poyais.

My agent has written to me from Edinburgh that a person in that city had received orders to have Mr Young's Honduras extract published in every Edinburgh paper. This, Sir, is a further proof of the malignant motives that have induced Mr Young to attack the Chief of Poyais. For the future I shall not consider myself called upon to answer the attacks that Mr Young may think proper to publish against Sir Gregor MacGregor and the settlement of Poyais, otherwise than by an appeal to the laws of England.

It is questionable whether the laws of England would have been applicable to this fracas among the Scots.

The Chief of Poyais (as he had now become) placed himself, however, beyond the laws of either England or Scotland and within those of France. He had discovered that there are scarcely any limits to human gullibility, and having perfected a formula for exploiting this, he could not resist using it again. In 1825, almost incredible as it appears, three whole years after that first ship had left Leith for the Mosquito Coast, a French expedition followed: and in France Gregor succeeded in raising a loan even larger than his British one — £300,000 this time. When he returned to London two years later it appeared that he had overreached himself, for he was flung into prison and made the sport of cartoonists.

But like Rob Roy, he was not the sort of person whom prisons were designed to hold. He extracted himself by guile, rather than force, and returned to France where he was imprisoned again, equally briefly. After this his only problem was to bear the expenses of royalty (or a chiefship) without any further augmentation of his resources. When his revenues were exhausted he simply submitted a memorandum to the government of Venezuela, explaining his difficulties. This most charming and hospitable of peoples welcomed him back with honour in 1839: he was granted money for his maintenance by a grateful nation and died six years later, a citizen of the country he had helped to liberate.

The Poyais madness was at its height when George IV paid his state visit to Edinburgh, in whose proceedings some people thought that the part which Clan Gregor played bordered on the weird. For it was the MacGregors who were given first place in escorting the royal regalia when the Honours of Scotland were paraded to and from the castle at the beginning and end of the King's visit, and the Chief of the recently outlawed clan who replied to the royal toast to the Chieftains and Clans of Scotland by lifting his glass to 'the Chief of Chiefs — the King.' He was Sir Evan MacGregor of MacGregor, a General like his namesake, and sometime Governor of the Windward Isles and Dominica opposite the Mosquito Coast.

The story of Rob Roy was staged, in a version adapted from Sir Walter Scott's novel, and the King attended a performance of it. The worldly and respectable audience evidently had no inkling that there was a real live Rob Roy in their midst, plotting to extract from Scotland's capital the last ounce of payment for what it had inflicted on his kindred over the centuries. The bogus Prince and counterfeit Chief made no appearance in the company of the real Prince and genuine MacGregor Chief, but he was busy enough behind the scenes.

As for the other members of Clan Gregor who were present on that occasion, it might have been expected that they would not care to revive clan sentiment for a name that had remained unused so long, so many of whose heirs had been long dispersed from the ancestral lands, whose clan memories were so tragic. But evidently they cared very much. Eight hundred and twenty-six of them, capable of bearing arms, solemnly affirmed that their Chief was John Murray, who accepted the office and became Sir John MacGregor Bart, Sir Evan's father. They founded a Clan Gregor Society in the year of the King's visit to Edinburgh, admitting MacGregor, Gregory and Gregorson as variant forms of their name. The Children of the Mist became in the end the clan that refused to die.

CHAPTER SIX

Gordons on the Make

By the time George IV visited Scotland there was one clan and one only whose very name had become ducal: that is, it possessed a Chief called Duke of Gordon. Furthermore, it was a generation since a Duke of Gordon had raised the body of men who were formed into the regiment called the Gordon Highlanders, and had designed the sett of their kilt with a yellow stripe that has become the clan tartan. The Gordons appeared to belong to the club of those Gaelic clans which had formed regiments of Cameron Highlanders, Macleod's Highlanders, Seaforth Highlanders; and the facts of history might well have given reality to this appearance. It was as early as the reign of King Robert Bruce that the first Gordon was planted in Huntly, and no later than 1445 when Sir Alexander Seton, having married the Gordon heiress, was created Earl of Huntly. But it has been observed already that while a Gordon clan soon proliferated in the north, its chiefs remained curiously detached from the Gaelic society they set out to dominate and exploit; while the vice-regal powers which successive Stewart kings gave to Gordon Chiefs in the north proved exceedingly damaging to the genuine Highland clans there.

A startling example of this occurred after James IV had died on the field of Flodden in 1513 with so many of his bravest subjects. The 3rd Earl of Huntly fled unscathed, accompanied by his younger brother Adam Gordon, to make the most of the fact that the new King James V was less than two years old. Huntly secured a place on the Council of Regency to reinforce his powers as royal Lieutenant in the north, and moved without delay upon a target that had been selected already by his father the 2nd Earl. It involved nothing less than the violent seizure of the earldom of Sutherland, and it involved such a complicated sequence of criminal acts that it is doubtful whether the enterprise could have succeeded but for the fortunate accident of Flodden.

The Southland of Earl Thorfinn the Mighty's former realm had been detached from Caithness, and erected into the earldom of Sutherland in 1201 for the house of Freskin the Fleming, who fortified it as a bastion of feudal power beyond the Moray Firth. It was not so extensive as the other segments of Thorfin's dismembered kingdom, Orkney and Caithness, which had been separated into independent earldoms as recently as 1472. But Sutherland lay nearer to the expanding power-base of the Gordons on the other side of the Moray Firth, and also it contained the seat of the bishopric of Caithness.

This northernmost diocese of the Scottish mainland had been erected to embrace not only Caithness and Sutherland, but also the enormous Mackay province of Strathnaver in the west, and there was a very good reason why its cathedral and episcopal palace were planted at Dornoch, on the low peninsula accessible to the Moray Firth and guarded in the north by the fortresses of the Sutherland earls. When St Margaret's son David appointed the first Bishop of Caithness from Dunfermline it is doubtful whether he was able to reside in his diocese at all. The second Bishop attempted to do so, and the local people blinded him and tore out his tongue. A third Bishop arrived, only to be roasted over his own fire. This was at the time when the region was demonstrating its hostility to the usurping sons of Queen Margaret in a variety of ways.

But the protection of the new Church establishment behind the feudal defences of Sutherland proved so effective that presently the bishopric became a favourite perquisite of royal Stewarts — not all of whom were legitimate, or of age, or even consecrated. By a happy chance, just such a worldly and amenable prelate was available to assist the Gordon Chief in his present plot.

It was based on the techniques used by Queen Margaret's sons to get rid of the legitimate heirs to the crown; calling the senior heir an idiot, the next a bastard, and the remainder merely wicked. In precisely the same order, Huntly proceeded by obtaining a 'brieve of idiocy' in 1494 against Earl John of Sutherland, a man who had possessed the wits to maintain himself in office in troubled times for almost forty years. Earl John had been married first to a daughter of the Lord of the Isles, by whom he had as his heir a son, also named John. By his second marriage he had a son Alexander: but he also produced a daughter Elizabeth, and if there is any evidence of idiocy to be found in his behaviour, it is that he should have permitted Elizabeth to marry Adam Gordon, younger son of the 2nd Earl of Huntly. For this was nothing less than an invitation to the

Gordons to dispose of the legitimate heirs and seize his earldom in Elizabeth's name, which is precisely what they did.

The 'idiot' Earl John appears to have been living at least until 1508 (though the suppression and cooking of evidence by the Gordons has created areas of uncertainty over what happened). His second wife was drawing widow's terce as a Countess as late as 1512, and this is of fundamental importance in view of the Gordon claim that her son Alexander was a bastard. Meanwhile it was necessary to bring a second charge of idiocy against the undoubted heir John, since his legitimacy was beyond question. This was done, and when John tried to obtain enfeoffment as Earl of Sutherland in 1512, he found himself barred, pending the brieve of idiocy that Huntly had laid against him in Edinburgh. The illegitimate royal Stewart currently occupying the bishopric of Caithness was so obliging as to administer the estate of the earldom in the meantime. The daring plan had reached this crucial stage when James IV and so many of his principal public servants perished at Flodden. The Gordons had had the devil's luck.

In the year after Flodden the brieve of idiocy was made effective against the legitimate heir John, and his sister Elizabeth, Adam Gordon's wife, was immediately served heir to the earldom. Her brother Alexander Sutherland complained through his procurator that he had been forcibly prevented from advancing his claim, which followed automatically from the dismissal of his elder brother's, and he fortified himself in his family's principal seat, the castle of Dunrobin on the coast of the Moray Firth a few miles north of Dornoch. Not until 1519 was he assassinated by Gordon agents, and his head displayed above the battlements of Dunrobin. Adam Gordon called himself Earl of Sutherland for the remainder of his life without ever obtaining a formal title, and his descendants possess the earldom to this day, although the true heirs were still contesting the Gordon usurpation at the end of the eighteenth century.

No sooner had the Gordons obtained this key position in the northernmost peninsula of Scotland than they turned their attention to the great region of Strathnaver which lay beyond it. If they could obtain a title of feudal superiority over it, they would secure as their vassals the numerous Mackay clan whose military potential had been demonstrated on so many occasions in the past: and the Campbells had already shown how effective such a dependent clan could be for Mafia purposes, by the use they had made of the MacGregors. The difficulty was that the Mackays possessed unassailable titles to their territory and an impeccable record of loyalty to the crown. Was it conceivable that the Gordons could undermine either, let alone both? It was.

All the evidence suggests that the Mackay Chiefs were acutely aware of the danger and had taken every precaution that was open to them. In 1411 the Mackays had attempted to restrain the army of the Lord of the Isles on its way to Harlaw. After the battle Mackay received a charter from MacDonald with the hand of his sister, which declared in Latin: 'We, Donald of Islay, Lord of the Isles have given, conceded and confirmed by this our charter to the noble Angus Aodh of Strathnaver . . .' — recognition of the Chief of Clan Aodh's title to the entire province. In 1506 his great-grandson secured registration of this charter by the Lords of the Scottish Council, who ordained that it should retain its validity 'in all times to come.' And James IV himself looked upon Mackay so favourably as to address him in Latin as 'nobilis vir Odo M'Ky de Straithnauer' — the noble man Aodh Mac Aoidh of Strathnaver; and in the Lowland tongue as 'our lowit squyar Y Mcky of Straithnauer.' Every single document confirmed the Mackay Chief's immemorial title to his province.

When Gordon of Huntly was appointed Lieutenant in the north, Mackay supported him in all the punitive expeditions that followed the forfeiture of the Lord of the Isles and the risings on behalf of his wretched grandson Donald Dubh. He took part in Huntly's expeditions to Lewis in 1503, 1505 and 1506. Nor would it have been easy to misrepresent the part he played, because Mackay was in separate communication with James IV, as his Treasurer's accounts reveal. They noted payments made 'to an man that brought writings to the King from Aodh Mackay by the King's command:' and four years later another courier was bearing 'writings from Mackay to the King.' It seems probable that the Gordon Chief needed Mackay's services as a Gaelic interpreter as well as a military commander.

The most remote of Highland chiefs on the Scottish mainland brought a contingent of his clansmen to fight for James IV at Flodden. Thereafter he witnessed the seizure of the Sutherland earldom before he died, evidently leaving sound advice to his heir as to the course he should adopt. It is unlikely that the Mackays would have felt any particular warmth for the house of Freskin that had been planted on their doorstep with its feudal powers, and John the new Chief entered into a treaty with the Gordon usurper even before Alexander Sutherland had been murdered. He was prepared to trade recognition of the bogus

Gordon title for acceptance of his own true one, and this he achieved in 1518 in the following words: 'It is agreed and fully accorded betwixt an noble and mighty lord, Adam Gordon, Earl of Sutherland on the one part, and an honourable man called John Mackay of Strathnaver on the other part . . .' Thus the Mackays protected themselves against the latest hazard.

They did it again when James V came of age and revealed his taste for extermination, summary execution and kidnapping. Mackay attended court and obtained a fresh charter to his lands under the great seal at Stirling in December 1539, and although this did not save him from being carried off to Dunbarton Castle during the King's punitive expedition in the following year, it did confirm his title to all the possessions 'held by our deceased illustrious predecessors.'

One final, essential precaution had been taken by the Mackay Chiefs. A favourite way of dispossessing people at this time was to show that their parents had married within a degree of cousinship that required a dispensation from the Church which had not been obtained. Consequently the children were technically illegitimate and incapable of succeeding to property. In tribal societies it could be particularly difficult to contract a marriage that did not expose the partners to this danger, and equally hard to obtain the necessary dispensation. Every known marriage of the Mackay Chiefs before the sixteenth century had been arranged with brides from other clans, but since the families of the Chiefs had intermarried generation after generation, the risk was ever on the increase. James IV's 'loved squire Aodh Mackay' had insured himself against it when he obtained a formal legitimation of his two sons under the Privy Seal in 1511, whose mother belonged to the ancient O'Beolan family from whom the first Earls of Ross descended.

Such were the obstacles that faced the Gordons in their take-over bid in Strathnaver. The steps by which they surmounted them make rather a bewildering story, but it is worth unravelling because it illustrates so well the way in which Stewart misgovernment fomented injustice, rapine, and a consequent hardening of clannish spirit in the tribal lands.

Clan Mackay fought for James V at Solway Moss in 1542, where Aodh son of Donald the Chief was among those carried off captive to London. There followed the death of the King, the succession of his week-old daughter Mary, Queen of Scots, and the appointment of Hamilton of Arran as Regent, a recognition that he was heir presumptive to the crown. This was the long-term effect of the downfall of the Boyds in the time of James III, whose sister Mary had been married to a Boyd and given birth to a son. After his untimely death the son had been murdered while she had been compelled to marry Hamilton, ancestor of the man appointed Regent to the baby Queen.

But Matthew Stewart, Earl of Lennox, claimed that the Hamilton line was illegitimate and that he was the true heir. So a dynastic conflict began, which became entangled in the rivalry between England and France, and also with the issue of the Reformation. The Regent Arran decided after some hesitation (for his mental powers were weak, his character indecisive and motivated solely by personal greed) to ally himself with the Catholics and France; whereupon Lennox espoused the cause of reform and the English interest. For this he received as his reward a wife who placed his family in line of succession for the English throne as well. She was the daughter of Queen Margaret Tudor, who had married the Red Douglas after the death of James IV at Flodden. If the children of Henry VIII of England should prove barren (which they did), the next heir to his throne would be the baby Queen of Scots, followed by any issue of the wife of Lennox. It is one of the notorious catastrophes of history that their eldest son was Lord Darnley whom Mary Queen of Scots married, thus ensuring — as she fondly hoped — that nothing could stand between her and the English crown. Such was the complex international situation, religious and dynastic, that the Gordons succeeded in manipulating, to the destruction of a Gaelic chief in remote Strathnaver.

In the year before the Battle of Solway Moss a nineteen-year-old Stewart youth who had not taken Holy orders, and never did so, was placed in the bishopric of Caithness. He was the brother of the Earl of Lennox, and their sister married the second Gordon Earl of Sutherland. She had already contributed one of the illegitimate children of her cousin James V. The teen-age Bishop entrusted the greater part of his episcopal properties — many of which lay in Strathnaver — to her husband the Gordon Earl, while he went to London to enlist Henry VIII's support for the rights of his brother Lennox against the claim of Hamilton of Arran that he was heir to the Scottish crown.

Donald, Chief of Mackay was in a more hideous predicament than he could have realised. His son a prisoner in London, Sutherland a nest of royal Stewarts with high ambitions, it is hardly surprising that he should have been lured into supporting their cause. His clan owed their security to past loyalty to the

house of Stewart, and even if Hamilton had been less disreputable, the claim of a Lowland family without friends or
influence in the north to the Scottish crown could not have
appealed to a Mackay chief. The only hostile move against the
Stewarts in his neighbourhood was Gordon of Huntly's attempt
to slip his brother into the bishopric of Caithness during the
young Stewart Bishop's absence; but this was merely the
hereditary kleptomania of the Gordons at work, not a party move.
After it had failed, the royal Lieutenant's brother made an equally
unsuccessful bid for the bishopric of Glasgow; though he persisted
in his spiritual aspirations, taking the title of Archbishop of
Athens before he was finally accommodated in the See of
Galloway.

Aodh, Mackay's son and heir, was released from his captivity
in London to join in an attack on Regent Arran in Glasgow, and he
also took part with the English forces that captured Haddington
in 1548, which resulted in the baby Queen's removal to France.
From now on, the Mackays were committed to the pro-English
Protestant party, and so long as the pro-French Catholic party
remained in power in Scotland, the Chief's heir could be indicted
for treason. When Donald Mackay died in 1550 and Aodh succeeded him, the Chief himself, holder of the Clan titles, was in
jeopardy. But the Protestant anglophile party did triumph in the
end, so why did Mackay's support of royal Stewarts in that party
bring about his ruin? Because the Gordons were studying every
move in the game, and seizing on each accident of circumstance
to ensure his downfall.

The pro-English cause was jeopardised at the outset by the
savagery with which Henry VIII of England overplayed his hand,
and its opponents found in the French Queen Mother, Mary of
Lorraine, the most able and steadfast Queen in Scottish history.
Huntly gave her his support at the moment when she gained the
ascendancy for her pro-French policies, and was rewarded with
the earldom of Moray. His cousin Gordon of Sutherland joined
him when the two men accompanied her on a visit to her daughter
Queen Mary in France. During their absence John Sutherland,
son of Alexander whose head had decorated the battlements of
Dunrobin, and consequently the legitimate claimant, was
murdered while those responsible were beyond the reach of
blame. Indeed, they were busy ingratiating themselves with the
young sovereign who knew so little about her country.

Mackay was the first cousin of the true heir to the Sutherland
earldom, and whether as an act of piety or of revenge, or simply

because he no longer had anything to lose, he now invaded Sutherland. This resulted in the first full-scale Gordon assault on Strathnaver in which, as the Gordon chronicler noted with satisfaction a few decades later, his clansmen 'invaded and spoiled, carrying from thence a great booty of goods and cattle the year of God 1551.' Thus the barbarism engendered by Stewart rule gradually engulfed this remote province.

But one form of booty the returning Gordon earls did not obtain, and that was the feudal superiority of Strathnaver, necessary to reduce the inhabitants of the province to the status of vassals. They had certainly planned to acquire this by the process of forfeiture for treason while they were in the auspicious company of the young sovereign and her mother in France. It would not have been necessary for them to resort to the alternative technique of a charge of bastardy, such as they had used to dispossess the Sutherland earls: yet by an extraordinary quirk of fate, this was precisely the weapon another used to cheat them of their latest prize while their backs were turned.

Aodh, Chief of Mackay could forfeit nothing if he had been incapable of inheriting anything. In October 1551 the Bishop of Orkney registered a precept showing that Aodh's grandparents had not been properly married, so that even his own father had been incapable of inheriting the title to Strathnaver. The telltale act of legitimation in the records of the Scottish Privy Council survives as a sufficient rebuttal to such a charge, but perhaps Aodh was advised that it would be in his best interests not to cite it in his defence. By 1553 the Bishop of Orkney had obtained the overlordship of Strathnaver which the Gordons coveted, and had bestowed the heritable use upon the Chief of Mackay.

It was an astonishing feat, performed under the noses of the Gordons, whose sense of outrage had not cooled by the time their chronicler Sir Robert Gordon recorded: 'Bishop Reid was a great favourer, of Mackay's house and family. He obtained from the Queen a gift of Mackay's lands in Strathnaver, fallen into Her Majesty's hands by reason of the bastardy of Donald Mackay, the father of Aodh Mackay; which gift Bishop Reid took in his own name, but to Mackay's use.' Lands in Strathnaver, wrote Sir Robert, son of a Gordon Earl of Sutherland. It is an invariable truth that to examine the areas in which people lie is to discover the best key to their characters and motives. From now on it became a fundamental practice of the Gordons to diminish the Mackay title to Strathnaver in such terms as this, while inflating their own. In particular, they juggled with the term Strathnaver itself, using it sometimes in its original meaning to define the entire province, at others to mean the river valley of the Naver from which the province derived its name, depending on whether they referred to Mackay's property or their own. Since time immemorial the Chiefs of Mackay had been described in every official document as rulers of the entire province of Strathnaver, not as owners of lands within it.

And Bishop Reid. Here was a man without either a clan or a dynastic name, a reforming churchman who built a fireproof library at Kinloss on the south side of the Moray Firth and who was described as 'a good man and of consummate wisdom.' Almost miraculously in such an age, his qualities had earned him a bishopric despite the competition of predatory Gordons and Stewarts in this area, and they also enabled him to stand up to the Gordons and beat them at their own game.

But the diocese of Caithness, with its headquarters in Sutherland and its unconsecrated bishop who was the Countess of Sutherland's brother, was able to compensate them for their disappointment. In the same year in which Bishop Reid of Orkney deprived them of the superiority of Strathnaver, Bishop Stewart entered into the first of the transactions by which his Church properties were transferred by degrees to the Gordons; not only in Sutherland, but in Caithness and Strathnaver as well. The reasons he gave to justify these acts of pillage are instructive. 'Because the said castles of Scrabster and Skibo and the palace of Dornoch are built in an Irish region, among fierce and unsubdued Scots, so that neither he nor his predecessors have been able to enjoy them without very great expenses, he, with the consent of the Dean and Chapter, appoints the Earl and Countess and their said heirs Constables of Scrabster and the palace of Dornoch for ever.' Nothing could reveal more clearly how totally unassimilated these people were in the Gaelic society they had come to expropriate.

Bishop Stewart suffered no deprivation by disposing of his episcopal property in the north, for he acquired in its place the priory and revenues of St Andrews in an environment that was far more congenial to him. Nor did Church affairs monopolise his attention. He married a daughter of the Earl of Atholl, though she divorced him on the grounds of impotence: which is surprising since he is known to have achieved at least one illegitimate child. He lived almost as long as Mary, Queen of Scots and his last years were a good deal happier than hers, for he 'colluded with the revellers of the town to hold the ministry vacant, and in meantime took up the stipend and spent the same at the golf, archery, good cheer.'

It was this fun-loving prelate who had visited Henry VIII in London while the Chief of Mackay was a prisoner there, offered to surrender Scottish places of strength to the English, and suborned Mackay into the actions that proved to be his ruin. For his part the royal Stewart Bishop was never called to account, neither did he lift a finger to protect the Celtic Chief whose property his brother-in-law was plotting to seize.

In 1554 Hamilton of Arran was persuaded to resign his regency on condition that no enquiry should be made into his massive peculations in office, and the Queen Mother took his place. She was almost immediately steered to Inverness by the Gordon Chief, where she learned of the 'enormities, slaughters and oppressions' — not of the Gordons, but of the Chief of Mackay. She summoned him to appear before her, and since this would almost certainly have led to his execution at the instance of the Lieutenant of the North, he disobeyed the order. The Earl of Sutherland was already prepared for this, and as soon as he had obtained the necessary commission from the Queen Regent he took an army through Strathnaver to the north coast, where he besieged the Mackay stronghold called Borve on its headland of Farr, reduced it to the ruin that it remains to this day, and hanged its commander. The Chief was tracked down and carried off a prisoner.

Then the Queen Regent disobliged the Gordons by failing to deliver their prize to them. Mary of Lorraine was a highly intelligent and fundamentally humane woman. The greatest problem of her regency was the growing influence of the Protestant reformers and the support these enjoyed in England, even during the reign there of the Catholic sovereign Mary Tudor. Yet the Gordons had hoodwinked her into ruining a Celtic Chief whose lands they coveted, in a corner of the kingdom totally immune from reformers and English influence, and one whose treasons (if such they could be called) had consisted in loyalty to the Stewart cause. Evidently she began to change her attitude after the facts had become clearer to her, for in 1555 a pardon was granted to Mackay under the Privy Seal for his offences ten years before. As though this were not ominous enough, when Bishop Reid died in 1558 and the superiority of Strathnaver reverted to the crown, she did not bestow it on either of the Gordon earls.

If she had not discovered it already, she was to learn now that Gordon loyalty was a fast-burning flame that required constantly

to be refuelled. The Gordon earls joined the Lords of the Congregation of Jesus Christ who opposed the Queen Regent's
regime, with English support, and used the cause of the
Reformation as a pretext to embezzle Church property. Elizabeth
Tudor had just succeeded to the English throne, who added to
the bonanza with gifts of money. The Earl of Sutherland celebrated his conversion in fresh transactions with Bishop Stewart.
In 1560 Queen Elizabeth sent an army into Scotland and the
Regent Mary died defeated in Edinburgh.

There followed a year in which there was no legal government
in Scotland, before Mary Queen of Scots returned to her realm.
The Chief of the Gordons, already Earl of Huntly and Moray and
Lord of Badenoch, became High Chancellor once more, and his
powerful position in a country lacking any strong authority
encouraged him to repeat the coup that had succeeded so well
in the rather similar conditions that resulted from the defeat of
Flodden. He conceived a plan to annex the lands of Findlater
(later erected into an earldom) for his third son John. They
belonged to the Ogilvies, a clan of great antiquity whose very
name is Pictish, deriving from *Ocel Fa*, which means High Plain.

Descending from the Celtic royal house, the ancestors of the
Ogilvies had occupied Angus, one of the little kingdoms in which
its collateral branches had been accommodated. By the tenth
century they were designated Mormaers of Angus, and when
Gillebride succeeded in 1144, he enjoyed the comparatively
recent title of Earl of Angus. It was he who bestowed on a younger
son, sometime before 1177, the property of Ogilvie from which
the clan has taken its name. When sheriffdoms were first erected,
the Ogilvie Chiefs were appointed hereditary sheriffs of Angus,
and a Sheriff Ogilvie was among those who were killed on the
Red Harlaw in 1411. His son Sir Walter built the strong tower of
Airlie from which his descendants took their title when they were
created Earls of Airlie in 1639.

Such was the ancient Celtic clan against which the Gordons
hatched their latest plot during that promising interregnum after
English troops had defeated the French forces in Scotland,
leaving a power vacuum. The English ambassador sent Queen
Elizabeth's Secretary William Cecil an account, describing how
Gordon of Huntly was so solicitous as to reveal to Ogilvie of
Findlater that his own son and heir was planning to deprive him
of his reason by locking him up and then depriving him of his
sleep. This technique provokes reflection on the way in which the
disinherited Sutherlands might have lost their wits (if they really

did so) before they were deprived of their earldom on those very grounds by the Gordons.

'This being revealed,' reported the ambassador, 'and sure tokens given unto his father that this was true, he thought just cause to be given unto him why his son should not succeed, and having no other issue, by the persuasion of his wife (who was a Gordon) gave the whole land unto John Gordon, who after the death of the said Findlater married her and so had right unto the whole living. To see also how God hath plagued the iniquity of the same woman, which in one month after her marriage John Gordon casteth his fancy unto another and locked her up in a close chamber, where yet she remaineth.' It was a shoddy reward for the part of Phaedra that she had played in dispossessing the Ogilvie heir, accusing him of having made sexual advances upon her.

Help reached her through the accident of remote events. In France Mary Queen of Scots was advised to place herself in the hands of her Catholic subjects in Scotland, amongst whom she was led to understand that the all-powerful Earl of Huntly was to be numbered. It was one of the more sensible decisions of this Queen of erratic judgement that she did no such thing. She chose instead the support of the victorious Protestant party and gave power to her illegitimate half-brother James Stewart, upon whom she bestowed the earldom of Moray. Ever loyal to the memory of her wonderful mother, she had neither forgotten nor forgiven Huntly's desertion of the Queen Regent in her hour of need.

With both Strathnaver and Findlater almost within the family's grasp, the Gordon Chief could not face the prospect of losing such a prize as Moray, and he resorted to open rebellion. The young Queen reacted with a decisiveness that evidently took him by surprise. She rode north to Inverness and there hanged the Gordon Captain of the Castle when he refused her admission. Then, advancing south-east towards Aberdeen, she brought an army against Huntly at Corrichie on Deeside. He died on the field, being 'gross, corpulent and short of breath.' His son John, whose ploys at Findlater were so near completion, was carried a prisoner to Aberdeen and there beheaded. Huntly's heir was also convicted of treason and imprisoned while the entire estates of the Cock of the North were forfeited.

So were those of the Gordon Earl of Sutherland, 'his dignity, name and memory to be extinct and deleted, and all his lands, offices and goods to be confiscated.' While Earl John of Sutherland fled abroad, Mary granted to Aodh, Chief of the Mackay, a fresh pardon for his offences during her minority. She even summoned him to accompany her on the visit to Queen Elizabeth that she was planning. It appears that she may have known of Mackay's sojourn at the court of Queen Elizabeth's father twenty years earlier. At the time it may have appeared conceivable that she intended to clear the tribal lands of the Gordon pest that her forbears had introduced into them in the mistaken hope that good order and respect for the royal authority would thereby be promoted.

But Mary never did succeed in meeting her cousin Elizabeth, so Mackay did not gain her ear. And justice in the Highlands was soon subordinated to the Queen's personal concerns. Her first backward step was to provide for Helen Stewart, Countess of Sutherland, 'knowing her to be an honourable personage, descended of good and noble lineage.' She was granted a living out of the forfeited lands, including Church property conveyed to her husband the Earl by her brother the merry Bishop. Next, the Bishop himself conveyed all the Church properties previously bestowed on the forfeited Earl to his disinherited son, who was further compensated with the lands of Aboyne in Huntly territory for what he had lost in Sutherland. James Stewart, Earl of Moray, observing Gordons creeping back beneath the Queen's skirts, tried to enforce the sentence of execution against Huntly's heir, but 'the Captain delayed to perform until he had first spoken the Queen; who hearing thereof, refused and disclaimed the warrant. And thereupon she commanded the Captain not to proceed against him till he had a warrant from her own mouth to that effect.'

Mary was to pay a terrible price for her habits of tergiversation, and her brother Moray would be the principal instrument of her ruin. But the Mackays were also to pay a dreadful price, and to continue paying it long after Queen Mary had lost her head at Fotheringay, and they were innocent of any offence except those for which she had granted a royal pardon.

In 1566 Mary married Henry Stewart, Lord Darnley, who shared with her the blood of their grandmother Margaret Tudor, and who consequently stood next in line of succession to the English crown. Her brother the Earl of Moray, his authority undermined when Mary gave her husband the status of King, raised an unsuccessful revolt that scared Mary into rehabilitating the Gordons as potential supporters. Huntly was restored to all his father's properties and appointed Chancellor; the Earl of Sutherland recovered his possessions under the Great Seal, and even the latest charter from Bishop Stewart received royal confirmation despite the scandal to reformers over such misappropriation of religious endowments.

But the Gordons desired more than this, and Mary gave it to them. Just before Christmas in 1566 she granted to the Earl of Huntly the feudal superiority of Strathnaver as it had been held by the Bishop of Orkney. She had sold the pass that the Mackays had defended for so many centuries.

It did not help her: only a few months later she was defeated and imprisoned by her rebellious subjects. But Huntly used the powers with which she had invested him to extract one further advantage before Moray compelled her to abdicate. The last Parliament of her reign endorsed her gift to him and recorded that the Queen 'granted and gave heritably to her trusty cousin and Councillor George, Earl of Huntly, Lord Gordon and Badenoch, her Highness' Chancellor, all and sundry the lands and baronies . . . which pertained heritably of before to umquile Donald Mackay of Farr . . . and pertaining to our Sovereign . . . by reason the said umquile Donald was born and deceased bastard without lawful heirs of his body gotten or lawful disposition made by him of his lands and goods during his lifetime.'

Even by Gordon standards of mendacity, this series of falsehoods concerning a Chief who had performed outstanding services to his sovereign is breathtaking in its range. There is no evidence that Donald Mackay had been born illegitimate through any technical irregularity in his father's marriage to an O'Beolan. But even if he had been, he could not have 'deceased bastard' since he was formally legitimised. Neither had it ever previously been asserted that his son Aodh, the present Chief, was illegitimate. The final enormity was to define a Mackay Chief who had been designated as proprietor of Strathnaver in all public documents during his lifetime as merely the owner of Farr where his ruined castle stood on its windy headland. But the Gordons required these lies to be placed on the statue book in order to obtain the *dominium utile* or actual possession of the Mackay country, now that they had been invested with the overlordship. The very first revolutionary Parliament which assembled after the deposition of the Queen expressed a lofty concern for means by which 'all Scotland may be brought to universal obedience.' Descending to details, this proved to be a euphemism for legalising the Gordon seizure of Strathnaver.

Unluckily, while this was in preparation, the Gordon Earl of Sutherland was poisoned by a member of his own family in

Helmsdale Castle, whose ruins still stand on the south side of the river mouth. His son and heir was fifteen years old and consequently required a guardian, just as the infant James VI did, and the King's guardian appointed the Sinclair Earl of Caithness, a natural choice since the Sinclair Earl was Justiciar of the North as well as the most nearly adjacent potentate. Nor did Caithness act in an exceptional manner when he took the young Sutherland Earl to his castle of Girnigo near Wick, to marry his daughter. It was one of the perquisites of wardship; and he enjoyed others when he travelled with his family to administer the estate of Sutherland during the remainder of his son-in-law's minority, taking up his residence in Dunrobin.

It would have been impossible for Huntly to meet this threat to the Gordon hegemony in any legal manner, however far-fetched. So he waited until the Justiciar Earl was absent in Edinburgh, then raided Dunrobin Castle, abducted his ward and carried him to the Gordon stronghold in Strathbogie, leaving the lad's Sinclair wife behind. For this crime no charge was ever preferred against the Earl of Huntly, and he soon added another with impunity. The Chief of Mackay, lacking any title to his lands, travelled beyond the Moray Firth to Elgin, where he made formal submission to Huntly as his vassal. From there he was induced to continue as far as Aberdeen, and here he obtained a charter at last after doing homage as 'leal, true and faithful man and servant' to the Cock of the North, in the presence of the young Earl of Sutherland.

Mackay's submission to Huntly introduced a new dimension to the Gordon policy of expansion in the north. Now that Clan Mackay had been reduced to the status of a vassal army at the Gordons' disposal, they could be launched against the next target, Clan Sinclair. But the Mackay Chief had made his submission to Huntly, not to Sutherland, and it was illegal according to Scottish statute to transfer a vassal from one feudal superior to another without his consent. This did not prevent the Gordons from doing it and getting away with it, but it presented an almost insuperable problem to Sir Robert Gordon their chronicler to explain plausibly how this had been done. One thing, however, he took no pains to conceal — that Mackay was enlisted to assault the Earl of Caithness as soon as he had been reduced to the necessary servitude.

Sir Robert suggested that Mackay had somehow contrived to become the vassal of two superiors at once. 'Mackay, upon his submission to the Earls of Huntly and Sutherland, and upon his faithful promise to assist Earl Alexander [Sutherland] against the Earl of Caithness in time coming, obtained from the Earl of Huntly the heritable right and title of the lands of Strathnaver for the sum of 3,000 pounds Scots money. Yet Huntly still retained the superiority of Strathnaver to himself.'

The promise to assist Alexander of Sutherland (who was not his superior) possessed no validity compared to the summons Mackay received on his return home from the Justiciar Earl of Caithness. In accordance with it he joined Sutherland of Duffus, the legitimate claimant to the Sutherland earldom, in an attack on Dornoch, where the castle that Bishop Stewart had handed to the Gordons and the tower of the cathedral held out for a week before both were captured. It seems probable that one essential purpose of this expedition was to rescue the daughter of the Earl of Caithness, left behind when her husband was carried off to Strathbogie.

While this was going on, the supposedly Catholic Earl of Huntly was using the novel machinery of the reformed religion in Edinburgh to obtain a divorce for Earl Alexander from his Sinclair wife. The grounds submitted were that she had committed adultery with the Chief of Mackay, who was not present to defend himself and had almost certainly not been informed of the charge. Otherwise, why was Mackay not accused when he was at the mercy of the Gordons in Elgin and Aberdeen? Yet Sir Robert Gordon the chronicler, who was Earl Alexander's son, later backdated Mackay's adultery to the time of the marriage in Caithness, if not earlier. 'An unfit match indeed, a youth of 15 married to a woman of 32 years, but a match fit enough to cover her incontinence and evil life which she led with Aodh Mackay, for the which she was afterwards divorced from Earl Alexander.' Either the Gordons possessed astonishing knowledge of the domestic secrets of Girnigo Castle, or the charge relates to the last months of Mackay's life, since he died in 1572. Alternatively, it is simply another sample of the habitual Gordon mendacity.

In the following year Earl Alexander came of age and returned to Dunrobin, bringing with him a wife no less bizarre than the one from whom he had been separated. Naturally she was a Gordon of Huntly: the fault of his first wife had been neither her age nor her adultery, but the fact that she was a Sinclair. His second had been married to the Earl of Bothwell, from whom she was divorced with indecent speed so that Bothwell could marry Mary, Queen of Scots. The grounds for that separation were the consanguinity of the partners, but since a papal dispensation had been obtained in advance, they had no validity, and Jane Gordon was still Bothwell's canonical wife in Catholic eyes, which Huntly's were alleged to be. Neither could she have married Earl Alexander without a further dispensation, even had she been free to remarry, since he was her cousin. But laws such as the Gordons invoked to embezzle the lands of Clan Mackay or to rid themselves of an unwanted Sinclair wife had no application to themselves. While they scoured the tribal lands for property that could not be inherited owing to a flaw in the marriage of the heir's parents, they took no more trouble to observe the most basic matrimonial conventions than they respected either the criminal laws of the land or those of property.

For the Mackays of Strathnaver the outlook was as bleak as it had ever been. There was now an adult Gordon Earl of Sutherland and a Mackay Chief who had succeeded at the age of eleven, possessing no title to the clan territories. They had reached perilously close to the predicament of the Children of the Mist, except that at least they possessed an undoubted Chief. He was one, furthermore, whose mother and grandmother were both Sinclairs, a circumstance that had never existed before, since it was comparatively recently that the great house of Sinclair had inherited its northern earldom and moved into the Caithness plain. The Earl of Caithness took Uisdean the infant Chief to the safety of Girnigo Castle, from where he returned to his own country at the age of eighteen with the Earl's daughter as the third successive Sinclair wife of a Mackay Chief.

The Gordon chronicler asserted that the Earl had abducted Uisdean with the intention of murdering him (just as he had murdered the late Earl of Sutherland in Helmsdale Castle, he added with his customary extravagance): in which case it is strange that he did not succeed in doing the same again. Instead, Uisdean emerged safely from Girnigo Castle once he had reached competent age, for which he showed himself consistently grateful to his protector until the Sinclair Earl's death.

But he returned to a troubled land, in which the Gordons were fomenting disorder between Mackays, Gunns and Sinclairs, with the object of finding a pretext to transfer the vassalage of the Mackay Chief from Huntly to Sutherland. How could yet another Stewart sovereign permit such enormities to continue?

The explanation is this. James VI had been taken from his mother as a baby to be crowned King and reared by Protestant divines, who made his early years miserable but taught him all the tricks that he later used to outwit them. In the new theocracy in which he was reared, he was told to his face that he was no more than 'God's silly vassal,' subject to the authority of the Almighty of which the clergy were the custodians. As soon as King James was old enough he set out to diminish these pretentions, and it was in pursuit of this object that he built up the power of the Catholic Gordons. He created Huntly a Marquess, a title that the Gordon Chief still enjoys today. Whether or not the King was already infected with anti-Gaelic prejudices, the Gordons certainly filled his ears with gruesome reports on the incurable barbarity of his Gaelic subjects and contributed to an aversion that became in the end pathological. It was essential to the Gordons that their victims among his Celtic subjects (amongst whom they made it emphatically clear that they were not to be included) should be reduced to the status of second-class citizens, deprived of their legal rights as the MacGregors were soon to be deprived by statute. So well were the King's prejudices against his Gaelic subjects fed that presently he was advising his son, 'think no more of them all than of wolves and wild boars.'

In Strathnaver the Gordons set out systematically to make good the accuracy of their accusations during the sixteen years in which the young Chief of Mackay sought to maintain his clan in their ancestral lands without any form of title. Finally, when their situation had become almost as precarious as that of the MacGregors, he submitted to the Gordon Earl who was not his feudal superior. As the Gordon chronicler recorded, 'a meeting was appointed between Earl Alexander and Mackay at Inverness. So having met there and conferred together, they appointed a second tryst at Elgin, where they passed a contract between them and made a perfect and final reconciliation in the month of November 1588.' Alexander released Mackay from the dues for Strathnaver which had accumulated during the past sixteen years, a small price to pay for securing the greatest Celtic clan in the far north as his vassals at last.

He also offered Mackay, already married to Elizabeth of Caithness and possessing a daughter by her, his own daughter as a second wife. Alexander himself had taken a Gordon wife while he was already married to a Sinclair one, and evidently he saw no reason why others should not share his experience, especially a Celtic chief to whom he wished to demonstrate the potency of his protection. Uisdean Mackay accepted this condition too, in circumstances that the Gordon chronicler, who was the girl's brother, veiled in a discreet silence. As for Mackay's legitimate wife and child, the Earl of Caithness her father raised the question of their rights two years later, only to receive Gordon of Huntly's macabre advice that he should seek a remedy in a legal manner. This is the last that is heard of them.

The long and intricate take-over operation in Strathnaver required one further adjustment to be made in a legal manner. When Mackay and Jane Gordon his bigamous wife produced a son, it became possible that this child might fall heir to the Sutherland earldom. To prevent this, the King was petitioned to grant a fresh charter, barring the Gaelic branch of the family from the succession, and it says much for the unity of views which James VI shared with the Gordons that he consented to this arrangement. Henceforth the earldom of Sutherland was never to be alienated from the surname of Gordon. Failing heirs of the Earl and of his brothers, it was to pass to a collateral branch of the Sutherland Gordons. If all these lines should fail, the earldom was to pass to the house of Huntly that had never hitherto enjoyed it, by a process of succession without descent. This stipulation served to destroy any pretention that the Gordon earls were Chiefs of Clan Sutherland, an office that passed to the Sutherlands of Duffus.

Before these arrangements were concluded, Gordon of Huntly had already become involved in an ambitious plan of genocide in Lewis. For this unfortunate island King James drew up his first scheme of expropriation in 1598 with twelve men who became known as the Fife Adventurers, and gave his cousin Stewart of Lennox a special commission of Lieutenancy with powers to help them in their attempted take-over. It failed because the five or six hundred hired troops whom the Adventurers transported to Lewis were beaten off by the islanders. To James VI, this constituted fresh evidence of the beastliness of the Gaels, and in 1602 he granted a fresh Lieutenancy to Lennox, and another to Huntly who possessed so much more experience in dealing with savage tribesmen. The King divided their responsibilities carefully and harangued a Parliament reluctant to co-operate with a tirade about the racial inferiority of Hebrideans. He caused the Privy Council to command the chiefs of every Highland clan to appear before it and find a caution for keeping the peace. At a time when the Adventurers themselves displayed a waning enthusiasm, Mackenzie of Kintail came forward with support for the project and was rewarded with membership of the Privy Council. Here the matter rested when James VI inherited the English crown in 1603 and departed for London.

Tormod MacLeod of Lewis travelled there in a desperate

attempt to dissuade the King from his monstrous enterprise, but his only reward was to be imprisoned in Edinburgh without trial for ten years. Another assault on Lewis was launched and failed: and now the King's anger knew no bounds, and the inevitable instrument of his vengeance stepped out of the wings in the obliging person of the Marquess of Huntly. James commissioned him to equip an expedition at his own expense, taking as his reward 'the whole North Isles except Skye and Lewis in feu.' Huntly's gratified response was that 'his Lordship offers to take in hand the service of settling the North Isles . . . and to put an end to that service by extirpation of the barbarous people of the Isles within a year.' That was the kind of language King James liked to hear.

But while it gratified him in London, it did not please the Lords of the Privy Council in Edinburgh who expostulated: 'anent the Lieutenancy, they think it likewise unreasonable that the King's power should be put in the hands of a subject to conquer lands to himself.' The powers of the Lieutenancy had rarely been used for any other purpose since they were first created, but they had not usually been defined so candidly. James ignored the protest and wrote to Huntly in 1607, reminding him that his orders were 'the extirpating of the barbarous people in those bounds,' and the planting of the isles with 'civil' people, in other words Lowlanders who did not speak Gaelic. He made this very clear by warning Huntly not to permit people from Badenoch or Lochaber to join the settlers.

Uisdean was among the mainland chiefs ordered to support this enterprise with armed men, and forbidden to accept any of the wretched fugitives in their territory. He is much to be admired because he refused to be a party to such a project, although he must have known that the Gordons would rush gleefully to have him denounced by the Privy Council and declared a rebel. In the event he was saved by the greed of Huntly, who tried to haggle with King James over the amount of feu duties. James revealed the power he held over the Cock of the North by responding with an attack on his Catholic beliefs. The Fife Adventurers decided during the impasse to cut their losses, and sold their interest to Mackenzie of Kintail. And so, for several centuries to come, the Hebrides were spared the Gordon presence, though they too had to endure it the end.

It is curious that the Gordons revealed their attitude and aims in this age as clearly as James VI himself did, and none more eloquently than Sir Robert Gordon, Alexander of Sutherland's son. As Tutor of Sutherland, that is, guardian for his nephew who inherited the earldom while he was still a child, he wrote the same kind of advice about his Celtic vassals as King James composed concerning his Gaelic subjects for the benefit of his son Prince Charles. Probably the Tutor was inspired by the King's example, though it would be hard to determine who influenced the other in the extreme racism that James shared with the Gordons. They agreed that the solution was to exterminate Gaels everywhere, and colonise their lands.

The Tutor advised his nephew the young Earl to adopt the following policy towards his uncle the Chief of Mackay. 'Use Mackay rather as your vassal than as your companion, and because they are usually proud and arrogant, let them know that you are their superior.' The master-plan (which was finally implemented in the nineteenth century) was to disinherit them entirely. 'If you shall happen to buy or purchase any lands in Strathnaver, use kindly the natives you find upon the land, that thereby you may purchase their love and alienate their minds from Mackay.' Kindness was to be temporary, designed merely to deceive. 'Be not too hard-handed to them at first, for by a little freeness and liberality you may gain them, which is the nature of all Highlanders. Yet by progress of time I wish you to send some of your own people to dwell amongst them.'

So he warmed to the theme of genocide. 'Use your diligence to take away the relics of the Irish barbarity which as yet remains in your country, to wit, the Irish language and the habit. Purge your country piece by piece from that uncivil kind of clothes, such as plaids, mantles, trews and blue bonnets. Make severe acts against those that shall wear them. Cause the inhabitants of the country to clothe themselves as the most civil provinces of the kingdom do, with doublet, hose, cloaks and hats, which they may do with less charges than the other. It is no excuse which some would pretend, alleging that uncivil habit to be lightest in the mountains.' Appropriately, it was a Gordon who protested against George IV's decision to wear the kilt in Edinburgh, saying that no sovereign had worn it in Scotland since the days of barbarism. Yet by that time a chief of the name had raised the Gordon Highlanders and ordained a regimental tartan for them.

Sir Robert Gordon the Tutor had not the faintest notion of the antiquity of the literature he was consigning to the flames when he wrote: 'the Irish language cannot so soon be extinguished. To help this, plant schools in every corner in the country to instruct the youth to speak English. Let your chief schools for learning to be at Dornoch.'

It so happened that Caithness, which it was Sir Robert Gordon's lifelong ambition to seize from its Sinclair Earl, was not a Gaelic region and never had been. Yet somehow he managed to convince James VI that its inhabitants could be compared to Celtic savages, after he had stirred up sufficient disorder there to lend colour to his accusations. It all started with a minor case of arson at Sandside on the north coast, in which it may well have been a Gordon agent who set fire to some corn. This was fanned into such a flame at the expense of the Earl of Caithness that the King was inspired to write: 'by the Godless and beastly behaviour of the said Earl, the country is come to that estate as not only our subjects of the more civil disposition are oppressed and enforced to leave it, but likewise is so evil disordered as no part of the Highlands or remotest islands of that our kingdom were ever more barbarous.' The Tutor of Sutherland duly received his commission of fire and sword against the Earl of Caithness, but was frustrated by the Mackay Chief, who declined to implement it.

Indeed, he reproved his brother-in-law the Tutor. 'As concerning the commission which the Council has desired you to take against the Earl of Caithness, the Earl of Caithness did know thereof long before and is on his guard, and has provided for his own safety: so that in my opinion it will be an longsome business, evil and hurtful for the countries and without profit to yourself.' But Gordon kept the pot boiling for another two years until the Privy Council gave him a commission that named Mackay explicitly, as well as 'earls, lords, barons, substantious feuars and landed gentlemen' of all the northern counties to assist the vendetta. The population of Caithness was disarmed in advance: 'a piece of battery' was even promised from Edinburgh. Thus protected, Sir Robert Gordon (who suffered in an exceptional degree from personal cowardice) advanced boldly into Caithness, where the Earl disappointed him by retiring to Orkney, too wise to commit treason by opposing a royal commission.

The Sinclair Earl of Caithness was a cultivated man who took an enlightened interest in architecture and expressed himself gracefully in an elegant hand. He asked Gordon 'to remember that he was a nobleman, a peer of the kingdom,' and 'that nothing could be laid justly to his charge but civil matters which concerned only his creditors, all other crimes alleged against him being mere calumnies; that he was the first nobleman that ever was proclaimed a rebel or challenged a traitor for debt.' His protest fell on stony ground. Gordon marched unopposed to his

castles, which contained the entire muniments of the ancient
earldom, charters dating back to the time when a Norwegian
king had authorised the Sinclair expedition to Greenland, cor-
respondence and administrative documents, including the writ
Caithness had shown to Mackay that would 'free himself from the
Earl of Sutherland's superiority,' and other deeds that stood in
the way of Gordon ambitions. It cannot be proved that Sir Robert
destroyed them all, but it is a virtual certainty. From the saga
period to the seventeenth century the history of Caithness is
almost an entire blank, and this vacuum is probably the most
formidable achievement of his destructive genius.

Its most satisfactory consequence was that Gordon's own
detailed and tendentious chronicle was freed from the risk of
contradiction in many of its libels on his neighbours. But it did
not gain him the earldom. Since Sinclair of Caithness had not
offered treasonable resistance to the royal commission, he was
able to return from Orkney, stripped of many of his powers and
responsibilities but still in possession of the coronet that the
Gordons coveted.

Neither did the Tutor of Sutherland ever succeed in finding
another. Yet he appears to have missed it by only a narrow
margin during the years in which Charles I ruled after the death
of his father James VI. The Gordons eventually succeeded in
ruining the Chief of Mackay so completely that he sold them the
central valley after which the province of Strathnaver took its
name, 'even from Mudale to Invernaver.' It was from the time of
this transaction that the Gordons used the term Strathnaver so
ambiguously, blurring the extent of their claim on the Mackay
country. By 1642 when it took place, Charles was scattering
peerages indiscriminately to friends and enemies alike, in an
attempt to gain support against the subjects who had rebelled
against his rule, and Sir Robert went to London to discover what
his loyalty might be worth. But King Charles merely erected his
property of Gordonstoun into a barony before he decided it was
time to forsake the Royalist cause, and so the ambitious Tutor
died Sir Robert Gordon, Baronet of Gordonstoun. Later his
property passed through an heiress to the neighbouring Chief of
Clan Cumming, so that the descendant of King Donald Ban is
today designated Sir William Gordon-Cumming, while
Gordonstoun has been transformed into a private boarding-
school.

The record of so many of the Gordon Chiefs should not be
allowed to obscure the achievements of members of the clan who

never entered the Highlands, any more than the story of Rob Roy should tempt us to forget the great academic dynasty of the Gregorys or the other distinctions of Clan Gregor. The greater number of Gordons, in all probability, do not descend from the Seton who married the Gordon heiress and founded the dynasty of the Chiefs of Strathbogie.

Eminent among these is the sept of Haddo whose representative Sir John Gordon came immediately to the support of Charles I when the Earl of Sutherland and the Marquess of Huntly failed him. He was taken captive and imprisoned in Edinburgh, where his place of captivity became known as Haddo's Hole: and he was the first of the King's supporters to be killed there by judicial execution. In the following century his family built one of the most splendid of early Adam masterpieces in Haddo House, and after they had been raised to the rank of Earls of Aberdeen they contributed a Gordon Prime Minister to the nineteenth century. This branch has since risen in the peerage, and its present head, Archie, Marquess of Aberdeen has consummated its many services to Scotland by handing the jewel of Haddo to the National Trust.

The Gordons of Sutherland had abandoned their surname in defiance of James VI's charter by the time their earldom was inherited by Elizabeth, Countess of Sutherland in her own right; so that she was also recognised as the Sutherland Chief. It was she who brought such enduring infamy upon her house by presiding over the Sutherland clearances to which Lockhart referred obliquely at the time of George IV's visit to Edinburgh. From Dunrobin Castle she sent fifty of her clansmen to contribute to the pageantry of the state visit, dressed in plaid and trews and carrying swords, and it was this that appeared such a cruel mockery of the thousands of her dependants who were being evicted from her estates in Sutherland to make room for sheep farms.

There has been an unhappy sequel which once again illustrates the tenacious, backward-looking attitudes of tribal societies. By chance the earldom of Sutherland has been inherited by another Elizabeth, Countess in her own right, who has lost no opportunity to express her regret over past deeds for which she is in no wise accountable. A few years ago, in a most graceful and imaginative gesture of reconciliation, she invited the Gaelic National Mod, the annual festival of Highland poetry and music, to convene in the castle of Dunrobin. It would surely have caused the Tutor of Sutherland to turn in his grave, if the language and culture that he was so determined to destroy had actually been permitted to capture the castle from which he scourged the Celtic lands. But his remains were not to be disturbed: the invitation was rejected with the greatest discourtesy.

CHAPTER SEVEN

The Doom of the Seaforths

There is no more spectacular story of the rise and fall of a line of Highland chiefs than that of the Mackenzies. It is all the more bizarre because it was prophesied by a Mackenzie seer, the only one in Scotland's story who can be compared, for the range of his predictions, to Merlin the prophet of Strathclyde a thousand years earlier. Before their downfall, the Chiefs of Clan Kenneth, Sons of the Bright One, had contrived to edge their way between the two spheres of influence of the Campbell and Gordon viceroys, and to snatch the outermost isle of Lewis as well as the greater part of the ancient earldom of Ross, which not even the great Clan Donald had succeeded in holding.

From their small beginnings around the sea-loch called Duich in which Eilean Donnan Castle stands beneath the range of the seven sisters of Kintail, the Mackenzies increased their power by service to the Kings of Scots, just as Farquhar MacTaggart had done in an earlier age. At the time when James III deprived the Lord of the Isles of the earldom of Ross, Alasdair of Kintail raised Clan Kenneth on the King's behalf to fight against Clan Donald and was rewarded in 1477 with that precious source of future security, a charter to his lands. His son Kenneth served James IV likewise, in the conflict that led to the downfall of the Lord of the Isles. When he died in 1491 he was buried in Beauly Priory north of Inverness, beneath a fine stone effigy that depicts him wearing a complete suit of armour. It was executed shortly after the capture of Inverness by Angus, son of John of the Isles, who was murdered there by his harpist, an episode in which the Mackenzies were once again prompt to bid for favour in royal eyes.

They won it. James IV erected Kintail into a barony for the Chief of Clan Kenneth, with the obligation to render a stag yearly. The stag's head was placed on the coat-of-arms of the Chief, and he became known by the title Cabarfeidh, which means Deer-Antlers. These have also become the clan badge, with the motto *Cuidiche an Righ*, the King's Share, again a reference to the stag. It seems unlikely that the name of a Celtic chief and a clan totem of this kind could really date from a feudal grant, and one registered as late as 1508. The sacred stag and the horned god belong to the same world of pagan Celtic myth as the boar, the cat and the mare. Heraldry arrived comparatively late in this society, with the military organisation that required it for purposes of identification in battle, and it seems probable that the stag's head is yet another of the motifs borrowed from a far earlier age.

A typical story of the troubled sixteenth century in which the Mackenzies played their cautiously adventurous part in competition with Gordons and Campbells concerns Mary MacLeod, who survived (almost miraculously it appears) to become the 10th Chief of Dunvegan. Mary Queen of Scots' mother gave her as a ward to Gordon of Huntly, yet another inducement to win that perfidious man's loyalty; while Campbell of Argyll succeeded in planting a Campbell husband in her arms. She had already fallen into the embraces of MacNeil of Barra, to whom it seems that she willingly bore a son. When she delivered a legitimate Campbell son there was considerably more consternation. It is scarcely surprising that the Mackenzies failed to compete successfully for such a prize, but noteworthy that they did contrive to hold her in Kintail against all comers for a while, though they failed to provide her either with offspring or a husband.

However, they enjoyed better fortune when Janet, daughter of the 9th Chief of Kintail, married Ruaridh MacLeod of Lewis, who had succeeded as Chief in 1532. She jeopardised clan interests when she bore a son, not to her husband, but to Judge Morrison, whose clan still held the hereditary office of Brieve in Lewis. He himself confessed that Janet's son Torcuil was his, and therefore could not be the MacLeod heir. Her behaviour, like Mary MacLeod's liaison with MacNeil of Barra, recalls the passionate love poem of an earlier century by one of the Campbell wives of Argyll, clearly not addressed to her husband, and suggests that Celtic women still asserted the parity with men that had astonished many in the remotest times. Presently Janet Mackenzie was abducted by the brother of MacLeod of Raasay: doomed to lead a dynastic way of life, she evidently contrived to make the best of it.

Ruaridh MacLeod of Lewis, still without a legitimate heir, next made a most auspicious marriage into the royal family. His second wife Barbara Stewart was sister of the man whom Queen Margaret Tudor took as her third husband. Their son was again called Torcuil, and he ought to have lived to achieve security for his clan after Mary Queen of Scots returned to begin her personal reign in Scotland and recognised him as her relative. 'Torcuil MacLeod, We greet you well,' she wrote to him in 1563. 'We are informed that some of the Isles are desirous to have you allied to them by marriage, and because you have the honour to be of the Stewart blood, we thought it expedient to give you advertisement that it is our will and pleasure that you ally yourself with no party in marriage without our advice . . .' In the same year Torcuil was drowned in the treacherous seas that surround his island, and it proved to be one of the worst disasters in its history.

MacLeod of Lewis had been singularly unlucky but he was still capable of repairing his misfortunes, as he proved when he married a daughter of Maclean of Duart, who bore him two sons. But these young heirs were menaced not only by the illegitimate Torcuil, offspring of Janet Mackenzie and the Brieve of Lewis: Ruaridh MacLeod had also begotten five illegitimate sons of his own. Two of these allied with the bastard Torcuil in an attack on MacLeod's castle in Lewis, and after storming it and imprisoning the Chief they carried away all the family charters to place in the safe-keeping of Mackenzie of Kintail. It was a spectacular coup.

By this time James VI had embarked on his personal rule, and had possessed ample opportunity to discover the cause of disorder in the Highlands, the lack or duplication of charters of ownership. Now MacLeod of Lewis had been reduced to the predicament of so many other chiefs, and he might as easily have enlightened the King as MacGregor or Mackay, for he is said to have lived to the age of ninety-four and died not earlier than 1595. But King James believed himself to be enlightened already, and we know what the guide-lines of his attitude were because he wrote them down for the instruction of his son. Mainland Gaels were barbarous compared with civilising non-Gaelic Gordons. But Hebridean Gaels were not to be regarded as human at all, and even barbarous mainland Gaels such as the Mackenzies might civilise them. 'As for the Highlands, I shortly comprehend them all in two sorts of people: the one, that dwelleth in our mainland that are barbarous, and yet mixed with some show of civility: the other that dwelleth in the Isles and are all utterly barbarous.'

Such was the simple formula which condemned MacLeod of Lewis to the same fate as the MacGregors were suffering. Instead of receiving justice and recovering his titles of ownership from the Mackenzies, he was summoned in 1583 to answer charges of having molested the bogus heir who had in fact risen in arms against him. When he failed to appear, he was put to the horn and brought captive before the Privy Council. In 1585, Torcuil the Mackenzie bastard made the shrewd move of placing himself in dependence on the Gordon Chief, the Marquess of Huntly whom the King favoured.

The true heirs to Lewis were the sons of MacLeod's third marriage with Maclean of Duart's daughter. From his mountainous island of Mull, the Maclean Chief was at this time assaulting the fertile little realm of MacDonald of Islay, once the seat of the Lords of the Isles. 'Fortune can give no greater boon than discord among our foes,' Tacitus had written one and a half thousand years earlier, describing the fatal inability of the Celtic tribes to combine in the face of a common danger, and their habits had not changed. The feud between Clan Maclean and Clan Donald, which would soon place both Islay and Mull in the hands of the Campbells, now produced its fatal repercussions further north. But once again, the traditional Stewart method of solving the problem played its malign part.

In 1589 James VI issued a full remission to Maclean of Duart and the MacDonalds for their past offences and invited them to Edinburgh to discuss the problems of their tribal areas. Here was an opportunity for the King to explore the true causes of the ills of Gaeldom. But as soon as they arrived they were imprisoned and charged with the very crimes for which they had received the royal pardon. While the Campbells were snatching what they could from the crumbling empire of Clan Donald further south, the Mackenzies seized this opportunity to mount their next coup.

They had turned their eyes on the region west of the Great Glen, between the Maclean lands of Morvern to the south and Kintail to the north and the isle of Skye across the narrow straits to the west. Here lies Glengarry, homeland of the MacDonald sept that still spells its name MacDonell, which is closer to the Gaelic original of the name. Like the island branch of Clanranald, it descended from John the Good, Lord of the Isles, by his first marriage with the mainland heiress of Garmoran. When he took as his second wife the Princess Margaret Stewart, they were obliged to be content with a smaller inheritance while the Lordship passed to a younger brother who was a king's grandson. It is all the more remarkable that these septs so often supported the Lordship in times of need, and exposed themselves to the same ruin that ultimately overtook it. Both Glengarry and Clanranald were among the chiefs carried off by James V, with the Chief of Mackay and Ruaridh MacLeod of Lewis, on his kidnapping expedition of 1540. In the capricious manner in which these things were resolved, MacLeod then received the charter to his lands that Mackenzie of Kintail had now stolen; Clanranald was retained in prison; Glengarry and Mackay were released without harm or benefit. Then, in 1574, Glengarry did receive a charter confirming his ancient title to his lands. The MacDonells of Glengarry had sufficient grounds for supposing that they were safe, particularly during the years in which Lewis became the principal magnet for speculative enterprise.

But there was that hiatus between the first assault on Lewis while James VI was still in Scotland, and the more drastic orders that he issued from London after he had ascended the English throne in 1603. This was when Tormod MacLeod travelled to London to plead that he was the elder son of the late Ruaridh MacLeod's marriage to Maclean of Duart's daughter, and consequently the legitimate heir to Lewis. No doubt he was able to explain that the Mackenzie claimant was the son of Morrison the Brieve, who had seized the muniments of Lewis by force. These incontestable facts appear to have made a brief impression on the King, which raises a presumption that Tormod was a handsome young man.

Agents were posted south to poison the mind of James against him, however, and these contrived his removal to Edinburgh, where Mackenzie of Kintail succeeded in keeping him in prison without trial (since there was no charge that could possibly be concocted against him) for ten years. Mackenzie was so hospitable as to pay the gaoler the cost of his maintenance in the Tolbooth. The most that Tormod was able to do about this was to petition that the money might be remitted to himself, 'to the effect that he may so use the same, as by a sparing diet he may reserve some part thereof to buy him clothes.'

With the Lewis situation stabilised in this manner, though its ownership remained unresolved, Stag-Antlers, Son of the Bright One, used his expertise in the corrupt processes of justice in Scotland's capital to proceed against MacDonell of Glengarry. The first stage consisted in laying a charge against him there which required Glengarry's presence to anwer: the second involved murdering two of his kinsmen in Glengarry, so that other preoccupations would prevent his attendance. Whether or not Glengarry even knew of the summons, he was engaged in taking reprisals when he found himself confronted by the third move in the plot. Cabarfeidh obtained a commission from the Chancellor of Scotland and the support of the Gordon Earl of

Sutherland in implementing it. There was a great deal of slaughter before he wrested from the MacDonells the castle of Strone and the lands of Lochalsh and Lochcarron. After that, it was a mere matter of sending the King the sort of details that confirmed his convictions concerning Celtic barbarity and lawlessness to obtain a charter to these prizes in 1607.

This was the year in which James VI ignored the protests of his Scottish Privy Council against permitting his subjects to conquer lands for themselves, and issued his fresh orders for the extermination of the inhabitants of the isle of Lewis: in which Mackay refused to take part, Huntly haggled so unwisely over the feu duties, and the Fife Adventurers withdrew, selling their interest in Lewis to Mackenzie.

Now he played his final card. It was a piece of extraordinary good fortune that the bogus claimant to Lewis, Brieve Morrison's son, left an only daughter as his heiress. The Chief of Kintail arranged that she should marry his brother Ruaridh (or Roderick), and after the death of her father in 1609 he successfully represented her as the lineal descendant of the MacLeods of Lewis.

This was the year in which another of James VI's strokes of what he called kingcraft was brought to a triumphant conclusion. At the same time as he had despatched Gordon of Huntly to Lewis, the King had launched an armament composed of Lowland levies drawn from the garrisons of Ireland against the southern societies of Gaeldom. They were commanded by Stewart of Ochiltree accompanied by Andrew Knox, Bishop of the Isles, who summoned the chiefs to meet the royal commissioner on the isle of Mull. It was the suggestion of the good Bishop himself that these men should be inveigled aboard a ship on the pretext that they were to be edified by a sermon from himself. Trusting the prelate where they might by now have been suspicious of a Stewart, they allowed themselves to be rowed aboard, and were immediately carried to the mainland and imprisoned.

MacNeil of Barra had been too wary to attend while Ruaridh Mór MacLeod of Dunvegan had sent his brother. But Maclean of Duart was in the bag together with the MacDonalds of Sleat and Clanranald, and there they remained throughout the winter, most of them in Blackness Castle, while the delighted King composed wide-ranging schemes for the future of their societies. Bishop Knox travelled to London to assist in the tripartite negotiations between the sovereign in England, his Privy Council in Edinburgh, and the captured chiefs in their castle in the west. These made grovelling submissions that won the Chiefs of

Sleat, Clanranald and Duart new titles to their lands on strict conditions. The chiefs of the west mainland were ordered to find security for keeping the peace, and most of them likewise submitted. The Mackinnon Chief was ordered to come from Skye, as well as MacLeod from Dunvegan. But he had not yet done so when the rest signed the Statutes of Iona in August 1609.

The King's style is recognisable in the preamble to these statutes, which states: 'the special cause of the great misery, barbarity and poverty into the which for the present our barren country is subject has proceeded of the unnatural deadly feuds which have been fostered amongst us in this past age.' It did not indicate what underlying causes had been fostering these feuds.

The statutes provided that masterless vagabonds were to be expelled from the islands, beggars to be treated as thieves. The greater number of Gaels could by now be fitted into one of these categories or the other. Bards were to be first placed in the stocks and then driven from the country: a measure that struck at the popular culture of the Gaels, even if it was not actually designed to destroy Gaelic literature and learning. Every gentleman was to send his eldest son to school in the Lowlands, a measure which helped as much as any other cause to create a class of alien landlords over the Gaelic peasantry of the Highlands, where once these had been the tribal fathers of their clans. These rules were subscribed by the Macleans of Duart, Lochbuie and Coll, by Mackinnon of the clan that had for so long provided the abbots of Iona, by MacQuarrie and the several MacDonalds. MacLeod of Dunvegan turned up to offer his obedience in the following year and got away with it.

The Mackenzie Chief, newly enobled, appears to have played little part in these proceedings except to stand as a relief cautioner for MacLeod of Dunvegan. But he calculated that James VI was so preoccupied with the southern Hebrides, and so favourably disposed towards himself as a Celtic chief who had proved to be civilised, that he might attempt a sleight of hand — especially as the Chancellor of Scotland was abetting him.

His trick was to seek a royal grant in confirmation of his titles to property at a time when so many other Gaelic chiefs were obtaining the same. Into those he slipped the island of Lewis with the other possessions of the MacLeods whose charters had been stolen by Janet Mackenzie's bastard son. But some spoil-sports among the Fife Adventurers warned the King, who angrily handed the title to Lewis back to these gentlemen, thus encouraging them to make one more attempt on the island.

With the rightful owner still imprisoned in Edinburgh on no particular charge and the bogus Mackenzie claimant dead, the desperate islanders managed to find one remaining son of Ruaridh, the last MacLeod Chief, brave enough to embark on a defence of their homes and lives. His name was Neil, and great must have been his astonishment when he found himself supported by none other than the Lord of Kintail. The help was given to him secretly, of course. Cabarfeidh sent his brother Ruaridh Mackenzie of Coigach to assist the Adventurers openly, while he undertook to provide from the mainland of Ross the essential shipload of supplies on which the gentlemen of Fife depended. By doing this he ensured that their expedition would founder when he informed Neil MacLeod when and where to intercept their supply ship.

So the Bright One had it both ways, as in his dealings with Glengarry. The Adventurers finally abandoned Lewis and sold their title to him. At the same time they returned with fresh complaints of the beastliness of the islanders and of Neil MacLeod in particular, in which no blame whatever besmirched the reputation of Lord Mackenzie of Kintail. On the contrary, he was able to effect his final conquest as a police action sanctioned by government, just as he had been able to do when he filched the lands of the MacDonells. James VI, who had so adroitly prevented him from obtaining his prize by less violent means, once reflected complacently in London: 'here I sit and govern Scotland with my pen, which my predecessors could not do by the sword.' To those of his subjects whom he did not confuse with wolves and wild boars it probably appeared a reasonable boast.

In Lewis there remained several of these to dispose of, especially Neil MacLeod and the other descendants of the late Chief Ruaridh, some of whom gathered with him on an impregnable isle called Berrisay which they had provisioned against such an emergency. Neil was still holding out on it when Cabarfeidh died and his brother Ruaridh of Coigach became Tutor of Kintail, as guardian to his nephew, the young Chief Colin.

A younger brother who had not inherited the Chiefship, but who exercised its powers for a space in the office of Tutor, was exposed to exceptional temptation to make the most of his short-lived opportunity, as Sir Robert Gordon did while he was Tutor of Sutherland. Mackenzie of Coigach his contemporary was at least as unscrupulous, and earned a reputation enshrined in the Gaelic saying that there were only two things worse than the Tutor of Kintail, frost in spring and mist in the dog days. His stronghold near Strathpeffer, called Castle Leod after the clan he helped to ruin, still contains his grim portrait and his living representative the Earl of Cromartie, whose entry in *Burke's Peerage* records that his ancestor the Tutor 'was instrumental in civilising the Western Isles and the more turbulent parts of the west coast of Scotland.'

The way the Tutor of Kintail carried out his civilising mission was by rounding up all the women and children of the men who had taken refuge on Berrisay and planting them on a rock within sight of the fugitives, who could see that their families were certain to perish when the tide rose. Neil MacLeod thereupon abandoned his place of refuge and the women and children were taken to safety. Neil escaped the Tutor's clutches for the present and found refuge in the home of that outstanding Chief Ruaridh Mór MacLeod of Dunvegan in Skye. MacLeod agreed to take him to James VI in London, in the hope that he might succeed where his brother Tormod had failed, in enlightening the King as to what was really going on in the tribal lands. Nothing was to prove more durable than this belief that the Chief of Chiefs, the Stewart to whom almost every clan was related by blood, was a source of justice, if only it could be reached. Many of the clans carried the conviction with them to Culloden.

Tormod had at least succeeded in reaching the King's presence before he was whisked back to his prison in Edinburgh, where he was still confined. His brother Neil was spared the fruitless journey, when the Tutor intercepted MacLeod in Glasgow with a summons to deliver him that Ruaridh Mór dared not ignore. So Neil was taken to Edinburgh and there hanged in the year 1613. Perhaps the Tutor hoped that Tormod would expose himself to execution also if he were freed: anyway, he could not be kept a prisoner without trial forever. So in 1615 he was released, and in 1615 left his country for Holland, where he died.

One thing the Tutor did not succeed in doing, although he attempted it; that was to deprive his nephew Colin of the isle of Lewis while he was his guardian. His claim to it was an altogether different one, although strictly speaking it was no claim at all. He was married to the heiress of the bogus claimant, Brieve Morrison's son by Janet Mackenzie. The bastard had indeed claimed to be the true heir, and had stolen all the writs and charters to the property without ever being brought to justice by a King who prated about introducing law and civility in the Highlands. But it was impossible to contradict the statement of the Brieve. All the Mackenzies had been able to do was to express their vexation by pursuing Clan Morrison with vindictive cruelty. So Colin came of age as proprietor of Lewis, whose sea-loch called Loch Seaforth he chose for his title when James VI raised him to the rank of Earl in 1623.

So it was (one may suppose) that the descendants of the Tutor escaped the fate prophesied by the Mackenzie seer in the pronouncement known as the Doom of the Seaforths. It is extraordinary that this very detailed prediction should be attributed to a man who died in the year before the Tutor of Kintail was born, half a century before the earldom of Seaforth was created, and years before the Mackenzies obtained any title to the island in which Loch Seaforth lies. He was known as Coinneach Odhar, or Sallow Kenneth, and in 1578 a commission was issued to the justices of Ross to 'apprehend, imprison and try Kenneth *alias* Kennoch Owir, principal or leader in the art of magic.'

James VI wrote a book on demonology and witchcraft before he left Scotland, after researches that enabled him to indulge another of his enthusiasms — the torturing of women suspected of practising magic. But at the time of Coinneach Odhar's execution he was too young to have developed such interests. It was after he had moved to London that he revealed his belief in second sight to Sir John Harington, one of his courtiers, in a reference to his mother. 'His Highness told me her death was visible in Scotland before it did really happen, being as he said "spoken of in secret by those whose power of sight presented to them a bloody head dancing in the air." He then did remark much on this gift, and said he had sought out of certain books a sure way to attain knowledge of future chances.' It was undoubtedly to gratify the King's tastes that Shakespeare wrote his play of *Macbeth*, whose witches use one recipe taken directly out of James VI's book on demonology.

There was no book containing the prophecies of the Mackenzie seer until a very much later age, and as oral tradition took up the theme of Coinneach Odhar, it moved him and his predictions into new times and fresh surroundings, just as it had done with the tales of the Ossianic heroes. At length his life story became planted with a wealth of detail in the century following that of his execution, and his prophecies were woven around the people of that age. But the fact remains that many of them were recorded long before they were fulfilled, and to this day there is scarcely a township or district throughout the vast territories once dominated by Clan Kenneth at the height of their power that cannot tell of a prophecy that came true, or of one awaiting fulfilment.

Some of them pass far beyond the clan borders. For instance, when the present Queen inherited the crown in 1953, it was the first time since the Union that the country possessed three Queens, since Elizabeth the Queen Mother and Mary the Queen Grandmother were both living. Coinneach Odhar's prophecy was by this time on record, that in the year of the three Queens there would be no difference between winter and summer, and everyone in the Highlands knew it. That winter thrushes nested on the north coast of Scotland in December, and in the same month raspberries were picked in Hampshire and primroses bloomed in Wiltshire. In the summer the seasons were reversed: Coronation day was colder than Christmas day, with sleet in London and snow that extinguished the bonfires on the north coast.

Another of the seer's predictions appears to have received a more apocalyptic fulfilment. A terrible catastrophe would occur, he warned, when it was possible to cross the river Ness dry-shod in five places, so that when Inverness town council discussed the building of a fifth bridge in 1937 it received a solemn warning in the local press of the consequences that Coinneach Odhar had foretold. Undeterred by such superstition, the town authorities built the fifth bridge, which was completed by the end of August 1939, a few days before the outbreak of the Second World War.

A more local fulfilment occurred in the ruins of Fortrose Cathedral on the Black Isle in Easter Ross. It was believed that if a wedding were ever to be held in these ruins, the graveyards of Fortrose would overflow. In August 1975 a local girl married an English naval officer in them according to the rites of the Episcopal Church, and immediately afterwards the number of local deaths increased astronomically. Of course all these happenings, great and small, can be attributed to chance, and there are many earlier ones which may be discounted because the prophecies were not on record before the fulfilment of them, even if everyone knew them. Until the predictions, originally communicated in Gaelic verse and prose, were recorded for examination in the light of later occurrences, no credibility could be claimed for Coinneach Odhar's gift of second sight.

Tradition is most suspect of all in its wealth of detail concerning his life, which it began by planting him in the wrong century. He was said to have been born in Uig in Lewis early in the seventeenth century. Here he received a divining stone that enabled him to see into the future while he was still an adolescent, and the fame it brought him led to his removal to the estate of

Brahan Castle, chief seat of the Earls of Seaforth until their doom was complete, and since then an eerie ruin. Ever since, he has been known as the Brahan Seer.

The Earls of Seaforth remained loyal to the Stewart dynasty to which they owed so much, and one of the most distinguished of them was the younger son of Colin, 1st Earl of Seaforth, who became known as Bloody Mackenzie. Sir George Mackenzie of Rosehaugh was an ornament of the legal profession in his age and author of the *Institutes* that form one of the pillars of Scots law. In the reign of Charles II he held the office of Scottish Lord Advocate, and in that capacity he was responsible for the prosecution of Covenanters. These religious fanatics were being persecuted with the same severity that they had inflicted on others in the time of Calvinist ascendancy, and after the revolution of 1688 once again restored the Calvinists to power, they were regarded as suffering martyrs, while those who had suppressed them earned epithets such as the one bestowed on Sir George Mackenzie.

It is interesting that he himself experienced the gift of second sight, and communicated examples of it to others — unless these stories are apocryphal. Yet he does not seem to have received any intimation of the impending doom of his own family. Dying in 1691, he lived long enough to see the fortunes of his house in eclipse during the rule of Cromwell, restored by Charles II, and finally endangered by the revolution that swept the last Stewart king from his throne. But the Mackenzie chiefs had overcome similar hazards in the past, and it would certainly have required second sight to predict that his entire line would actually be extinguished. This was what Coinneach foresaw, while the author of the *Institutes* could not.

The central figure in the prophecy is the grandson of Colin, 1st Earl of Seaforth, who was Kenneth the 3rd Earl, nephew of the Lord Advocate. Earl Kenneth remained loyal to the Stewarts during the rebellion against Charles I, was imprisoned during the Commonwealth, and released after the Restoration. He married his cousin Isabella Mackenzie, descendant of the grim Tutor of Kintail and sister of the 1st Earl of Cromartie. According to the legend of Coinneach Odhar's life, she was living in Castle Brahan while her husband was absent on an embassy to Paris. Becoming uneasy over the Earl's delay in returning home, she sent for the Brahan Seer and asked for news of him. Coinneach consulted his divining stone, and then told the Countess baldly that her husband was safe and well. But where was he; who was in his company; what had Coinneach actually seen? Coinneach remained reticent, which greatly increased the curiosity of the Countess of Seaforth. She commanded him to describe the clothes her husband was wearing, the people to whom he was speaking. Finally she goaded him into describing in detail the dissipations that were detaining him in Paris, and in particular the beautiful women whom he was entertaining so intimately.

In her rage, and perhaps because the Chief had been accused in public of infidelity, she ordered that the Brahan Seer should be rolled down a hill in a flaming tar-barrel lined with spikes. As a final twist to the story, the Earl arrived home just too late to save him: and before Coinneach Odhar died, he pronounced his last prediction, the Doom of the Seaforths.

Thus the legend, and it is supported by not a single iota of historical evidence. The record of proceedings against Coinneach Odhar is to be found amongst the state papers of almost exactly a century earlier, although those of the seventeenth century are far more ample, and might be expected to contain evidence of the judicial execution of a warlock, if there had been another seer of the same name. That would not have been unlikely in a society in which the gift of second sight was so widely credited, and as for the similarity of names, it was the most common in use in the clan, and shared by Cabarfeidh himself. Yet there is not a tittle of evidence to suggest that there were two Coinneach Odhars.

The paradox is this. The Brahan Seer's prophecy was extremely detailed and far-reaching, and it was set down in writing some time before its fulfilment. Not only did it enjoy as general a currency in the Highlands as his prophecy of the coming of the railway there and the construction of the Caledonian Canal in the Great Glen, but it was being discussed in advance by such men as Sir Walter Scott and Sir Humphrey Davie.

Assuming that the Doom of the Seaforths could only have been predicted by the sixteenth-century seer, is it relevant that no earldom of Seaforth existed in his lifetime? It seems not. If a person can slip out of the straitjacket of time, he can presumably see into any age, and not merely beyond the smoke of a burning tar-barrel. Some of the pictorial images that flash before his inward eye may lack clarity or intelligibility, which will be reflected in his account of them. What the Brahan Seer saw of the Caledonian Canal was the sails of sea-going ships passing up the Great Glen. He would not have understood the mechanism of the railway engine, and consequently spoke of carriages without horses. It is hard to conceive how he could have discovered that the Mackenzie Chief had become Earl of Seaforth unless his visions were accompanied by a sound-track, but this detail of the prophecy might have been added by oral tradition like the story of the cruel Countess and the tar-barrel. It can be discarded without undermining the extraordinary precision of the remainder.

The house of Seaforth would be extinguished in sorrow, so ran the prophecy. Its last Chief would be deaf and dumb, the father of four sons who would die before him. His possessions would be inherited by a white-hooded girl from the east, who would kill her sister. As though these facts were not startling enough, there would be other signs to herald their approach. In the lifetime of the last Earl of Seaforth there would be four Chiefs, of Gairloch, Chisholm, Grant and Raasay, of whom one would be buck-toothed, another hair-lipped, the third half-witted and the last a stammerer, and all would be the friends of the last Lord. Each of those details were on record before the Doom was fulfilled, and not one of them failed to come true.

Kenneth, 4th Earl of Seaforth succeeded his father in 1678 and remained loyal to James VII ten years later when that monarch fled from the country after its invasion by his son-in-law William of Orange. King William had brought with him the Scots Brigade from Holland under the command of General Hugh Mackay of Scourie, a cousin of the Mackay Chief. Appointed Commander-in-Chief in Scotland by the usurping King, Hugh Mackay garrisoned Castle Brahan in his name. But after resistance to the new regime had collapsed in the Highlands, Cabarfeidh was restored to safety among all the other chiefs who made their reluctant submission to King William. He died one year before the Dutch King, leaving William the 5th Earl to live under the threat of doom.

The measure of Earl William's power in the north can be gauged by the fact that when the Jacobite insurrection occurred in 1715 he set out to support it from Castle Brahan with no less than 3,000 men under his command, including MacDonalds and Rosses as well as his own clansmen. Near the Kyle of Sutherland they were set upon by a force raised by the Earl of Sutherland, and the outcome of the affray is immortalised by one of the most spirited of Gaelic rants, the boastful song of victory known as *Cabarfeidh*, the invincible Deer-Antlers. The raiding Mackays were there, the song declares, until they took to their heels. The Munro Chief, Laird of Foulis, was so foolish as to confront

The Hunterston Brooch found at Hunterston, Ayrshire *c.* 1700 A.D. A silver-gilt brooch made is Scotland or Ireland.

'The Book of Kells'. Claimed to have belonged to St Columba. This copy of the Gospels is a highly illustrated and elaborate version.

St Fillans Crozier. 14th century
silver gilt reliquary containing
a bronze head.

Dunstaffnage Castle. One of the principal strongholds of Ewen MacDougall,
the third MacDougall chief.

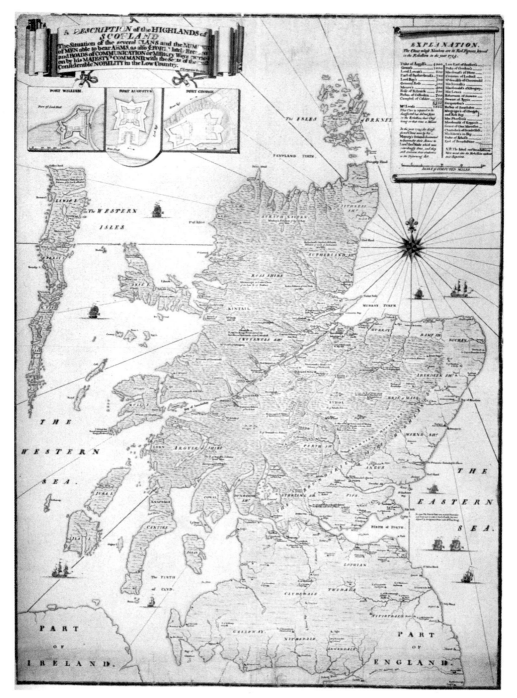

A map by C. Lempriere 1731, showing how the clans were distributed in Scotland, the three forts in the Great Glen and the road through the Highlands.

Kilchurn Castle, Loch Awe. Founded by Sir Colin Campbell of Glenorchy, mid 15th century.

Tomb of Alexander McLeod at Rodel. This tomb was made in 1528, 20 years before he died.

ABOVE: The clarsach or Highland Harp played at public performances and family gatherings. This particular harp was given by Mary Queen of Scots to Beatric Gardyne of Banchory.

LEFT: Effigie of the warrior Bricius MacFingore, a MacKinnon chief, buried in Iona.

ABOVE: Sir Duncan Campbell,
first Lord Campbell 1546–1631.
Portrait by Jameson.

RIGHT: Francis Nacnab, 12th
Laird of MacNab 1735–1816.
Portrait by Sir Henry Raeburn
R.A.

James IV of Scotland 1473–1513, was responsible for establishing a faculty of medicine at Aberdeen University.

James V 1513–42. James V was crowned when he was less than two years of age. This painting from the Seton Armorial shows him with his first wife, Madeleine.

James Graham, First Marquis of Montrose 1612–50. Portrait painted by George Jameson.

Eileen Donnan, the fortress in Loch Duich. This fortress became the responsibility of the Mackenzies who left in the hands of Clan MacRae for protection.

Duart Castle, Mull, which had been owned by the Macleans, and then later seized by the Campbells in the later part of the 17th century.

Fort Augustus. The fort seized by the Duke of Cumberland. Watercolour by T. Sandby.

Black Watch Soldier of 42nd Regiment of Foot 1742.

Alasdair MacDonell of Glengarry. Portrait painted by Raeburn.

The Canongate, Edinburgh August 1822, during the procession of George IV.

'The March of the Clans' by Turner, painted for George IV's visit to Edinburgh.

David Allan's painting of a piper playing in a Highland cottage. Painted late 18th century.

A coatee of Murray of Atholl tartan. This particular one was specially made for George IV's nephew, Sir Augustus Frederick d'Este, son of Duke of Sussex.

R.R. McIan's print of Lamont clan tartan 1845.

R.R. McIan's print of MacAlister tartan.

R.R. McIan's print of MacAuley clan tartan.

Cabarfeidh, and so were the Roses of Kilravock on the other side of the Moray Firth: the clansmen of both names are dismissed in the rant as a lot of silly old men. Neither the Frasers nor the Grants stood their ground, while the Forbes Clan ran headlong all the way to Culloden. But the boastful celebrations at Castle Brahan with which the song ends proved to be short-lived. The 5th Earl escaped to France after the rising had failed, yet had the temerity to return in support of the next Jacobite attempt in 1719. But the prophecy of doom had allowed for no such misfortunes as these, and the house of Seaforth proved immune to their consequences. The attainder of the Mackenzie Chief was reversed in 1725, and the 5th Earl departed unscathed to his fathers in 1740.

There were writings on the wall, but they did not match the well-known prophecy. The forfeited title of Seaforth had not been restored when the attainder was reversed, so that the 5th Earl's eldest son had to be content with the courtesy title of Lord Fortrose. But he represented Ross in several Parliaments, enjoyed the honour of his Chiefship and the immense properties that belonged to it, and supported the Hanoverian government in the 1745 rebellion. Most importantly, he left a son to succeed him when he died in 1761, which went far to remedy the misfortune that one of his brothers died unmarried while the other was drowned without leaving an heir.

Then in 1771 the earldom of Seaforth was restored to his son, so that it was once again possible for the prophecy to be fulfilled to the letter. But first the restored Earl was able to give his name, the tartan of Clan Kenneth and the deer-antlers totem world-wide renown, by raising the regiment called Seaforth's Highlanders. When he died without direct heirs, the Chiefship and its vast estates passed to the descendant of a younger son of the 3rd Earl and his Countess, to whom the Brahan Seer was said to have uttered his doom-laden prophecy. He was killed on active service in India in 1783, after he had possessed for only two years the great inheritance that he never returned home to enjoy. He was succeeded by his younger brother, whom everyone knew to be the last of his line and consequently the natural target for a prediction that had remained unfulfilled so long, that many by now had perhaps lost faith in it.

Since he did not descend from the restored earldom of Seaforth, but only from the earlier one that had been forfeited, he was raised to the British peerage in 1797 as Baron Seaforth of Kintail, a variant that might perhaps have been expected to avert the omens. Although he was rendered deaf by an attack of scarlet fever as a schoolboy, this did not prevent him from rising to the rank of Lieutenant-General, which is the more surprising because his deafness caused him difficulty in articulating properly. He married and produced a family of four sons and six daughters, and no doubt faced the prophecy of doom with equanimity, although he could see that by now three of its conditions had been met. He was the last of his line, he was deaf and dumb, and he possessed four sons.

Then these began to die, one after another. The last survivor was sent to the south of England to be nursed during his last lingering illness, and a daily bulletin on his health was sent to Lord Seaforth at Castle Brahan. One of these was so much more favourable than those that had arrived earlier that the household began to rejoice. But the family butler shook his head, saying, 'no, he'll never recover. It's prophesied that Lord Seaforth must outlive all his four sons.' And so he did, before he followed them to the grave in 1815, missing by only a few years the pageant in Edinburgh at which the house of Seaforth ought to have been making such a brave show.

His eldest daughter was married to Admiral Sir Samuel Hood, who held the command in the Indian theatre until he died at about the same time as her father. So when she returned in widow's weeds to fill the role of Chief of Clan Kenneth, she arrived as a white-hooded girl from the east. In the grounds of Castle Brahan she was driving her younger sister Caroline in a carriage when the ponies took fright, and she was unable to restrain them from bolting. Both ladies were thrown out, and Caroline sustained injuries from which she died. Thus the white-hooded lass killed her sister. It was she who sold the isle of Lewis to Sir James Matheson, the beginning of the end of the vast estates of Seaforth.

So the Chiefship of Clan Kenneth passed finally to the descendants of the Tutor of Kintail, who were created Earls of Cromartie and live still in the Tutor's castle near Strathpeffer.

CHAPTER EIGHT

Campbell's Kingdom

It was not the Gordons, nor the Mackenzies, but the Campbells who advanced down the centuries to the most powerful position of all among the clans, earning themselves in the process a reputation for perfidy and unscrupulousness that has passed into Scottish folklore. For the most part they were acting as others did, given the opportunity, and their greatest crime was that they were so much more frequently successful. This they owed to the gift for strategy and tactics of so many of their chiefs, who seem to have possessed in an uncommon degree a sense of the direction in which events were moving, of the course of unfolding history, which enabled them to remain so often in the van of circumstance. Where the great Clan Donald were so frequently to be found in opposition to the tide of events, which swept away their redoubts one after another, the Campbells displayed a hereditary flair for joining the winning side.

Their origins were far more modest than those of the house of Somerled, and when Neil the Campbell Chief supported Robert Bruce and married his sister he had not placed himself in a more favourable position than MacDonald, who also supported the Bruce cause. Neil's son Colin Mór was the first Chief on record to obtain a charter for the clan lands of Lochawe, a comparatively modest endowment. His descendant the Duke of Argyll is named Mac Cailein Mór — Great Son of Colin — like the Chiefs of Clan Diarmaid before him, as though the greatness of their progenitor was an hereditary quality.

Certainly they set about enlarging his patrimony with a skill that no other clan could emulate, until they had constructed a chain of power bases stretching from Moray in the north-east to Ayr in the south-west, and were poised to assault the island world formerly dominated by Clan Donald. The links in this chain are commemorated to this day by the Campbell earldoms extending from Cawdor in Moray through Breadalbane, past the Argyll dukedom to the earldom of Loudoun in Ayrshire.

The three ancillary earldoms were all based on lands obtained with the hand of an heiress, and Loudoun was the first to fall into the bag. Colin Mór of Lochawe succeeded in winning the daughter of Sir Reginald Crawford of Loudoun, Sheriff of Ayr, for his younger brother Duncan, and when Crawford died in 1303 the property was theirs. It was not until 1601 that the descendants of the Campbells of Loudoun took their first step into the peerage, but in the meantime they enjoyed the hereditary office of Sheriff, which was a most useful asset.

Meanwhile Archibald the son of Colin Mór, who succeeded as Chief of Clan Diarmaid in 1343, was rewarded with many forfeited lands for his loyalty to David II, Robert Bruce's son, during the troubles of his reign. Archibald's grandson Duncan moved even closer to the Stewart dynasty which succeeded after David II's death, marrying the daughter of Regent Albany while he was ruling the country during James I's captivity in England. This was to prove a hazardous connection, for although Duncan of Lochawe's marriage to a first cousin of the King led to his elevation to the peerage as Lord Campbell in 1445, it also exposed him to James I's hostility when he returned to take his revenge on the relatives who had been enjoying his patrimony while they did nothing to ransom him from prison. Lady Campbell's own brother and two of her nephews were executed; but her husband the Campbell Chief was far too clever to be caught in the wrong company, and so his line continued to flourish until his grandson was created Earl of Argyll by James II in 1457.

By this time the Campbells had gained the territories which were to form the earldom of Breadalbane, and to expose them to such infamy as the persecutors of Clan Gregor and the Fletchers. It was during that lawless period when James I was a captive in England and Mac Cailein Mór became Regent Albany's son-in-law that he obtained the heiress of Mariota of Glenorchy, descendant of the royal house of Alpin. Thereafter, her cousin Gregor of the Golden Bridles and his descendants fought their long losing battle to hold their lands in Glenorchy by the sword, until they were swept away and John of Glenorchy was created Earl of Breadalbane in 1677.

Marriage with another heiress brought the district of Lorne to the 1st Earl of Argyll, that loch-indented land facing the mountains of Morvern and Mull which is named after the kindred of Lorne in the far-off days of the kingdom of Dalriada. It had belonged to the MacDougalls until their fatal opposition to Robert Bruce, and had since passed to the Stewarts. When John Stewart of Lorne begat only two daughters as his heiresses, Colin of Argyll married one of them, his uncle Colin of Glenorchy the other, and

John of Lorne bequeathed his lordship to the Campbell Chief.

The highest offices of state accompanied this second royal Stewart marriage. James III, a somewhat lazy man in matters of government, with a far greater interest in architecture and the arts, evidently singled out Mac Cailein Mór from among his relatives and Gaelic subjects as the one best qualified to represent tribal Scotland in his administration. He was appointed Justiciar, Chamberlain, Sheriff and Baillie by royal charter in 1473. He thereupon abandoned his old headquarters, the picturesque castle of Innischonaill on its island in Loch Awe, and established a new base at Inveraray on Loch Fyne, which was erected into a burgh of barony in 1474. Innischonaill became a sinister Campbell prison, while the family of Glenorchy built their castle of Kilchurn at the western end of the Loch from which they could dominate the valleys of Glenorchy, Glen Lyon and Glenoe to the east. But most ominous for the future, James III also granted to the 1st Earl of Argyll a commission of Lieutenancy with vice-regal powers extending throughout Argyll, Lorne and Menteith, and this dangerous authority was extended both to the Campbell and the Gordon Chiefs again by James IV.

The 2nd Earl of Argyll was appointed Justice-General of Scotland in addition, and it was he who combined his judicial powers with his clansmen's thuggery to snatch the inheritance of of Cawdor from within the Gordon sphere of influence.

The ancient thanage of Calder or Cawdor in Moray passed on the death of John of Cawdor to his posthumous daughter Muriel. The girl's mother was the daughter of Rose of Kilravock, one of the clans lampooned in the Mackenzie rant of the 1715 rebellion. Then they had fought on the opposite side to Clan Ross, with whom they have no connection despite the similarity of name. The Roses do not derive from the territory of Ross on the other side of the Moray Firth, but take their name from the lordship of Ros near Caen in Normandy. It belonged to William the Conqueror's brother Odo, Bishop of Bayeux, whose tapestry is the most celebrated of all his possessions. It seems almost certain that one of the Bishop's knights was the ancestor of Hugh Rose, established in Kilravock by 1282, whose family were destined to preserve one of the most complete collections of historical records that survive from any castle in Scotland. They shared the fertile lands of Moray with such neighbours as the Brodies, the Cummings and the Calders, and when Isobel of Kilravock was left a widow by her husband John of Cawdor and then gave birth to a daughter, she determined that this baby would marry a Rose when she grew up, and no property-hunting Campbell.

But the Justice-General not only obtained the wardship of the baby heiress from James IV; he also secured an influence over her grandfather Rose of Kilravock, who was faced at this time by a criminal prosecution on a charge of robbery. Even if he had been brought to trial and convicted, this would have provided no evidence that he had not been framed. Neither can it be proved that the Justice-General was using blackmail to restrain Muriel's grandfather while he made his next move. All that can be said with certainty is that Argyll eased Kilravock's personal embarrassment; and Kilravock displayed a remarkable indifference to what occurred next.

In 1499 Mac Cailein Mór sent sixty of his clansmen to Cawdor to kidnap the little red-haired Muriel when she was only four years old. Tradition relates that her mother Isobel branded the child with a red-hot key so that she could be sure of identifying her later, and that her nurse bit off a joint from one of her little fingers, just to make certain. A party set off in pursuit of the kidnappers, and it was said that the sons of Campbell of Inverliver, who led the expedition, dressed up a corn-stook as Muriel and defended it until they were all killed while the rest of the party made their escape with the baby heiress. Someone pointed out that if Muriel were to die, many Campbell lives would have been lost in vain; and was told that she would never die so long as a red-haired lass could be found in the Campbell country. In the event it appears that the real Muriel survived with her brand-mark and her missing finger joint. She married the 2nd Earl of Argyll's third son John, the ancestor of the Earls of Cawdor.

Cawdor Castle, one of the most remarkable in Scotland that is still inhabited by the descendants of its builder, possesses a tower which dates from the time of Muriel's grandparents. It was said that in 1454 the Thane of Cawdor dreamt he would build a new castle wherever a donkey loaded with a box of gold should stop, in the self-willed way of donkeys. The Thane tried out the efficacy of his dream, and when the donkey chose a hawthorn tree as its resting-place, Cawdor built his new castle round it. In the vaults of his stronghold the trunk of this tree still stands.

Cawdor was the last of the four Campbell earldoms to be created. It was not until 1796 that John Campbell was created Lord Cawdor, whose son was raised to the rank of Earl. But while the Breadalbane castle of Kilchurn is now a ruin and the heiress of Loudoun lives in England, Cawdor Castle is still the residence of Muriel's descendant.

The 2nd Earl of Argyll died fighting for his king on the field of Flodden; so did Sir Duncan Campbell of Glenorchy and his brother. While the Campbells used their high offices for their own ends, their chiefs gave a brave example to clansmen who were prepared to sacrifice their lives defending a corn-stook. A similar constancy followed the espousal of the Protestant cause in Scotland by the 4th Earl, who was the first of his rank to commit himself in this way. Although he died in 1558, two years before the Church of Rome was abolished in Scotland by Act of Parliament, he had left his clan once again in the lap of his country's destiny.

Yet for all their statesmanship and sincerity in their religious beliefs, the Campbells acted in the ensuing century in a manner that has left an indelible stigma on their name. The 7th Earl of Argyll, who succeeded in 1584, was one of the most cruel and perfidious of chiefs: not for nothing did he become known as Archibald the Grim. The trick by which he lured Alasdair MacGregor of Glenstrae to his death in Edinburgh with seven of his clansmen is only by a narrow margin the most despicable of his deeds. Not far behind him in villainy was Colin Campbell of Glenorchy, who sat in the Reformation Parliament of 1560 but was not too preoccupied by religion to produce ten legitimate children as well as a number of bastards. The enormous families of these Glenorchy Campbells must have been one of the inducements that led them to evict the old inhabitants so ruthlessly. Colin's son Sir Duncan of Glenorchy lived until 1631 and sired eighteen legitimate children, one of whom, Sir Colin, was among the justices appointed in 1633 to hunt down the MacGregors. A single son of Sir Colin alone produced fifteen children.

One of this vast progeny of Glenorchy received an exceptional inheritance when his remote cousin was created Lord Campbell of Loudoun in 1601, and died leaving only a solitary granddaughter as his heir. Sir John Campbell of Lawyers, a sept of Glenorchy, married her and was created Earl of Loudoun. The episode illustrates the clannish team spirit to which the Campbells owed their success in such measure. Had the MacDonalds repaired the fragmentation of their clan and hunted in a pack as the Campbells did, their fortunes might have been very different. Their inability to do so, combined with their loyalty to the Catholic religion, was now to bring fresh disasters, in which the Campbells were the instruments of their ruin.

The King Priam of this sad story was Angus of Islay, who succeeded his brother in 1569 as the Chief of the southern

MacDonalds; those of Antrim as well as the Mull of Kintyre, Islay and its adjacent isles. His mother had been a Campbell of Argyll, but this does not seem to have profited him, for he remained all his life incurably guileless, though not lacking in the grandeur of the descendants of Somerled. The most important island potentate in his neighbourhood was the Chief of the Macleans, to whose family his wife belonged, and both Angus and Maclean might have been expected to build upon this alliance a structure of mutual defence against the encroaching Campbells. But Angus inherited a feud with the Macleans over the ownership of the Rinns of Islay, and in his attempts to heal it he was no match for his unscrupulous brother-in-law Sir Lachlan of Duart.

In his simplicity he accepted an invitation from Sir Lachlan to discuss their differences in Castle Duart, only to be locked up on his arrival and held prisoner until in 1586 he surrendered the Rinns of Islay. Angus of Islay now invited Maclean to visit him in his castle of Dunyveg, and it is hardly credible that such an astute rogue would have walked into such an obvious trap unless, for ulterior motives, he wished to be imprisoned in his turn. Angus detained him as a reprisal for his own treatment at Duart, and it was the signal for Archibald the Grim to obtain a commission from James VI to intervene. Angus was evidently trusting by nature, and he may have supposed that his cousin Argyll was acting in his interests now, as he was to suppose later so fatally. He delivered Sir Lachlan to Archibald the Grim, who took the opportunity to occupy Castle Duart, although future events reveal that he had determined to capture the MacDonald lands before assaulting Mull.

What followed is extremely puzzling. Argyll took the Maclean Chief to the King, who lectured him severely, then released him. Yet Sir Lachlan returned to invade Islay again, using shipwrecked men from the Spanish Armada to augment his own clansmen. This should have served to place the full weight of royal authority, delegated to Archibald the Grim, at the disposal of the injured Chief of the southern MacDonalds, and so it would have done, had Mull been Argyll's primary objective. But since it was his policy to ruin MacDonald first, he represented that Angus had failed to hand over some Maclean hostages to him, and so plausible was his misrepresentation of what had occurred that James VI actually handed more MacDonald territories to the Maclean Chief. This advanced Campbell interests a further step, by stirring up deeper animosity in the islands. At about this time Campbell of Cawdor moved in from the wings to purchase some lands in the isle of Gigha from the embarrassed MacDonald Chief.

In 1591 Angus of Islay and Maclean were commanded to travel to Edinburgh to meet the King, where they were immediately imprisoned, and released only on finding securities. Campbell of Cawdor stepped forward once more, to stand surety for Angus, while the Chief's own two sons were retained by James VI as hostages. His elder son James impressed the King sufficiently to receive a knighthood from him, and there matters might have rested if the Campbells had allowed them to.

But of course they did not, and in 1593 poor Angus of Islay found himself accused of treason for trivial reasons that were by no means clear to him, and forfeited in the following year. Taking advantage of the King's apparent predilection for his son, Angus renounced all his rights to Sir James and submitted himself to the royal will, appearing personally before the King and Council in Edinburgh in 1596. Once again the dangers of peace began to stalk the southern Hebrides. They were dispersed by Sir Lachlan Maclean in 1598, when he once again invaded Islay. Whoever incited him to do it, he ruined two clans by his act, and his own life was the least that was lost by it. Sir James, back in Islay to safeguard the rights that his father had renounced to him, was hit by an arrow and left for dead on the field. When he recovered, he emulated his father's passive attitude, suggesting that he should surrender the Mull of Kintyre to the crown (which might keep this peninsula out of the clutches of the Campbells) and that the castle of Dunyveg in Islay should be occupied by a royal garrison. Again Sir John Campbell of Cawdor moved from the wings, bringing his sister to Sir James of Islay as a wife.

Whatever the real motive in proposing this match, it could certainly have lent weight to a suspicion that Sir James was plotting in the Campbell camp against the devoted father who had already surrendered all his property to him. There had been differences between Angus and his heir in the year of Maclean's last invasion, and the Campbells built on them until in 1603 the MacDonald Chief was induced to arrest his son and hand him over to Campbell of Auchinbreck, who delivered him to Archibald the Grim. Appropriate allegations were submitted to the Scottish Privy Council, while James VI was on his way to become King in London, and Sir James was committed to Blackness Castle. Argyll proposed himself as crown tenant of Kintyre, received the neighbouring island of Jura in addition, and at once set about evicting their inhabitants.

Faced with the appalling consequences of his simplicity, Angus of Islay wrote to the King in London 'beseeching your Majesty for the cause of God to respect my age and poor estate, and to let me know your Highness's own mind signed with your Majesty's own hand.' He evidently understood by now that a diabolical influence stood between him and his sovereign, poisoning communications between them. Archibald the Grim, dominating the Scottish Council in the King's absence, ensured that this continued. He had already done much to barbarise the mainland Gaels, and as he fomented disorder in the Hebrides and reported its details to the King in lurid colours, he undoubtedly contributed to the King's extravagant opinion that the islanders 'are all utterly barbarous, without any sort of show of civility . . . think no more of them all than of wolves and wild boars.'

He must have observed for himself that James of Islay whom he had knighted was nothing of the sort, and we have about sixteen of the letters the young man wrote in English as evidence of his high standard of education in what was to him a foreign language and culture. Only one of his Gaelic letters survives as evidence of his bilingual literacy, but it suffices. He made several attempts to escape from Blackness Castle, the final one in 1607 in company with Lord Maxwell, when he tried to jump over a wall encumbered by his fetters, and was captured after suffering a leg injury. Two years later he was tried for treason in Edinburgh, condemned to death and all his possessions forfeited. The sentence was not carried out, however, and after languishing in captivity for six years before his trial, he remained a prisoner for another six years with the death sentence hanging over him.

During that time the Campbells gained almost all that Archibald the Grim had been striving so unscrupulously to achieve. In the words of the MacDonald bard Iain Lom, 'you stole green, pleasant Islay from us by trickery, and Kintyre with its fertile plains.' Argyll was already tenant of Kintyre: in 1612 Angus of Islay sold what remained to Campbell of Cawdor for a mere 6,000 merks. After he had died in 1614 a warrant was issued to execute Sir James, now Chief of the southern MacDonalds, under the sentence that had been passed six years earlier. But this time he did succeed in escaping from his prison, with the help of MacDonald of Keppoch, and for a time he attempted to recover his lost patrimony. But Argyll brought an army to scourge the MacDonald lands (including government troops for which he found himself bound to pay £7,000), and Sir James of Islay was compelled to flee to Ireland. There Argyll pursued him until he made his escape to Spain. In 1620 he was allowed to return to London, pensioned by James VI, and granted a pardon in the following year. But he was never allowed to return to his own country, and died in England in the first year of Charles I's reign, the last, disinherited Chief of the great Clan Donald to have reigned at Dunyveg in Islay.

In securing the superiority of Islay, Sir John of Cawdor did not become the vassal of Mac Cailein Mór, since he held his ill-gotten fief directly from the crown. Neither did Archibald the Grim, crown tenant of Kintyre, win a fresh regality through his punitive expedition, such as might have been transformed into a fifth Campbell earldom. And his next act was one that imperilled the entire clan structure of which he was the head. His son Lord Lorne was eighteen years old when he accompanied Argyll on his expedition against the MacDonalds in 1615: he was not yet twenty-one when his father became a Roman Catholic convert and fled the country, never to return. Suddenly the leadership of Scotland's most powerful and most hated clan passed to a minor who was not even bolstered by the prestige of the chief-ship.

It would be edifying to record that Archibald the Grim had been purged by remorse, and that he spent the remainder of his days seeking to make amends for the seeds of evil he had sown in Gaeldom. Remorse he may have felt, but there is no evidence that he was preoccupied by more than his soul's salvation. Even his own clan was left to shift for itself; and it is truly remarkable how successfully it did so in the troubled times that lay ahead.

This was very largely due to the qualities of his son Lord Lorne, the future Marquess of Argyll, and the corner-stone of his success was to keep the Campbells on course as the pioneering clan of the Scottish Reformation despite the defection of their Chief. His task became particularly difficult after 1633, when Charles I paid his first visit to Scotland as sovereign, and revoked the titles to Church lands that had been embezzled since the Reformation, in order to re-endow the Episcopal Church in Scotland.

John Knox himself had fulminated against the misappropriation of properties that he wished to see employed for the support of a reformed ministry and to endow a system of universal education. But Calvinist divines also asserted that Jesus Christ should reign in Scotland, a euphemism for claiming that they should rule. So the self-styled Lords of the Congregation of Jesus Christ had a double motive for leaping off the Calvinist bandwagon, before they found themselves deprived either of their offices or their Church properties by men who could even call James VI to his face 'God's silly vassal.' When Charles I threatened to recover the Church endowments from Scotland's aristocracy he made the first fatal move that was to cost him his life. Many of the country's most influential men at once recovered their religious zeal and gave their support to the Calvinist ministry which opposed an episcopal form of Church government and a liturgical form of service.

Charles was evidently aware that the Campbells comprised something resembling a state within the state, as the paramount clan in the tribal lands. Yet he could not seek the support of the Campbell Chief in promoting the kind of Church in which he believed, since Mac Cailein Mór was a devout Catholic living in exile in London. For reasons of his own he did not build up the authority of Sir John Campbell of Cawdor either, as an alternative supporter, but gave an earldom to the Glenorchy Campbell who had married the Loudoun heiress in Ayrshire. He also ingratiated himself with the Glenorchy and Argyll Campbells during that visit to Edinburgh in 1633, by sanctioning measures against the MacGregors more vicious than any which the Scottish Parliament had enacted previously. He had taken to heart the advice his father had given him, saying that while the islanders were to be treated like wolves and wild boars, the mainland contained some barbarous Gaels (MacGregors) and some civilised ones (Campbells). The effect of what King Charles did in 1633 was to strengthen the clan that would become his most powerful enemy in Scotland during the approaching rebellion, and to provide the young deputy-Chief Lord Lorne with an effective partner in the Earl of Loudoun during this period of conflict.

In Edinburgh a National Covenant of resistance to the new religious order was drawn up in Edinburgh, and the Gordon Earl of Sutherland, gorged with the properties of the diocese of Caithness, hastened to place his signature on it. But Lord Lorne did not commit himself, preferring to join the deputation that went to London in an attempt to persuade the King to withdraw his unpopular measure. Charles rejected their advice, but such was Lorne's discretion that the King retained confidence in him, and even commanded him to sign the Covenant. The King also ignored the recommendation of Mac Cailein Mór that he should arrest his son, saying that if he permitted Lorne to return to Scotland he would live to regret it. Shortly afterwards the 7th Earl of Argyll died, and Lorne was invested as the Campbell Chief just when he had most need of the powers of this position. When the first revolutionary Assembly of the Presbyterian Church met in Glasgow, it was he who stepped forward to direct its proceedings, which threw down the gauntlet of open defiance to royal authority.

Archibald, 8th Earl and 1st Marquess of Argyll, was probably the most outstanding of all the Campbell Chiefs. In placing his clan unequivocally in the camp of the Covenanters, he ensured its ultimate triumph, once the Calvinist revolution of the Lowland Scots was consummated. At the same time he doubled the animosity of all those clans which adhered to the Catholic faith or to the Episcopal Church that James VI had planted in Scotland, and the most prominent of these were the MacDonalds whom the Campbells had so deeply wronged. If King Charles were to grant commissions of fire and sword to the wolves and wild boars whom the Stewarts had scourged in the past, Mac Cailein Mór would have to mobilise his clan to protect its territories. The MacDonalds were now a weakened and fragmented confederation, but in northern Ireland they possessed a leader who enjoyed the status of Earl of Antrim, and as early as the time of Lorne's visit to London King Charles was already negotiating with him to return the Mull of Kintyre to the MacDonalds, which it would have been a simple act of justice to effect in any circumstances.

From the moment when Argyll committed his clan to the Covenant, he began mobilising forces against its private enemies. He prepared an invasion of the MacDonald stronghold in northern Ireland. He called up his vassals to mount guard over Kintyre and Lorne. With an army of 5,000 men and a train of artillery he himself led an expedition through Mar, Atholl and Badenoch in the name of the Covenant, and such was his conduct that he felt obliged to obtain an indemnity from Parliament on his return for 'all manner of burnings and the putting of people to torture and death.' He invited the Murray Chief, the Earl of Atholl, to meet him, then kidnapped him. In the folklore of Scotland the most memorable of his atrocities was the destruction of 'The Bonnie Hoose o' Airlie,' immortalised in a Lowland ballad.

This was the seat of the Chiefs of the Ogilvie Clan, who had already suffered the depredations of the Gordons in their attempt to seize the lands that subsequently formed the earldom of Findlater. In the interval they had been harassed by Archibald the Grim, who launched the MacGregors against them in 1591 in an attempt to lay hands on their territory of Glenisla. It was still there for the taking when in 1640 'Argyll most cruelly and inhumanly enters the house of Airlie and beats the same to the ground . . . plundered, robbed and took away . . . men, tenants and servants, their whole goods and gear . . . and left nothing but bare bounds of such as they could consume or destroy or carry with them. And such as could not be carried away was despitefully burnt up by fire.'

Unhappily for his victims, King Charles still hoped to win the great Campbell Clan to his side when he returned to Scotland in 1641, creating Argyll a Marquess, the Earl of Loudoun Lord Chancellor, endorsing the statute that condoned Argyll's crimes and most fatally of all, both for himself and for the victims of the Campbells, granting Argyll a military commission to act against rebels. Charles hoped that his concessions would win him the Scottish army of the Covenant in his conflict with his English subjects, but he returned empty-handed, and Argyll even sent Loudoun after him to inform the King that the Covenanters sympathised with the attitude of his English opponents.

King Charles did gain one adherent among the Covenanters to whom he had conceded so much without obtaining anything in return. James Graham, Earl of Montrose, later justified his change of sides by declaring: 'when the King had granted you all your desires, and you were every one sitting under his vine and under his fig tree, that you should have taken a party in England by the hand, and entered into a league and covenant with them against the King was the thing I judged it my duty to oppose to the yondermost.' As soon as Montrose showed signs that he might defect, Argyll moved swiftly to have him arraigned before Parliament, where Montrose treated his peers to a stylish defence containing the famous boast: 'my resolution is to carry along with me fidelity and honour to the grave.' Argyll pressed the case against Montrose, but his point of view could not yet be defined as a crime, and he was released from prison on the day before King Charles left Edinburgh. The proceedings had sufficed to keep this persuasive youth away from the King's ear, but Argyll's failure to destroy Montrose at this juncture was to prove the fatality of his own career.

James Graham derived his name from the English manor of Grey Home which is to be found in William the Conqueror's Domesday Book. It was carried to Scotland in time for William of Graham to witness the foundation charter of the abbey of Holyrood in 1138. In the following century Sir Patrick Graham brought it to the Highlands when he married into the Celtic dynasty of Strathearn. He also enrolled it amongst the names of

Scottish patriots when he died fighting against the English at the time of King John Balliol's downfall, leaving a nephew to give his life two years later in battle under William Wallace. Sir Patrick's descendants were raised to the earldom of Montrose, and James succeeded to this title when he was only thirteen years old. He was little older when he prophesied the career that would eclipse all the military achievements of his forbears.

> As Philip's noble son did still disdain
> All but the dear applause of merited fame,
> And nothing harboured in that lofty brain
> But how to conquer an eternal name,
> So great attempts, heroic ventures shall
> Advance my fortune or renown my fall.

He was twenty-five years old when he jumped on a barrel at the signing of the National Covenant in Edinburgh to demonstrate his support for it, and someone called out, 'James, you will never be at rest till you are lifted up above the rest in three fathoms of a rope.' Argyll saw to the literal fulfilment of that prediction, but not before Montrose had destroyed the Campbell power in its meridian.

Clarendon the historian, who knew both men, described the rivalry that was to destroy them both. 'Montrose had always a great emulation, or rather a great contempt of the Marquess of Argyll (as he was too apt to contemn those he did not love); who wanted nothing but honesty and courage to be a very extraordinary man, having all other good talents in a very high degree . . . The people looked upon both as young men of unlimited ambition and used to say that they were like Caesar and Pompey; the one would endure no superior, and the other would have no equal.' In character and appearance they were poles apart: Argyll, short, red-haired and of unprepossessing appearance, careful of his personal safety to the point of cowardice, yet cruel in offensive action when he had overwhelming strength on his side; and as devious as any Campbell Chief had ever been in his conduct. Montrose by contrast was tall, handsome and winning in his manners. The openness of his mind found graceful expression both in prose and verse; and even when his judgement was at fault he could sway others by the elegance with which he could use the English language. Above all, his courage was to become the wonder of Europe.

But in his early Covenanting days he had imperilled the King's cause that was to become his own by gravely affronting that vain northern potentate the Marquess of Huntly, Cock of the North. When Huntly was invited to support the Covenant, he replied grandly: 'my house has risen by the Kings of Scotland. It has ever stood for them, and with them shall fall.' He had evidently forgotten the conduct of his ancestor on the field of Flodden. 'If the event be the ruin of my sovereign, then shall the rubbish of his house bury beneath it all that belongs to mine.' In fact the Cock of the North generally scuttled at the first sign of danger, and succeeded in earning almost identical epithets from both sides in the conflict. The Covenanters referred to him as 'that feeble, effeminate, foolish atheist,' while Charles I dismissed him as 'feeble and false.'

His cousin the Earl of Sutherland played perhaps the most despicable part of anyone during this period, ostensibly supporting the Covenant and repeatedly submitting accounts for the expenses of his imaginary services, while he exploited every eventuality to enrich himself and ruin his neighbours. But for the restoration of Charless II in 1660, the Mackay country might not have been privileged to wait until the nineteenth century for the Sutherland clearances.

With Sutherland protesting his loyalty to the Covenant and doing nothing to assist its cause except when it happened to serve his own interests, and Huntly declaiming his fidelity to the King with equally little effect, the Gordons were in a state of considerable disarray when their turn came to be scourged by Mac Cailein Mór, especially since Huntly was married to Argyll's sister, and their son and heir Lord Gordon was an enthusiastic supporter of the Covenant. While Argyll swept through the Gordon territories of the north-east, Huntly fled all the way to the Mackay country on the north coast, prepared presumably to take ship to an even more distant destination, should it be necessary to save his skin. It was left to the gallant Sir John Gordon of Haddo to risk his life for the honour of his clan, and forfeit it to the vindictive Campbell Chief who despatched him to his death in Edinburgh.

But at last nemesis had caught up with Mac Cailein Mór and his Campbells. In Ireland there was a gigantic MacDonald youth called Alasdair Mac Cholla Chiotaich — known as Colkito — whose father Argyll had locked up in one of his castles. Six feet six inches in height, Alasdair had joined the revolt in Ireland when he was only eighteen years old, and could see that the Campbells, having driven his clan from their lands in Scotland, were now using the pretext of religion to pursue them to their Irish refuge. In July 1644 he set sail for Scotland with rather less than the force that the Earl of Antrim had been promising to King Charles, little over a thousand men, together with their wives, families and priests. But when they landed in Mull and crossed to the mainland, it sufficed to efface all other responsibilites from the mind of Argyll, and spur him westwards to concentrate on the protection of his clan. Colkito took his men beyond the northern confines of Campbell's kingdom, from Ardnamurchan to Badenoch, and they might have been an illusory danger but for the fact that they were joined by the man who was to prove himself the most brilliant soldier in Scotland's history, James Graham of Montrose.

King Charles kept Montrose straining at the bit until Royalist fortunes in England were at a low ebb and the army of the Covenant was free to fling its full weight against any insurrection in Scotland. Montrose returned to his own country in disguise, with only two companions, without any army or weapons, but with the precious commission appointing him the King's General in Scotland hidden in the lining of his saddle. He was sometimes recognised but never betrayed as he made his way towards the Highlands, seeking news of the whereabouts of Colkito and his MacDonalds. Finally he traced them to the braes of Atholl, where the Covenanters had already called out the local clans, Stewarts and Robertsons, to resist them.

The opposing forces were on the point of conflict when Montrose rode into the MacDonald camp, unfurled the royal standard that he carried, and was received with acclamations. Then, displaying the charismatic powers that were to operate like a magic wand during the months ahead, he strode amongst the Stewarts and Robertsons, persuading them that he represented the legitimate government which the MacDonalds also served, and reconciled the three clans into a single fighting force. This might have been more difficult, had not Argyll given the Atholl clans a taste of Campbell methods four years earlier, when he had burned down the house of Airlie and seized the Earl of Atholl. Now Lord Ogilvie was among his supporters, and as the little army marched towards Perth it was reinforced by men of Clan Graham, who had been more recent victims of the Covenanters.

With these men who possessed no cavalry and little ammunition Montrose won the first of his astonishing victories against a Calvinist army twice as strong in numbers, reinforced by a troop of cavalry, and fighting under the devout slogan 'Jesus and no Quarter.' The Saviour showed his displeasure by leaving Scotland's third city in the hands of Montrose with all its essential supplies. The Ogilvies of Airlie came to join him, and a Gordon contingent from the north. Chancellor Loudoun hurried to London to minimise the effect on his cousin's credit, but he arrived too late. The apparently invincible tribal prince of the north was seen to be insecure in his own reserves. Montrose had suspected that Mac Cailein Mór aimed to dethrone King Charles in order to set up King Campbell, and at the moment when Montrose struck he was indeed the most powerful man in either kingdom. Sweet was the revenge of the MacDonalds when they destroyed that power.

The Lowland Calvinists, who saw their great Gaelic Chief humbled, were too besotted by their religious dogma to understand that what had occurred was the latest act in a tragedy of clan conflict centuries old. They believed that it was divine punishment for sin, though the Minister came nowhere near the Campbell Chief in his diagnosis. 'We had the most free and strange parley that ever I heard, about the evident sins of the Assembly, the sins of Parliament, the sins of the army, and the sins of the people.' Meanwhile Montrose, having defeated his first Covenanting army, hurried to Aberdeen to face his second of the three that remained in the field in Scotland. He sent a herald to the city under a flag of truce, accompanied by a drummer-boy, demanding its surrender. As the herald returned with a rejection of this demand, someone on the city wall shot the drummer-boy in full view of the army of Montrose. The Calvinists gave no quarter to their enemies in any circumstances, believing that these were warring against God: this was the sole occasion in his military career when Montrose permitted his men to emulate the barbarity of their opponents. The city was stormed and sacked. Within four weeks of his return to Scotland, a fugitive without an army, Montrose had destroyed two of the four armies of the Covenant.

Now Argyll himself advanced against Montrose, with 2,500 men and no less than 1,500 cavalry. He swept through the Gordon lands of the supine Marquess of Huntly, devastating them as he went. He destroyed the corn, drove off the livestock, requisitioned the horses, placed a colossal reward on the head of Montrose. But when he tried to catch up with the little Royalist army he was led an endless goose-chase through the wilds of Badenoch until his men deserted and he returned to Edinburgh in disgust to resign his commission. Then he retired to his private kingdom in the west, the great Campbell province that he and his predecessors had carved out of the lands of their neighbours.

That winter Montrose and his MacDonalds descended upon it to revenge Argyll's recent cruelties as well as their earlier wrongs. They passed through Glenorchy where the MacGregors had been hunted like vermin, through Lorne and Argyll to the very gates of Inveraray, from where Mac Cailein Mór escaped in a fishing-boat — he who had so recently held the destiny of three kingdoms in his hands. Wishart described the MacDonald revenge. 'They range about all the country and lay it waste. As many as they find in arms going to the rendez-vous appointed by their lord they slay, and spare no man that was fit for war . . . Then they fire the villages and cots, and lay them level with the ground; in that, retaliating Argyll with the same measure he had meted unto others, who was the first in all the kingdom that prosecuted his countrymen with fire and sword.'

So the ancient tribal vendetta moved towards its climax. It had been fomented by Stewart kings from the start, building up the power of the Campbells as the ruthless supporters of their own authority. Now a Stewart sovereign had been rejected by his English-speaking subjects in both Scotland and England, and in his extremity he had handed the scourge to those very Gaels who had endured its stripes for so long. Had either the King or these Gaels possessed sufficient insight, they would have realised that this novel alliance between them was the kiss of death for both. The prospect of a sovereignty based upon the power of the country's Celtic peoples had been receding ever since the death of the High King Lulach in 1058, and could never be restored. It was not so much that the King's supporters were Catholics opposed by Calvinists, as that they were Gaels with an alien language and an archaic tribal structure of society.

But at least the clans would topple the paramount chief who owed his powers to collaboration with the English-speaking Lowlanders.

Montrose did not linger in the Campbell country, but made his way north in midwinter towards the Great Glen. Argyll came after him by sea, and planted his army at the castle of Inverlochy, whose ruins still stand near to Fort William. There was every hope that Montrose was now trapped between the Campbell forces at the southern end of the glen and the garrison composed of Frasers and Mackenzies at Inverness. Yet other clans still joined his standard: Macphersons from Badenoch, MacDonalds of Keppoch, Glengarry and Clanranald, Macleans of Duart and

Lochbuie who had not always seen eye to eye with one another in the past, Stewarts of Appin. But the numbers of the Royalists could not match those of Argyll, cosily encamped around the fortress of Inverlochy in that frosty February, for he had been lent 1,500 Lowland soldiers to reinforce his 2,000 Campbells.

Montrose bridged the gap with one of his most astonishing feats of surprise and endurance. He took his men up into the trackless, snow-bound wilderness of mountains south of the Great Glen, in which it was hardly possible for a living creature to survive, and brought them to the heights above Inverlochy from which no danger could be expected. His men spent the night there without even lighting a fire to warm themselves, lest they should betray their presence: and in the dawn they swept down upon the army of Argyll and destroyed it.

In the camp of Montrose was the rapier-tongued MacDonald bard, Iain Lom, who had already lamented the Campbell seizure of Kintyre. A descendant of the Lords of the Isles and of the royal house of Stewart, the passionate spokesman of his clan, he celebrated the outcome in one of Scotland's most famous martial songs.

'Early on Sunday morning I climbed the brae above the castle of Inverlochy. I saw the army arraying for battle, and victory on the field was with Clan Donald.' Generally Iain Lom was not slow to take up arms himself, but on this occasion he chose the role of spectator saying, 'if I should be killed, who will immortalise your victory?' He did it in the most savage anti-Campbell poem that his language contains.

'Many a warrior with cuirass and cavalry saddle, as good as ever was in your clan, was not allowed to escape dry-shod, but had to learn to swim at Nevis estuary. Many a warrior with helmet and bow and slender straight musket lay stretched at Inverlochy, and the darling of the women of Kintyre was among them.'

The men of Argyll's army were taken totally by surprise as they were preparing their breakfast. Their Chief witnessed the catastrophe that followed from his war galley in the loch, and long before the carnage was over he was speeding out of sight as fast as sail and oar could carry him, to the safety of his castle at Inveraray. It was only later that he learned how 1,500 of his clan had perished. 'When the great work of blood-letting came to a height at the time of unsheathing of slender swords, the claws of the Campbells lay on the ground with sinews severed.'

Although Iain Lom celebrated Montrose on other occasions, it was the MacDonald hero Colkito whom he extolled on this occasion. 'Alasdair of the sharp cleaving blades, you promised yesterday to destroy them; you directed the rout past the castle, an excellent plan for keeping in touch with them. Alasdair of the venomous blades, if you had been accompanied by the heroes of Mull, you would have restrained those who escaped you when the dulse-eating rabble was in flight. Alasdair, son of handsome Coll, expert at breaking castles asunder, you routed the sallow-skinned Lowlanders, and if they had drunk kail, you knocked it out of them. Were you familiar with Goirtean Odhar? Well was it manured, not by the dung of sheep and goats, but by the congealed blood of Campbells. Perdition take you if I feel pity for your plight, as I listen to the distress of your children, lamenting the company which was on the battlefield, the wailing of the women of Argyll.' So ends Iain Lom's fierce song of victory, which recalls so chillingly the hatred that the Campbells inspired.

Montrose marched up the Great Glen towards Moray, where the Chief of the Grants joined him with 300 of his clansmen. The Earl of Seaforth had been avoiding offence to the Covenanters because Argyll was by now claiming his title to the island of Lewis, and he was anxious to deprive the Campbell Chief of any excuse to bring a charge of malignancy against him, as an excuse for seizing his property. At first he fled at the approach of Montrose, then he brought the Mackenzies to the royal standard. The Chief of Mackay in the far north would certainly have rallied his clansmen to Montrose despite the fact that they were Protestants; but he was already a prisoner in Edinburgh while the Cock of the North still skulked in Mackay's house at Tongue. The other Gordon chieftain, the Earl of Sutherland, had held a colonelcy of horse and foot in the army of the Covenant since 1643, and had by now been entrusted with the defence of the far north. But he used his commission exclusively to plunder his neighbours as the fortunes of the war gave him opportunity, and invariably vanished at the least sign of danger.

The honour of the Gordons was saved by two of Huntly's sons, and especially by Lord Gordon, the Campbell Chief's nephew, who had previously followed his uncle into the Covenanting camp. Recently, he had incurred particular odium by aiding Mac Cailein Mór in the devastation of the Gordon country, but he now made amends by riding into the camp of Montrose, bringing 500 Gordon infantry and over 1,500 horsemen. When he died in battle later that year, it was remarked: 'never two of so short acquaintance did ever love more dearly.' With the accession of the Gordons, Montrose had welded a confederation of clans and chiefs such as had scarcely ever been seen in Scottish tribal history, and under his command they won victories during 1645 that became the wonder of Europe.

Neil MacMhuirich the bard chronicled them in classical Gaelic, and he noted how people recalled the previous time a Highland host of this magnitude had come to fight for the rights of MacDonald of the Isles in 1411 at the field of the Red Harlaw. While his patron MacDonald of Clanranald was on the march, 'they met an honourable old man who was telling them stories and historical affairs, and along with other stories he related, he said that the Mearns had not been wasted since the time it was spoiled by Donald of Islay, the year he fought the battle of Garioch or Harlaw against Duke Murdoch: "and I suppose, young man, that you are descended of him, if you be the Captain of Clanranald."' He was indeed the senior descendant of the Lords of the Isles, and this anecdote reveals how traditional tribal thinking remained, and how remote from that of the men of Westminster or the Covenanters in Edinburgh.

Montrose swept south to capture Dundee, and was surprised by an army of the Covenant while his men were roaming the town, exhausted by the battle and many of them far from sober. Never did his personal magnetism achieve a more stupendous result. Rounding up his soldiers, he marched them out of one gate of Dundee as the enemy were entering the opposite one, and yet brought them to the safety of the hills, after forcing them to perform a feat of marching and counter-marching that lasted for three days and two nights. 'I have often heard those who were esteemed the most experienced officers, not in Britain only, but in France and Germany, prefer this march to his most celebrated victories.' Such was the admiring comment. As soon as his men were sufficiently rested, Montrose brought them back to destroy the army which had so nearly trapped him in Dundee.

Montrose had by now crippled the capacity of the Campbell Chief to dominate the affairs of two kingdoms, and extinguished the dream of the Covenanters to impose Calvinism on the English as the price of their support. When Cromwell defeated the army of King Charles at Naseby, it was no longer needed. What Montrose could not do was to bring his army into England to retrieve the fortunes of the King. He did win one final victory at Kilsyth on the borders of the Lowlands, in which the gallant old Earl of Airlie led the cavalry, and this gave him brief control of Glasgow and Edinburgh, where the Chief of Mackay was among the prisoners whose release he secured.

But when he tried to cross the Lowlands, none would join his standard: the appearance of a Celtic army in their midst filled English-speaking people with horror, irrespective of their religion or politics. Beside the River Yarrow, Montrose was surrounded by a force which outnumbered him three to one. He wished to die with his men, but was persuaded to flee while these surrendered to General Leslie on being given quarter for their lives. The Calvinist ministers who accompanied the army of the Covenant persuaded him to break his military oath in the name of their terrible god, and Patrick Gordon described the manner in which they enforced the divine laws they had come to safeguard. 'With the whole baggage and staff . . . there remained none but boys, cooks and a rabble of rascals and women with their children in their arms. All those, without commiseration, were cut in pieces, whereof there were three hundred women that, being natives of Ireland, were married wives of the Irish. There were many big with child, yet none of them were spared. All were cut in pieces, with such a savage and inhuman cruelty as neither Turk nor Scythian was ever heard to have done the like. For they ripped up the bellies of the women with their swords, till the fruit of their womb . . . fell down up the ground, weltering in the gory blood of their mangled mothers.'

In some cases 'they were thrown headlong from a high bridge; and the men, together with their wives and sucking children, drowned in the river beneath; and if any chanced to swim towards the side, they were beaten off with pikes and staves, and thrust down again into the water.' Thus were the horrors of Ireland brought to Scotland: and it is only fair to notice that the English on at least one occasion treated Welsh women and children in the same manner, hearing them speak the unintelligible Celtic tongue about the kitchen fires of an army camp.

Soon afterwards King Charles surrendered to the Scottish rebels without laying down any conditions for the safety of those who had risked their lives so bravely on his behalf. Montrose wrote to him, 'I humbly beg your Majesty to be pleased to consider that there is nothing remembered concerning the immunity of those who have been upon your service.' Gratitude was an uncommon virtue among the royal Stewarts, and anyway Charles was by now in a weak bargaining position. Montrose retired abroad, the holy men of Edinburgh offered their burnt offerings in a holocaust of executions, while the Covenanting leaders negotiated to hand the King to the English and bring back their army from Newcastle in return for arrears of payment amounting to £300,000. Since this sum bears no relation to the modern value of money, it suffices to say that Argyll obtained one tenth of it for himself, while the Earl of Sutherland swooped south to make his own claim for his alleged losses, and for his supposed services.

After the English had executed King Charles without consulting his Scottish subjects, there occurred the final act in the tragedy of Scotland's Caesar and Pompey. With hereditary deceit, young Charles II commissioned Montrose to invade Scotland on his behalf at the same time as he entered into negotiations with Argyll. Consequently, when Montrose was captured and taken to Edinburgh to be executed under a statute passed long before by the rebel Parliament, his enemies possessed the royal authority for this act of revenge, which Argyll enforced to the full.

The window in which Argyll sat in Edinburgh High Street to witness his rival's humiliation can still be seen there. Montrose was mounted on a high seat in a cart drawn by four horses, his arms tied so that he would be unable to defend himself against the missiles of the crowd, in a journey that lasted for three hours. But the charisma of Montrose protected him to the end, contrasting even in these circumstances with Argyll's shoddy lack of dignity. 'In all the way there appeared in him such majesty, courage, modesty, and even somewhat more than natural, that those common women who had lost their husbands and children in his wars, and who were hired to stone him, were upon the sight of him so astonished and moved that their intended curses turned into tears and prayers; so that the next day all the Ministers preached against them for not stoning and reviling him.'

Whether by accident or design, the cart stopped beneath Argyll's window: for a moment the eyes of the two men met, then the shutter slammed shut. But an Englishman had seen it, standing in the crowd, and he called out that 'it was no wonder they started aside at his look, for they durst not look him in the face these seven years bygone.'

The Calvinist divines, from whom Montrose had at least saved the English, if not his own fellow-countrymen, came to his prison to pester his last earthly moments, but he retained his faith that he was amongst the Calvinist elect, and cared nothing for their excommunication. As he ended his final poem, addressed to the Almighty,

I'm hopeful Thou'llt recover once my dust
And confident Thou'llt raise me with the Just.

The Provost of Edinburgh expostulated against the indignity of the sentence against such a man. 'What need of so much butchery and dismembering? Has not heading and publicly affixing the head been thought sufficient for the most atrocious state crimes hitherto?' But Argyll was adamant that Montrose should be quartered after hanging, his limbs displayed in each of Scotland's main cities. So when Charles II landed at Aberdeen to become Scotland's Covenanted King, a limb of the faithful servant he had betrayed was among the first sights to greet him there. Argyll himself placed the crown on the young King's head, as though the privileges of the royal Clan Duff now belonged also to the Campbell Chiefs. But Cromwell soon destroyed the attempt of the Scots to restore the Stewart monarchy. Charles fled abroad again, the country was placed under military rule, and the clans were safe from Mac Cailein Mór until Charles II returned to London in 1660.

He might have remembered with gratitude the great Chief who had crowned him so many years before, and Argyll came to London to attend him in case he had forgotten. But Charles had not forgotten the humiliation he had suffered at the hands of Argyll and the other religious zealots, nor the manner in which they had treated Montrose. Argyll was sent back to Edinburgh for trial, and while the limbs of Montrose were collected for a magnificent state funeral there, the Campbell Chief was condemned for treason and executed despite the loyal attempts of his cousin Loudoun to save him. Today, in the church of St Giles which Charles I erected into a cathedral, the remains of the two great leaders whom his civil war destroyed rest beneath splendid memorials in opposite transepts.

Both had lost and won. The confederation of clans that had fought under Montrose did stem the tide of Campbell aggression, when it was aimed at the uttermost bounds of Lewis. But in northern Ireland, where Argyll maintained a Calvinist army to batter the last stronghold of the Catholic MacDonalds, he succeeded in bolstering the colonial policy of James VI, who had planted Scottish Protestant settlers there. So he must share with that King some of the responsibility for the present situation in Ulster.

Before his death, Argyll told his son, 'my thoughts became distracted and myself encountered so many difficulties in the way, that all remedies that were applied had the contrary operation. Whatever, therefore, hath been said by me or others in this matter, you must repute and accept them as from a distracted man of a distracted subject in a distracted time wherein I lived.' Characteristically, he expressed himself tortuously and with less than honesty to the last. There was nothing distracted about the manner in which he had steered his clan back on course after the defection of his father, and then used every opportunity to increase Campbell power. Nor was this an ignoble course, judged from his standpoint. For the Campbell power was his weapon in promoting a religion in which he sincerely believed, and in dominating the politics of Britain to Scotland's advantage. In the end his policy triumphed, but not before his heir had suffered the same fate as his own.

The title of Marquess was lost with his conviction for treason, but his son succeeded as Earl of Argyll and in 1663 the forfeited estates were restored to him. This proved exceedingly unfortunate for the Macleans of Duart who had supported Montrose so gallantly, and whose clan territories in Mull had been one of the nearer targets of the Marquess-Chief. The companion of Montrose had died a few weeks after the execution of Charles I, and his son Sir Hector Maclean had been killed fighting for Charles II a few years later, so that when the new Campbell Chief renewed his father's assault on Mull, he was faced by a Maclean Chief only sixteen years old.

Mac Cailein Mór possessed a court judgment from the unruly period between the death of Cromwell and the restoration of Charles II, vesting both the feudal superiority and the actual ownership of the Maclean of Duart lands in the Campbell Chief, so that the unfortunate islanders were placed in the same position as the MacGregors of an earlier century when they had no alternative but to fight for their home-acres. Gradually the 9th Earl of Argyll turned the well-oiled screw of judicial procedures. In 1672 he obtained an order against the Maclean Chief for the rents and feu-duties of his clan lands; in 1673, a decree for the Chief's removal from his castle; in 1674, letters of ejection.

Then a natural disaster struck the Macleans, when their twenty-seven-year-old Chief died, leaving an infant heir. In 1675 Argyll obtained fresh letters of ejection against the baby's guardians, and it was now that the clan began to resort to force in their own defence, ignoring a summons to come to Inveraray and sample Campbell justice there. Macleans seized a Campbell stronghold in the Treshnish Isles. Argyll was empowered to use the militia of Argyll, Bute and Dunbarton to enforce a commission of fire and sword against them, and in the face of such overwhelming odds they surrendered. Campbells took over Castle Duart and the Maclean territories including the distant and fertile island of Tiree.

The result is well illustrated by the treatment which the Revd John Beaton received, a Protestant Episcopal minister in Mull, as he described it to the Scottish Privy Council a few years later. He was destitute, he reported, 'through the general devastations and herships committed by the Campbells in Mull, there being taken from him at one time thirty-eight great cows and eighty sheep, six goats and all his plenishing, household furniture and victuals.' Beaton represented the immensely ancient learned family whose library of Gaelic manuscripts was at least as precious as that of the MacMhuirichs. When 'the house itself was broke up, spoiled and robbed of all that was therein, in high contempt of His Majesty's authority and laws and of the petitioner's sacred function,' much of this collection perished.

Beaton represented the Episcopal Church that Charles II had restored on his return to his kingdom: the Campbell Chief adhered to the Calvinist cause to which his great-grandfather had committed his clan as early as 1558. In the course of the conflict that rumbled on between these two religious factions, Argyll was tried for treason and sentenced to forfeiture and death soon after he had completed his take-over of the possessions of Clan Maclean. He escaped death when his daughter-in-law came to visit him in prison accompanied by a servant, and he walked out behind her, disguised in this man's costume, and fled to Holland.

The Macleans enjoyed a respite of sorts, since the Campbell claims against their property now fell to the crown, but the Campbells were not evicted from Duart or their other positions of strength. Then Charles II died in 1685 and his natural son the Duke of Monmouth stepped forward as a Protestant champion, opposing the succession of the Catholic James VII. Mac Cailein Mór returned from exile to raise an army of 3,000 Campbells in the Protestant cause, and Macleans and MacDonalds eagerly joined the force that the Scottish Privy Council levied to oppose him. This time Argyll reached the scaffold, declaring before his execution, 'I die not only a Protestant, but with a heart-hatred of Popery, Prelacy and all superstition whatever.' The religious bigotry he had inherited from his father is barely redeemed by its sincerity.

Over forty years earlier his father had devastated Atholl and imprisoned its Earl. Now the Murray Marquess of Atholl led the MacDonalds and Macleans into the lands of the Campbells whose Chief had just been executed. They hanged several of his relatives, imprisoned many of his clansmen in gaols that had been filled of old with victims of the Campbells, and compensated themselves handsomely for the pillage they had suffered in the past. Many Campbells in the United States today descend from those who were transported to the American plantations after the failure of Monmouth's rebellion.

Prominent among the leaders of Atholl's punitive expedition into Argyll was the Chieftain of a small sept of the MacDonalds known as MacIain, whose clansmen inhabited a region containing a kind of natural fortress called in Gaelic the Valley of Mist — Glencoe. Three years later, when William of Orange came to seize the throne of his uncle and father-in-law James VII, MacIain was naturally one of those who came forward amongst the other MacDonalds and the Macleans, MacGregors and Stewarts, as much to oppose the Campbells as to support the rightful king. And this time they were very unlucky indeed.

One of the instruments of their misfortune was the son of the house of Glenorchy who had been created Earl of Breadalbane. Anyone who is puzzled by Charles II's restoration of property to the 9th Earl of Argyll and indifference to the fate of the Macleans, who had served his father so faithfully, is likely to find his promotion of John Campbell of Glenorchy even more extra-ordinary. This man, having no more MacGregors to hunt on his own ground, had made a bid for a more distant objective in Caithness. Here the Sinclair earls had barely escaped from Gordon clutches before the great rebellion, and lived in relative tranquillity since the house of Sutherland found itself under a cloud after the Restoration. This seemed to Campbell the younger of Glenorchy to offer a promising vacuum which he might fill, and so he contrived to make himself the principal creditor of George Sinclair, 6th Earl of Caithness.

On the Earl's death in 1676 John Campbell made 'gross and fraudulent misrepresentations' which somehow enabled him to pass himself off as Earl of Caithness, as though peerages could be bought and sold or used to settle debts. He even went so far as to invade Caithness and evict the true Sinclair heir from his castle of Keiss. So far from paying any penalty for his crimes, he merely had his patent of nobility revoked by the King, who cured his disappointment by creating him instead Earl of Breadalbane, which is all the more bizarre since his father Sir John of Glenorchy in Breadalbane was still very much alive.

That astute observer John Mackay, a government agent, remarked: 'it is odds, if he lives long enough, but he is a Duke. He is of fair complexion, and has the gravity of a Spaniard, is as cunning as a fox, wise as a serpent, and as slippery as an eel.' Whether or not he would succeed in winning a dukedom, he might very well transform himself into the Chief of Clan Diarmaid. Mac Cailein Mór was an exile whose father and grandfather had both been executed for treason, while his great-grandfather had died in exile and disgrace. The Calvinist cause to which he was committed had enjoyed only a brief ascendancy during the period of over a century since the Reformation, and its adherents were still a minority, most of them Lowlanders.

From the ease with which William of Orange triumphed in the Glorious Revolution of 1688, it may appear obvious that he was bound to win. In backward-looking Gaeldom it did not look so certain. The legitimate Stewart succession had never been overturned, and even when it had been interrupted by Cromwell's interregnum, the rightful king had returned in the end. An Episcopal Church had been restored after only a short interval, and the Roman religion in which most MacDonalds and other Christians had always believed was at last being relieved from persecution in Scotland. When the alternative of a revival of Calvinist persecution under a usurping King also involved the return of a dreaded Campbell Chief from his exile, it is not surprising that the clans rallied to the cause of James VII with unusual unity, while the wily Breadalbane in their midst hedged his bets.

After the 9th Earl of Argyll's head had been placed on the same spike of the Tolbooth in Edinburgh that had held those of Scotland's Caesar and Pompey, his son fled to the Hague and returned with William of Orange. It was he who administered the oath to King William in London, after expressing his appreciation that William had come to relieve 'our religion, liberty and property from the very brink of ruin.' Religion was to be the weapon for restoring Campbell property, as it had been the means of increasing it in the past, as the very oath which Argyll read out, and the King repeated after him, emphasised. 'We shall be careful to root out all heretics and enemies to the true worship of God.' That included people like the Episcopal Minister John Beaton in Mull, whose library the Campbells had already burned, as well as the majority of the Campbells' neighbours. The Law, as well as religion, was placed at Argyll's disposal: he was given authority to sue the judges who had sentenced his father.

Meanwhile a second Graham emerged as leader of the Jacobite clans, John of Claverhouse, Viscount Dundee. His very name would have attracted them, even if he had not possessed the charm and the capacity for decisive action of a Montrose. He had already made himself hated and feared by the faithful remnant of the Covenanters who would not recognise the authority of an uncovenanted king, and who assassinated an archbishop in the name of their religion. As the day of their final triumph approached, Dundee prepared to lead into battle the MacDonalds of Clanranald, Keppoch, Glengarry, Sleat and Glencoe, the elderly Stewart of Appin's son with two hundred of his clansmen, MacNeils from the far isles, MacGregors, Robertsons and Farquharsons. Sir Ewen Cameron of Lochiel brought a thousand of his clansmen, and the menaced Macleans of Duart, to whose clan his wife belonged, had as urgent a motive as any to be present. But the unity which the clans so rarely achieved except in the extremity of a lost cause could not survive the death of their leader. Dundee led them to victory at Killiecrankie against the forces of King William, but after he had been killed in battle the clan federation disintegrated.

The Earl of Breadalbane's father had died two years before the revolution, leaving him Chief of the Glenorchy sept. When Dundee summoned him to support King James he ignored the call, but he did not send any of his clansmen to fight for King William either, and even instructed them to meddle with neither side. So when MacIain, Chief of the MacDonalds of Glencoe, returned home through Breadalbane after the Battle of Killie-crankie, he was traversing the lands of an ancient enemy who had not put himself under the protection of either of the contending kings. The MacDonalds passed up Glen Lyon, whose laird was Breadalbane's insolvent nephew Robert Campbell, driving the valley's cattle, horses, goats and sheep before them to the heights of Rannoch moor and down into the natural fortress of Glencoe. For the present the Earl of Breadalbane uttered no protest and attempted no reprisal. He sat tight in his castle of Kilchurn, plotting his next devious move.

On the one hand he kept in touch with the Jacobites, on the other he suggested to King William that he was the most suitable person to win the Highland clans to his allegiance by distributing money to their chiefs from the public purse. This was agreed, and £12,000 was set aside in London for the purpose. James VII's Generals, Barclay and Buchan, came to meet Breadalbane in his castle of Achallader in the summer of 1691, together with a number of Highland chiefs. These included Camerons, Macleans, Stewarts and MacDonalds, amongst whom were MacIain from Glencoe with his sons. All of them undertook to suspend hostilities for three months in an agreement which recognised them as men holding commissions from the previous sovereign, not as rebels against the present one. No mention was made of the reward they might expect for transferring their allegiance.

But the duplicity of Breadalbane was revealed when it was leaked to King William's government that the terms of the truce were subject to the agreement of James VII, that it should be void if he were to invade Britain, and that Breadalbane himself had agreed to join the Jacobites with a thousand men if King William were not to accept the terms to which the chiefs had agreed publicly. Henceforth not even a Campbell in his right mind would have trusted Breadalbane.

As the regime of King William steadily consolidated its power, not only in London and Edinburgh but also in Highland garrisons such as Inverlochy, a desire spread among the Jacobite Highland chiefs to be relieved of their allegiance to the King who had fled, and an emissary was despatched to him, asking for a discharge from his service. Nothing could have displayed the old-fashioned Highland honour in a more graceful light, these men, like Johnnie Armstrong of old, asking grace at the graceless face of a Stewart king. For James VII havered interminably, thinking of nothing except his own interests, while William had meanwhile required every chief to swear allegiance to him by the New Year of 1692. It was during this ominous interval that Breadalbane planted in the mind of one of King William's ministers a stratagem for cowing the clans into submission that would also revenge his private wrongs at the hands of the MacDonalds of Glencoe.

By the time a reply came from James VII, discharging his subjects from their allegiance, only a few weeks remained in which to take the oath to King William. All the same, they would have sufficed MacIain if he had not made a dreadful mistake. He was an old man who remembered the years when Colonel Hill had been garrison commander at Inverlochy Castle in the days of Cromwell, a tactful professional soldier with whom he had formed a warm acquaintance. After the revolution Colonel Hill was appointed to Inverlochy once more, but only in a military capacity this time, without his former civil authority. So when MacIain rode the short distance from Glencoe to Inverlochy at the very last moment to take the oath of submission, Hill told him that he was unable to administer it. The nearest place where MacIain would be able to make his submission was Inveraray, far to the south.

Alarmed by now, MacIain and his companions hastened through appalling winter weather to the Campbell capital and reached there on 2 January, only to discover that Sir Colin Campbell of Ardkinglas, the Sheriff Depute, had left to celebrate the New Year holiday and was not yet returned. Yet when he did so, he accepted MacIain's oath of allegiance to King William and Queen Mary although by now it was 6 January. After all, he was not the only MacDonald chieftain who had been unpunctual. The young Clanranald was allegedly storm-bound in the Hebrides; Keppoch, Sleat and Glengarry were also dilatory. But a conspiracy, instigated by Breadalbane, had singled out the MacDonalds of Glencoe for an act of genocide, partly as a warning to other Highlanders, partly as a private act of Campbell revenge. Ardkinglas placed MacIain's name on the list of those who had taken the oath which he forwarded to the Scottish Council. Another Campbell crossed it out.

Yet the ultimate blame for the atrocity which followed is due, as so often in the history of the clans, to a distant king and his Lowland servants. It was the Secretary of State, Dalrymple of Stair, who acted upon Breadalbane's nefarious suggestion concerning the MacDonalds of Glencoe, and advised the King on 16 January: 'If MacIain of Glencoe and that tribe can be well separated from the rest, it will be a proper vindication of the public justice to extirpate that sept of thieves.' The MacDonalds of neighbouring Glengarry, Dalrymple recommended at the very same time, should be granted indulgence although their Chief had also failed to take his oath in time. King William signed the instructions to exterminate the inhabitants of Glencoe both above and below the order.

At the beginning of February a detachment of soldiers marched into the glen. They belonged to the Earl of Argyll's regiment and were led by Captain Robert Campbell of Glen Lyon. So even if the majority of the troops were not Campbells, many of them Lowlanders who could not even understand the language of the local people, the outcome of their presence would be attributed for ever to Clan Diarmaid. The MacDonalds welcomed them trustingly, since they believed that the submission of their chieftain had been accepted, and they were billeted throughout the homesteads of Glencoe.

Ten days later, Campbell of Glen Lyon received this command.

'You are hereby ordered to fall upon the rebels, the MacDonalds of Glencoe, and to put all to the sword under seventy. You are to have special care that the old fox and his sons do upon no account escape your hands.' At five o'clock on a morning of thick snowfall the massacre was carried out. The aged chieftain was shot as he was getting out of bed: his old wife had her clothes torn off her, the rings bitten from her fingers, and was thrown out to die in the snow. Some escaped, to perish in the freezing corries above the glen. But others vanished into the snow-curtained darkness of the long Highland winter's night, to find safety in the homes of distant neighbours, and among these were the two sons of MacIain. In fact the attempt to exterminate the MacDonalds of Glencoe was bungled, and a high proportion of them escaped. Partly this was due to a failure to block the eastern end of the glen before the massacre began. But tradition and probability suggest that many of the soldiers had no stomach for such a breach of trust, such a violation of the Highland code of hospitality, and found means of warning or aiding their victims.

It is the intention, not the statistical result, that has immortalised the massacre of Glencoe in the annals of infamy, enshrined in a haunting little Gaelic song: 'People of our glen, get up quickly! They have broken their oath to us, and they are going to repay our hospitality with murder and arson.' Even though many of the inhabitants of the glen escaped, every one of their homes was destroyed in a Highland February.

At first there was anger in official quarters that the extermination in Glencoe had not been complete and there was a proposal that the survivors should be deported. But as news of the atrocity spread in London, Paris and Edinburgh, men in high places developed a growing compulsion to screen themselves from blame by finding a scapegoat. King William himself, who had signed and countersigned the order for the massacre, ordered an enquiry, and its commissioners dutifully exonerated the monarch. The orders of Dalrymple of Stair, they decided, had exceeded the King's intentions and were the 'cause of the slaughter which, in effect, was a barbarous murder.' The tortuous machinations of Breadalbane were investigated and he was imprisoned and threatened with impeachment. But probably there were few who understood the full extent of his responsibility for the massacre of Glencoe, although he lived to a great age, hated and despised.

Mac Cailein Mór was not implicated, although men of his regiment had carried out the massacre. He petitioned King

William for restoration of the rank of Marquess that had been bestowed on his grandfather, was created a Duke instead, and died a year after his sovereign. It was left to the 2nd Duke to support the Treaty of Union in 1707 which established the Calvinist Church of Scotland, and protected Scots law as an independent judicature within a United Kingdom. So Campbell's kingdom was in the end preserved amongst the institutions that this Gaelic clan had done so much and risked so much to support.

CHAPTER NINE

Clan Clergy

At the end of the seventeenth century the clans still retained the reputation that a Roman author had bestowed on their forbears when he wrote: 'the whole race which is now called Celtic or Gallic is madly fond of war, high spirited and quick to battle.' It is a matter of debate whether they had retained this quality as a response to government policy, as a life-style endemic in all tribal societies, or as a luxury rather than a necessity.

The Romans also remarked that the Celtic peoples were deeply religious and superstitious, and their spiritual life had been controlled by a hereditary priesthood within the tribal framework. After their conversion to Christianity they had created a form of Church organisation unique in Europe, based on little monasteries that were maintained by particular clans like the orders of Druids in pagan times. After the Roman system superceded that of the Celtic Church and celibacy of the clergy was enforced, a hereditary priesthood was no longer possible, though the Mackinnons contrived to provide abbots of Iona over a period of centuries from the ranks of their laity.

When the Roman Catholic Church was abolished in Scotland by Act of Parliament in 1560, it was open to the new reformed religion to restore the old principle of hereditary vocation so dear to the Celtic peoples. They might even have evolved a new clan like the Macnabs (Sons of the Abbot), MacPhersons (Sons of the Parson), or MacTaggarts (Sons of the Priest). The Latin word *clericus* had passed into Gaelic, meaning someone who could read and write, a capacity that was for long confined to those in Holy orders in most parts of Europe, and today there is a Clergy tartan closely resembling one for the name of Clarke, however that name is spelt. But the Clarkes did not blossom into a religious or even a secular clan.

Several clans did, however, evolve a hereditary clergy in the traditional way, although these did not adopt a particular name from their founder, and the story of their achievements serves to counter-balance the tales of strife which hostile Scottish governments loved to collect, and the Gaels themselves preserved with equal enthusiasm in their oral traditions.

A typical example of the way in which martial and religious vocations went hand in hand in one small clan is furnished by the Munros. At the time when the Marquess of Argyll was maintaining an army in Ulster during the rebellion against Charles I, a cousin of the Munro Chief, who spelt his name Robert Monro, was the General of the Covenanting forces there. Previously he had served in the Thirty Years War in Germany in the regiment that Charles I had permitted the Chief of Mackay to raise as a force of mercenary clan soldiers, and in 1637 he had published a record of its services which is unique in the annals of that war. 'If you ask why I wrote these observations,' he explained, 'it was because I loved my comrades; if why I published them, know it was for my friends.' Robert Monro's cousin the Chief also served in Mackay's regiment, and rose to the rank of Colonel. Their tradition has continued down the centuries. It was a Munro who claimed to have fired the first shot in the American War of Independence in 1775.

The Munros inhabited Ferindonald, Gaelic for Donald's Country, a singularly fertile area that extends from Ben Wyvis to the shore of the Cromarty Firth in Easter Ross. It is supposed that Donald was the name of the clan's founder, while tradition asserted that their name derived from Roe Water in Derry, and that they were related to the Beatons and came from Ireland to Scotland in the same circumstances at the end of the thirteenth century. The clan's Gaelic name *Rothach* means Inhabitant of Roe, a locality that cannot be found on a Scottish map.

The Munro Chiefs emerge first in historical record holding their lands from the Celtic Earl of Ross, and after the extinction of this independent authority the Munros held directly from the crown. By this time their stronghold was established at Foulis overlooking the Cromarty Firth, where the present Chief still lives, in a seventeenth-century mansion that is one of the architectural jewels of the North. A fire lit on the topmost tower of the old castle of Foulis could evidently be seen far and wide by clansmen living in the surrounding basin, so that the gathering-cry of the clan became *Caisteal Folais na theine* — Castle Foulis ablaze. Since the introduction of heraldry they have made a use of the eagle's head similar to the adoption of the stag's antlers by the neighbouring Mackenzies, while the crest used as the clan totem displays the entire bird. Generally it is difficult to trace the precise origin of symbols that appear so much older than the science of heraldry, but in the case of the Munros it seems to be the eagle which the Earls of Ross adopted to attest their ownership of Buchan, that flew into Ferindonald as their mascot.

The clan endured its share of misfortune during the troubles of the Middle Ages, but emerged from them relatively unscathed. Robert their Chief met his death in 1369, fighting in support of his overlord the Earl of Ross, but a century later they were in possession of a crown charter to the barony of Foulis, a most precious form of security. By this time too they had contributed an early sample of the art of piping, the tune called *Blar Bealach nam Brog*, the Field of Shoe-Pass, in commemoration of a local conflict.

The Munros, like the Campbells, became early and enthusiastic supporters of the Reformation despite the remoteness of the clan from the Lowlands in which the seed was sown. This may have been due partly to their location, between the Gaelic west and the outposts of southern power and influence which in those days were so largely maintained by sea, and could reach such a safe anchorage in the Cromarty Firth on their doorstep.

The clan had already reared a celebrated cleric on the eve of the Reformation in Donald, son of Alasdair Munro of Kiltearn, who spelt his name Monro like the author-soldier of the following century. Donald became Vicar of Snizort and Raasay in 1526, and was appointed Archdeacon of the Isles in 1549. His contemporary George Buchanan, who was himself rated one of the outstanding scholars of Europe, described Donald Monro as 'a pious, diligent and learned man, who travelled all over these islands and viewed them correctly.' He was contrasting Monro to all the absentee (and in some cases unconsecrated) churchmen of those degenerate days. Monro by contrast earned his promotion to Dean of the Isles by touring them thoroughly and writing the description of them on which his fame rests today. In 1560 he conformed to the reformed religion and was appointed Minister of Kiltearn, and it was possible that he might have founded a dynasty of clergy. But he maintained his celibacy to his death, unlike those of his brethren who had not even observed it in the days of Popery.

It was observed in 1570 that Donald Monro was 'not prompt in the Scottish tongue:' in other words, he was not fluent in Gaelic. There has frequently been difficulty in discovering when the Highland chiefs and their nearest relatives ceased to speak the language of their clansmen, and there has been comparable uncertainty as to the language most commonly used on the east side of Scotland, especially in such an area as the Monros inhabited. To this day it is spoken beside the Moray Firth, while it was never a native tongue of the coastal communities of Caithness. Evidently a minister required Gaelic in Kiltearn, otherwise Donald Monro's weakness would not have been remarked upon, and certainly the Chief's family generally spoke it, since Sir William of Foulis' son William was Minister of Dingwall by 1561, and the nephew of a Munro Chief Minister of Tain in 1599. In both charges Gaelic must have been required. How much more so in distant Strathnaver, by then already a target for the missionary activities of kinsmen of the Munro Chiefs.

During the years in which the old Church hierarchy was gradually dismantled and a new ministry introduced, there were many areas of the Highlands in which people grew up without any Christian instruction whatever. In a society possessing such ancient traditions, many of these reverted to pre-Christian beliefs and practices. The evidence of witch trials all over Europe prove that these were not peculiar to the Scottish clans, but belonged to a widespread cult. Nor did its devotees belong to the most ignorant and untravelled members of the community. The royal Stewart Earl of Bothwell was the leader of a coven in the reign of James VI, who himself published a book on the subject before he left Scotland. Another practitioner was a chief of the very clan which had embraced the reformed religion with such early enthusiasm.

In 1589, the same year in which the Earl of Bothwell employed his coven of witches at Berwick in an unsuccessful attempt to encompass the King's death by magic, Hector Munro of Foulis invoked the same powers to save his own life at the expense of his half-brother George Munro of Obsdale. Being gravely ill, he lay down in a grave at midnight wrapped in blankets over which fresh turf was lightly laid. A witch then hastened to consult the head of the local coven and returned with the message that 'Mr Hector was her choice to live and his brother George to die.' The Munro Chief thereupon recovered, his brother died in the following year, and the unfortunate witch was strangled and burned at the stake for her pains.

These happenings are a startling contrast to the activities of the Chief's cousin Robert Munro of Coull, son of William of Coull, who had become Minister of Cullicudden in about 1580. Robert went to Farr in Strathnaver in 1589, and for the next thirty years and more he administered the enormous parish single-handed, as far as Durness in the extreme north-west. His younger brother Hector had a far easier life as Minister of

Edderton in Easter Ross. The prosperity of this clerical sept became apparent when Robert in Strathnaver was able to lend money to the Mackay Chief, a debt that was returned in due course. Another Robert Munro of the Coull branch became Minister of Dingwall in 1574, in succession to William of Foulis.

But the clergy of Coull were outshone by the Munros of Milntown and Pitlundie. One of these was appointed Chancellor of Ross in 1586, and in the Synod of Ross this branch had filled the parishes of Suddie, Fortrose and Kiltearn by the end of the sixteenth century. The son of the Revd George Munro of Pitlundie, Minister of Fortrose, became Minister of Rosemarkie. In 1609, Robert Munro began a ministry at Rosskeen that lasted for nearly half a century. In the Synod of Caithness three of John of Pitlundie's sons found parishes; David at Latheron in 1634, Alexander at Golspie in the same year, preceded by their younger brother John at Reay in 1628.

But it was Alasdair, son of Hector of Milntown and brother of the Minister of Rosskeen, who was to earn the most lasting fame, and his recruitment appears to have resulted from the unexpected arrival of an influential prophet from the south, Robert Bruce of the great house of Airth.

After Robert I's son David II had died without leaving heirs, the Bruces had passed from the national stage for a space, but they continued in various lines, of which the Clackmannan house provides the Bruce Chief today in the person of the Earl of Elgin and Kincardine. A junior branch of Clackmannan established itself at Airth Castle, now a sumptuous hotel, and by the time of the Reformation its lord was Sir Alexander Bruce, married to a member of the Catholic Livingstone family. Sir Alexander played the open-handed prince in his castle and even took the law into his own hands in Edinburgh, where James VI himself failed to bring Bruce to justice when he raised an affray that led to murder.

The full-blooded patriarch and his devout Catholic wife had five sons, of whom they were so eccentric as to name two Robert; one of these became a Catholic priest, the other a Calvinist minister. The latter was said to have seen the light of his new faith in the Wallace tower of Airth Castle, where William Wallace was believed to have rescued one of his relatives three hundred years before. Robert Bruce received further inspiration when he went to hear John Knox preaching in his old age, and he followed Knox in the pulpit of St Giles there. His own preaching became legendary, and James VI came to listen to his cousin's exhortations. When the King brought back his Danish bride, it was Bruce who annointed her at her coronation.

But like other members of the new theocracy, he made sweeping claims on behalf of God's spokesmen at the expense of 'God's silly vassal,' and on one occasion actually reduced King James to tears. There were quarrels at Holyroodhouse between the cousins. James repeatedly demanded that Robert Bruce should beg forgiveness on his knees and Bruce as often refused. As James was setting out from the palace of Holyroodhouse in 1603 to mount the English throne, the two men said an affectionate farewell, but still Bruce did not kneel or ask pardon. The King thereupon sentenced him (from a safe distance) to banishment. So this man with the background of a courtier and the aptitudes of a statesman made his unexpected appearance in Inverness.

As James VI no doubt anticipated, it was difficult for Bruce to communicate his uncompromising Calvinist views in a region where Gaelic was the spoken language, since no Bruce of Airth is in the least likely to have understood the tongue at any time. All the more essential to his purposes were the Munros, whose bilingual gentry had already generated such an enthusiasm for the same mission that a Provost of Tain declared in 1605, 'the greatest number of the said ministry are Munros.' Among these was Alasdair of Kiltearn, where the Dean of the Isles had held his final charge until his death some fifteen years before Alasdair was born. Dean Munro had been described as deficient in Gaelic: not so Alasdair of Kiltearn. He was already surrounded by his Milntown relatives in the ministry. After he had been inspired by Robert Bruce to follow the same vocation, he followed the Dean's literary example in a direction that reminds us of the overriding problem of the reformers.

It had been a principal objective of the Protestants throughout Europe to make the Bible available in all vernacular languages, and to dispense with liturgical forms of worship in Latin. James VI authorised the English version of the Bible that escaped further tinkering until recent times. But there was no translation into Scottish Gaelic, which was by this time sufficiently different from Irish to make the Gaelic translation of the Protestant Bishop Bedell in Ireland unserviceable. Alasdair Munro tried to remedy this by turning Bible stories into Gaelic poetry that his parishioners could memorise, and although only two samples of these compositions survive, they suffice to prove him no mean poet. When he went to Strathnaver in about 1635, to take over the enormous parish that Robert Munro of Coull had administered for so long, he planted a tradition of Gaelic religious verse that was to bear wonderful fruit in the Mackay country.

In the manner of his race, he also planted his own descendants as custodians of his vineyards. His son Hew followed him in Strathnaver, while another son became Minister of Alness in Ross, where he was described as 'a man of great readiness and considerable learning.' His daughter Christine married John Mackay, and their son William became Minister of Dornoch, where the cathedral of the diocese of Caithness had been planted in Catholic times. It fell into ruin, but was restored early in the nineteenth century. This kind of clerical succession through the female line was not uncommon, as in the case of the chiefship.

When James VI introduced the office of Justice of the Peace in the far north, the new ministry was given secular authority in many cases, useful as a supplement to their ghostly powers. The roll of justices for 1634 lists three Gordons and two Mackays for the sheriffdom of Sutherland and Strathnaver, as might be expected in the lands of a Gordon Earl and Mackay Chief. Far more remarkable is the fact that it also contains the names of three Munro ministers, including Alasdair the poet. In Caithness likewise there were two Munro ministers, the sons of John of Pitlundie, at Latheron and Reay. Of course in their native sheriff-dom of Ross it was not only the ministers of Clan Munro who were appointed justices.

Lest too overpowering an odour of sanctity be attributed to the Munro ministry, it should be mentioned that James Munro was appointed Minister of Dunnet in Caithness in 1685, and absconded in 1689 'on account of immoral and flagitious conduct.' He was still being charged to appear before the Presbytery in 1698, but failed to do so. Earlier, John Munro, Minister of Tarbat in Easter Ross, incurred the wrath of the Privy Council, which ordered his suspension in 1624 'for his contemptuous rebellion and disobedience.' This sounds like the kind of independent behaviour that earned Robert Bruce similar disapproval, on the part of a clergyman of somewhat comparable standing. For John Munro was several times a member of the General Assembly of the Church, and of a social rank that made him an eligible husband for the daughter of a Mackintosh Chief.

As a rule, these Munro ministers can be traced back to the clan heartland, but there is an odd exception in John Munro who was born in Uist in the Outer Hebrides and became chaplain to the Mackay Chief at Tongue. There he was able to preach in the fine new building erected by Lord Reay, which remains the parish church to this day. His son George returned to become minister in South Uist, which is still partly Catholic and partly Protestant, with Lewis to the north a bastion of the Calvinist faith and Barra to the south staunchly Catholic. This alignment has much to do with the Franciscan missions that were sent to the Hebrides during the hiatus after the Catholic Church was abolished in 1560, without any effective ministry being put in its place; a misfortune that also helps to explain the re-emergence of the witch cult in Scotland.

One of these missionaries was the Irishman Cornelius Ward (a name derived from the Gaelic for Son of the Bard), whose arrival in the Hebrides coincided with that of Alasdair Munro in Strathnaver. He reported to Rome that in 1635 he made fifty converts to the Faith in Skye besides instructing 116 Catholics in that island. However, the MacLeods eventually became predominantly Calvinist, as their island remains to this day, and this led to the emergence of a remarkable sept of MacLeod clergy.

Their progenitor was Donald MacLeod of Swordale, not himself a minister, but a man of notable piety and brother of the Minister of Kilfinichen whom Dr Johnson described as the 'clearest-headed' man he met during his excursion in the Hebrides. Donald of Swordale's son Norman became Minister of Morvern in 1775 and subsequently Moderator of the General Assembly. His son Norman followed him in the ministry and earned undying fame by the book he published in Gaelic called *Caraid nan Gaidheal,* Friend of the Gael, which was once to be found beside the Bible in every Protestant Highland home. It is a monument to Dr Norman MacLeod's respect for the Gaelic heritage of his race, which he attested in the remark that even 'the superstition of the Highlands, dark and wild as it may appear, had a happy tendency in forming the character of the Gael.' He also made a metrical version of the Psalms in Gaelic for the use of the Established Church of Ireland, and such was his enthusiasm for his Celtic heritage that Lord Cockburn said of him: 'if his heart was seen, I am sure it would be dressed in a kilt.'

In 1836 he was elected Moderator of the General Assembly like his father before him, and when Queen Victoria paid her first visit to Scotland he preached before her at Blair Atholl and was subsequently appointed one of her chaplains. His younger brother John followed him as Moderator of the General Assembly, while his own son John succeeded to his parish of Morvern, another son Norman became a chaplain to Queen Victoria and

Moderator of the General Assembly, and his nephew Norman was called to follow him in the church of St Columba in Glasgow when he died as minister there. Even by the clan standards of the country, this is a remarkable record, and it has continued to this day. In the fourth generation there were three ministers of the Church of Scotland, and one who strayed into the Episcopal Church of England. The most famous in the fifth generation is George MacLeod, former Moderator of the General Assembly, founder of the Iona Community, and now Lord MacLeod of Fuinary.

The saddest example of a clan clergy whose development was stunted by an accident of history is that of the learned Beatons. In 1657 died John Beaton, probably the last of the hereditary physicians of this clan, in the isle of Mull, and was buried on Iona. It was his second son John, born in 1640, who trained as a minister and obtained the parish of Kilninian in the north of Mull during that period of strife between the Macleans of Duart and the Campbells, and kaleidoscopic religious change. In Beaton's youth the Episcopal Church planted by James VI was swept away by the Presbyterian opponents of Charles I. Then Cromwell defeated the Presbyterians who tried to impose their system on the English under a Covenanted King. In 1660 Charles II returned to restore the Episcopal Church. It was in the following decade that John Beaton entered his charge in Mull.

The varying fortunes of the religious sects were inseparable from those of the rival Chiefs, Maclean of Duart and Campbell of Argyll. When Mac Cailein Mór was executed for treason in 1661, Maclean gained a short breathing-space, as short as Stewart gratitude. Once the Argyll estates were restored to his heir, the assault on Duart was resumed, until it fell in 1679. The next Campbell Chief was forfeited in 1681, though his clansmen remained in possession of the Maclean strongholds and lands of Mull. Such were the circumstances in which John Beaton sent his pathetic petition to the Privy Council, describing his destitution, after Campbells had raided his home and burned a great part of his library.

He saved a trunk-full of his precious manuscripts, but he could not save his post when the revolution of 1688 brought in a Calvinist Dutch King, and the exiled Campbell Chief returned from exile to be raised to the rank of Duke. In 1702 a successor was appointed to the parish of Kilninian while the ousted Episcopalian, John Beaton, was described as 'a poor sojourning clergyman.' The comment was a sympathetic one, written by Edward Lhuyd,

Keeper of the Ashmolean at Oxford, to whom Scotland owes a debt for seeking out Beaton and making a catalogue of his priceless papers before so many of them disappeared. He found the sojourning clergyman at Coleraine in Ireland in 1700, where he asked Beaton to read from the Irish Bible, and made a record of his pronunciation. Beaton also transcribed some ancient Gaelic writings which Lhuyd preserved with the note: 'what follows written in Irish, Dr John Beaton, a man most skilled in the history and language of Scotland, faithfully extracted from an ancient vellum manuscript.' Lhuyd wrote these comments in his native Welsh.

He also made a list of the books that Beaton had lost at the hands of the Campbells, and of those that remained we know that he did not mention them all because he concluded by remarking that there were 'many more books.' The greater number he saw have disappeared since, although all might have been saved if a single member of any of Scotland's four universities had shown the same interest as the Welsh scholar from Oxford. The National Library of Scotland's ancient collection known as the Broad Book or Gaelic Manuscript 1 survives as a sample of what the Beaton corpus of learning once contained. Until recently the National Library did not even know to whom it had once belonged. The very date and place of death of the last of the learned Beatons are unknown.

The contempt of Lowlanders for the rich Gaelic heritage of which they knew nothing underlay their attitude to its custodians, whom they regarded as barbarians. But many of the Gaels themselves were influenced by the reformed religion and by the prejudices of their Lowland compatriots to adopt the same attitude. It was expressed in Gaelic in these words soon after the abolition of the Catholic Church in 1560. 'Great is the blindness and sinful darkness and ignorance and perverseness of those who teach and write and compose in Gaelic, since with the view of obtaining for themselves the vain rewards of this world they are more desirous and more accustomed to preserve the vain, extravagant, false and worldly histories concerning the Tuath de Danaan and the Milesians' (bodies of extremely ancient legend); 'Finn son of Cumhail and his Fingalian heroes; and many others which I shall not mention here.'

The author of this attack was John Carswell, Minister of Kilmartin in Argyll when the Roman Church was abolished, and later appointed Bishop of the Isles. At least Carswell set out to put something in place of these vain and worldly treasures, as he explained in Gaelic: 'to write and to teach and to compose the sincere words of God and the perfect way of truth.' A Plato determined to ban the works of Homer, Carswell composed a Gaelic catechism for his evangelical enterprises, and went on to issue the Liturgy of John Knox in Gaelic, published in 1572 with those severe strictures.

Among all the clan clergy, none played a more active part in promoting Bishop Carswell's objectives than the Campbells, partly because their Chief had espoused the reformed doctrine so early and was a figure of such importance, partly because the hereditary principle operated to perpetuate Carswell's personal influence. His daughter Christine married Neil Campbell, who took over the parish of Kilmartin from the Bishop in 1574, and of their sons, Donald succeeded to Kilmartin in 1628, while Neil followed his grandfather as Bishop of the Isles and John was appointed Bishop of Argyll. So this dynasty maintained its religious ascendancy right through the period of episcopacy imposed by James VI and Charles I. When the Scots revolted against the episcopal policy of King Charles, Bishop Neil was called to be Minister of Campbelltown in 1642, though it is not certain that he took up his charge in the troubled times that followed. Bishop John's son Alexander represented the fourth generation of this dynasty by becoming the Minister of Inishail.

By this time another Campbell sept had taken up the literary task begun by Carswell. Its founder was Dugald Campbell who became Minister of Knapdale in 1620, shortly after his Chief Archibald the Grim had become a Catholic convert and fled abroad. Dugald was followed in Knapdale by his son Duncan, while his other son Patrick ministered to the parish of Glassary. Here Patrick was followed by his son-in-law Donald Campbell, while Duncan's son took charge of Killean. It was this family that co-operated so enthusiastically in the task of translating the Old Testament into Scottish Gaelic.

They were assisted by the hereditary clergy of a quite different clan, with whom the Campbells did not always enjoy such amicable relations. So the story of this association serves as a reminder that all the sensational tales of conflict between the clans give a far from complete picture of their everyday lives, and in many instances a misleading one. This third group of ministers who helped the Campbells in the composition of Gaelic religious texts were Camerons.

The Camerons occupied the mountainous territories north of the Stewarts of Appin and the MacDonalds of Glencoe, dominated by Scotland's highest mountain, Ben Nevis. Straddling the south-western end of the Great Glen, their lives were affected inevitably by the strategic pass that brought discord to their doorstep. Successive governments had maintained garrisons in their midst at Inverlochy Castle, and after the revolution of 1688 a new one was erected and named Fort William in honour of the new King.

Successive Cameron chiefs had faced the threat of the two royal Lieutenants, Campbells and Gordons, competing for control of this area. In 1547 Ewen Cameron of Lochiel had been beheaded by an Earl of Huntly. But Mac Cailein Mór had succeeded in establishing himself as feudal superior of the lands of Lochiel.

During the era of the rebellion against Charles I, the restoration of Charles II and the revolution which placed King William on the throne, it was the good fortune of the Camerons to be ruled by a Chief who lived for ninety years at a time when there were five successive heads of the house of Argyll. As the vassal of Archibald the Grim, the 17th Chief, Sir Ewen Cameron of Lochiel began life in difficult circumstances, complicated by the fact that his mother was a Campbell of Glenorchy and he was born in Kilchurn Castle. Archibald the Grim was by this time a Catholic living in exile, but his son kept Ewen a hostage for the peaceable behaviour of his clan right through the period of the Montrose wars, to Ewen's lifelong regret. When he escaped from the power of the Marquess of Argyll at the age of eighteen, he immediately espoused the cause of Charles II and was among the last to remain in arms for the Royalists in the Highlands. Finally he capitulated to Cromwell's General Monck, who marched down to London a few years later to stage-manage the restoration of the King. Ewen Cameron of Lochiel accompanied him, to receive a knighthood while Monck was created a Duke.

An Episcopalian, he was among the Highland chiefs who fought for James VII at Killiecrankie, and narrowly escaped the fate of the MacDonalds of Glencoe by making his belated sub-mission to William and Mary personally in London. But his descendants inherited his Jacobite sympathies and fought for Prince Charles Edward at Culloden. His clan was not one to which the Synod of Argyll might have been expected to look for recruits to the Calvinist ministry or help in preparing its devotional literature.

But at the time when the Catholic Church was abolished in 1560 there had been a priest who conformed to the new order called John Cameron, thought to have been a brother of the 16th

Chief of Lochiel. He was appointed to the parish of Dunoon, where he was followed in 1591 by Ewen Cameron. So this clerical dynasty, bearing the name of a subordinate, resentful tribe whose members for the most part adhered to a different sect, became established in Argyll. Ewen Cameron was followed by John, 'a person of great probity and learning,' who succeeded him sometime before 1610. Whether these three were grandfather, father and son is a matter for surmise, but John was certainly followed by his son Ewen at Dunoon, while his other son Neil became Minister of Inverchaolain. Ewen also took part in public affairs as a Commissioner in the Assemblies of the Civil War, while both of them were colleagues of the Campbells in the work of translating the scriptures. So was John Cameron, grandson of the Revd John of Dunoon, after whose death in 1680 the succession passed through his daughter Mary who married John MacLaurin, Minister of Kilmodan.

The studies of all these men, as well as their pastoral duties, were repeatedly imperilled by outside events, particularly after the restoration of an Episcopal Church on Charles II's return in 1660. Patrick Campbell, Minister of Glassary and son of Dugald of Knapdale, was arrested after the passing of the Test Act in 1681. That was the year in which Argyll himself was convicted of treason and escaped from prison to take refuge abroad. Patrick Campbell was liberated on a surety of 5,000 merks but ordered to leave the kingdom. James VII's Toleration Act of 1687 enabled him to return, though it did not reconcile him since the Act granted toleration to Catholics also. But he lived to see the final triumph of Calvinism before he died in 1700 'with much peace and rejoicing,' to receive the obituary of 'a faithful Minister of Christ who continued steadfast in the times of persecution.'

The hazards for the Cameron clergy were potentially different, since their Chief was an Episcopalian and a Jacobite. Yet when John Cameron, Minister of Dunoon, was deprived in 1660 and hailed before the Privy Council for his 'seditious carriage,' Sir Ewen of Lochiel stood cautioner for him. It is interesting that he should have been sent to the castle of Inverlochy in Cameron territory to serve a term of imprisonment. Dying in 1680, he did not witness the day of triumph.

Such were the dangers and difficulties facing these men as they collaborated in the composition of the Gaelic texts that would serve as a guide to 'the perfect way of truth.' They were mobilised by the Synod of Argyll, and in addition to the published Liturgy of John Knox, translated by Bishop Carswell, they possessed the encouragement of a Gaelic version of the Catechism of John Calvin, published in about 1630. This was once believed to have been the work of Carswell also, but the theory has now been disproved. While the authorship remains uncertain, suspicion falls on Athairne MacEwen and his son Neill, of the clan that had for long provided the hereditary bards to the Campbell Chiefs. John MacMarquess in Kintyre is an alternative candidate. Whoever it was, he was a competent Gaelic scholar, but not one of the Cameron or Campbell clergy who were busy in other fields at this time.

In 1649, the year of Charles I's execution, the Synod of Argyll appointed seven ministers to make a Gaelic version of the shorter Catechism, as the General Assembly had approved in the previous summer, 'for catechising such as are of weaker capacity.' In 1650 a new list of eight ministers was drawn up and given the additional responsibility of translating *A Brief Sum of Christian Doctrine*. In the following year the Gaelic version of the shorter Catechism that is now attributed to Dugald Campbell in Knapdale and Ewen Cameron the Commissioner was approved by the Synod.

In addition, books of the Old Testament were distributed to various members of the syndicate for prose translation, as well as batches of the Psalms to be turned into metrical Gaelic. Dugald in Knapdale was allotted the first eighty. He was given besides the book of Ecclesiastes, and set about collecting material for other parts of the Old Testament as well. In all this work he received the help of his son Duncan Campbell who followed him in the charge of Knapdale. Ewen Cameron in Dunoon had other psalms to turn into verse, while Neil Cameron in the parish of Inverchaolain received the first book of Chronicles as his share. John, grandson of the original John Cameron in Dunoon and his eventual successor there, is known to have assisted Dugald Campbell in Knapdale when he was young, both with the Scriptures and with the Psalms. The work prospered with admirable team spirit. In 1653 the shorter Catechism was printed and so quickly sold that a second edition was soon called for.

The Psalms proved as strong a magnet to these literary clergymen as they had done to English littérateurs in Elizabethan times. But the Gaelic enthusiasts faced a particular difficulty, in that their verses had to be fitted to unfamiliar Lowland tunes and cast in a metre 'strange and unknown to the Gaelic tongue.' The fact that Gaelic is a stressed language added to the complications. In 1658, the year of Cromwell's death, the translators submitted their first fifty Psalms to the Synod, who found them 'defective in syllabilization,' and arranged a seminar in Campbelltown to solve the problem.

Here Dugald Campbell had the benefit of John MacMarquess' advice, described by the Synod as 'an old man able in the Irish song,' possibly author of Calvin's Catechism in Gaelic also. More remarkably, a minister called David Simpson was summoned to help, a man who had come to Argyll in 1651 after graduating at St Andrews, 'willing to apply himself unto the study of the Irish language that he may be instrumental for the propagation of the Gospel in the Highlands.' Evidently he had applied himself so well that he was now qualified to give expert assistance to his Highland brethren in their native language. With these men sat the Revd John Stewart from Kingarth, and Dugald Darroch who ministered to the Highland congregation in Campbelltown: for this burgh near the southern end of the Mull of Kintyre was one in which both of Scotland's languages were spoken, Gaelic and English — or, as people were now calling them, Irish and Scots.

On his return from Campbelltown, Dugald Campbell handed over the corrected version of what is now known as the *Caogad* or Fifty, to be printed. Twelve hundred copies of them were published in Glasgow in 1659, with a Gaelic epistle from the Minister of Knapdale urging the reader to pray that this spark of Gospel inspiration might fill the Highlands with 'a glowing fire full of light and heat.' Immediately the Synod pressed on with the task of completing the set of Gaelic metrical Psalms and also translating the entire Bible, for which it considered Dugald Campbell especially well qualified by his knowledge both of Hebrew and Greek: 'because of his skill both in Irish and in the original languages.'

The restoration of Charles II in 1660 put all these plans in jeopardy. At the last meeting of the Synod of Argyll before Episcopacy replaced it, the Minister of Knapdale was ordered to superintend both tasks. His son Duncan, who would eventually follow him in Knapdale, was expelled from his present parish of Glenorchy, which may have given him greater freedom to assist his father. By 1673 when Dugald Campbell died, the pair had almost completed the translation of the Psalms.

But now an Episcopalian rival was at hand with his own version, which he petitioned the Privy Council for permission to publish in December 1673. His name was Robert Kirk of the parish of Balquhidder, and it was said that he had sat working through the night for months in his attempt to beat the Campbells to the winning post. His text was placed before a committee of churchmen for their consideration, and these no longer contained representatives of the dynasties of former translators, since Duncan's brother Patrick Campbell had been evicted from his manse like himself, while John Cameron had died after being imprisoned in Inverlochy Castle.

In 1684 Kirk's Psalms were published under a Privy Council order which gave him a monopoly against all comers for the next eleven years. But in the event his version was never reprinted; and ten years later, after the revolution that brought William of Orange to the throne, the Synod of Argyll was able to publish its final and complete version of the metrical Psalms.

For a time it was feared that this was lost, and one of the first recommendations of the Synod of Argyll after it was able to convene again was 'to the ministers who are to attend the next General Assembly to inquire at Edinburgh for the copy of the Irish Psalms which was fitted for the press, having been among others of the late Earl of Argyll's papers.' This Campbell Chief who was executed like his father before him had taken good care of the Gaelic Psalms despite his other preoccupations. They were found among his papers and 'by a plurality of votes' the task of seeing them through the press was bestowed on John MacLaurin, Minister of Kilmodan, who had married the daughter of the late John Cameron, imprisoned for sedition in Inverlochy Castle.

So the tribal network finally triumphed after all. Dugald Campbell was on the editorial board, from the parish of Kilmartin that Bishop Carswell had occupied at the Reformation, and where his grandson Donald Campbell had succeeded him in the fullness of time. Duncan Campbell was among the editors, successor to his father in the parish of Knapdale. Their work was fulfilled when the General Assembly of the newly established Church of Scotland adopted the 'complete paraphrase of the whole Psalms in Irish metre, approven and emitted by the Synod of Argyll . . . together with a translation of the Shorter Catechism of this Church in Irish.'

These cultivated, property-owning Campbells and Camerons were of course joined by men of many other clan names of the west, just as the Munros were in the north. And while some were preoccupied with the task that had been a principal objective of the Reformation throughout Europe — the translation of the Scriptures into vernacular languages — other members of the clergy invested their learning in different fields. For instance

Alexander Campbell, appointed Dean of Lismore in 1604, preferred to compose a chronicle of events in the Highlands up to the year 1542, in Latin. Colin Campbell by contrast, who became Minister of Ardchattan in 1667, took a profound interest in mathematics and astronomy and corresponded with Isaac Newton, who remarked on one occasion, 'I see that were he amongst us, he would make children of us all.'

Ultimately the Calvinist ministry softened its attitude to the ancient profane learning of the Gael, and a few of the clergy even joined the devoted band of people who set out to rescue the oral traditions which formed such an important part of this rich heritage, especially after the destruction of manuscripts. Prominent amongst these was John Gregorson Campbell, who became Minister of the island of Tiree in 1861 and died there unmarried thirty years later. During those decades he assembled folklore collections which were published in a succession of books of profound value to Gaelic culture: traditional tales of the *Feinne* or Fingalians, Highland superstitions, witchcraft practices and examples of second-sight.

The Campbell Chiefs also continued their time-honoured respect for their people's culture at a time when so many Highland chiefs were becoming totally anglicised and alienated from their clansmen. John Francis Campbell of Islay set the supreme example, collecting the *Popular Tales of the West Highlands* which he published himself, and encouraging all who were engaged in the same work. He issued the first collection of Ossianic ballads to be published, with their conversations between the aged Ossian and St Patrick, and their episodes remembered from Viking days. Above all, he helped to rekindle pride in the Gaelic heritage which Highlanders had been taught to despise, and in this he received the active support of the 8th Duke of Argyll, who himself sent one of his estate workers, John Dewar, through the islands and mainland to add to these great collections of traditional lore. The Dewar manuscripts, like those of the Revd John Gregorson Campbell (and the Gaelic Psalms of an earlier century) were lovingly treasured by Mac Cailein Mór. If no other Highland chiefs committed such depredations as those of the Campbells, none of them did so much to preserve what is precious in Gaeldom either.

No exact comparison can be made between this record and that of the clans who remained Catholic. The priesthood, being celibate, could not become a hereditary vocation. From 1560 until the nineteenth century the Catholic Church was subjected to penal laws and its adherents to intermittent persecution. One of the stated reasons for singling out the MacDonalds of Glencoe for extermination was that they were believed to be Papists, although it appears more probable that they were really Episcopalian Protestants. But so was the Revd John Beaton, whose treatment illustrates the Calvinist attitude that an Episcopalian was no better than a Papist. The common denominator of Gaelic belief in these rival faiths was its piety.

Amongst the Catholic clergy during the ministry of John Gregorson Campbell in Tiree, none is remembered with greater admiration than Father Allan MacDonald of Eriskay. He was first appointed to South Uist in 1884 in a time of deep distress throughout the island kingdom of MacDonald of Clanranald. A chief had succeeded as a minor in 1794 to estates from which he derived the staggering rent of £25,000 a year. Instead of investing any part of this for the welfare of his clansmen, he used it to buy a rotten borough in Parliament and dissipated his entire fortune in the English metropolis. When he became bankrupt he sold the Clanranald islands one after another. South Uist went to a purchaser of Gordon blood in 1828, who immediately set about evicting its inhabitants from the fertile land in the island. Those who did not emigrate lived on in poverty and insecurity, until the first of the Acts was passed by Parliament to protect the Gaels from eviction by absentee landlords, two years after Father Allan's arrival in South Uist.

At first Father Allan's parishioners included the inhabitants both of South Uist and of the little isle of Eriskay, two miles across the sea to the south. But finally he was appointed to be resident priest in Eriskay, where he earned the devotion of the islanders, emulated the Minister of Tiree in his folklore collections, and also composed devotional poetry in Gaelic of a very high order. He died tragically early in 1905, but his poetry and other literary remains have been edited and preserved by Dr John Lorne Campbell of Canna, one of the islands sold by the worthless Chief of Clanranald. And Mrs Campbell of Canna (Margaret Fay Shaw) has immortalised the heritage of Father Allan's parishioners in her own collection of the *Folksongs and Folklore of South Uist*.

CHAPTER TEN

Clan Dress and Music

When George IV visited Edinburgh in 1822 there was widespread complaint there that the kilt and the bagpipe occupied 'a great deal too much space.' Such complaints are rarely heard today when they occupy very much more space still, for the Lowlanders have now adopted the dress and musical instrument of the Gael as essential emblems of the Scottish nation. Very different had been their attitude in earlier times, when both had been generally despised as symbols of Highland barbarity.

Foreigners often commented on the dress that Sir Robert Gordon of Gordonstoun was so eager to abolish: the description of a French visitor in 1556 is typical. 'They wear no clothes except their dyed shirts and light woollen coverings of several colours.' Their legs were left bare in this costume, as a cleric of the diocese of Caithness reported in 1542. 'We of all people can tolerate, suffer and away best with cold, for both summer and winter (except when the frost is most vehement), going always bare-legged and bare-footed.' He signed himself a 'Redshank,' evidently a Lowland term for Highlanders who dressed in this way.

There is no evidence that the Gaels in Scotland continued the Irish practice of marking the *leine* (long linen shirt or tunic) with stripes to indicate the rank of the wearer. Anyway, the *leine* gradually went out of use in Scotland during the seventeenth century, while 'coverings of several colours' that the Frenchman saw grew in size and significance. At the Battle of Kilsyth in 1645, Montrose instructed his soldiers to throw away their plaids in the summer heat, and knot the ends of their shirts between their legs before they fought. But many of these men were MacDonalds from Ireland, while the Hebrideans in his ranks had perhaps not yet been affected by the ruin of the Irish linen trade caused by the Elizabethan conquest.

By this time wool was becoming generally available, although it had been a rare commodity in the Highlands. So the rug grew into the enormous plaid that a Gael could pleat round his waist in ample folds and secure with a belt, leaving sufficient material above it to draw over his head when it rained. At night he could roll himself in it, and increase its warmth by dipping it first in water. The plaid expanded to as much as five feet in width and twelve to fifteen feet in length, and so took the place of the *leine* as a covering for at least a portion of the thigh.

But far more of the thigh remained exposed than the modern kilt leaves bare, as an Englishman noted in 1730, before the dress had been outlawed by Act of Parliament. 'A small part of the plaid, which is not so large as the former, is set in folds and girt round the waist to make it a short petticoat that reaches half-way down the thigh, and the rest is brought over the shoulders and then fastened before, below the neck.' The grounds for calling its wearers Redshanks were as valid as they had been two centuries earlier. 'The stocking rises no higher than the thick of the calf, and from the middle of the thigh to the middle of the leg is a naked space.' There was little need in those days for anyone to enquire what, if anything, was worn beneath the kilt. 'For the most part they wear the petticoats so very short that in a windy day, going up hill, or stooping, the indecency of it is plainly discovered.'

Some degree of decency was, however, ensured by the wearing of a purse resembling those commonly hung at the waist throughout Europe, at least from the Middle Ages. It was secured by a thong round its top whose ends hung down by the weight of terminal knots. A third thong which secured the flap could hang between them. Generally this purse was of leather and round in shape, but worn with the belted plaid and hung by a strap to lie on the lower part of the stomach, it became flattened to the shape of the *sporan* (which is simply Gaelic for purse) as people still wear it today. The Celtic love of ornament has embellished this entirely functional object: though as to its secondary function, the logical French defined it as a *cache-sexe* rather than a *porte-monnaie*.

In the seventeenth century, the Englishman William Sacheverell was commissioned to make one of many attempts to raise the contents of an Armada galleon that still lies in Tobermory Bay off the isle of Mull, and he observed the local dress with less hostility than the nefarious Gordon of Gordonstoun. 'It is loose and flowing, like the mantles our painters give their heroes. Their thighs are bare, with brawny muscles. Nature has drawn all her strokes bold and masterly; what is covered is only adapted to necessity.' Sacheverell would have agreed with the French definition of the sporan. 'What should be concealed is hid with a large shot-pouch.'

In remote pagan times the Celts of Europe had attracted comment by wearing skin-tight trousers among strangers who then dressed themselves in a form of tunic that ended at the knee. In Ireland, where they remained unconquered by the Romans, the aristocracy affected the Roman fashion from which the modern kilt derives. They were determined, it seems, to be different in all circumstances; and so the Gaelic aristocracy continued to be, after the kilted garment known as the belted plaid had become the usual form of attire throughout the Highlands. They formed a taste for wearing skin-tight trousers once more, at a time when the fashionable male elsewhere dressed himself in baggy breeches with stockings below them. The Highland tights, which covered the feet in a single garment reaching to the waist, was called in Gaelic *triubhas*, spelt *trews* in the Lowlands. An English observer noticed in 1730: 'few besides gentlemen wear the *trowze*, that is, breeches and stockings all of one piece and drawn on together; over this habit they wear a plaid, which is usually three yards long and two breadths wide, and the whole garment is made of chequered tartan.'

The word tartan, which describes something so peculiarly Scottish, is in fact French, and *tartaine* in its original meaning contains no reference either to design or to colour, but simply defines a type of material. Yet it was already changing its meaning in Scotland as early as 1538 when James V ordered material for a form of Highland dress. 'Heland tertane to be hoiss,' noted his Treasurer. It was in 1556 that the Frenchman Beaugué noted the variegated colours of the woollen plaid, while in 1578 Bishop Lesley hinted that multiple colours were simply a taste of the rich. 'All, both nobles and common people, wore mantles of one sort (except that the nobles preferred those of several colours).'

A few years later George Buchanan, a Gael himself who was one of the outstanding Latinists of Europe, suggested in that language that the delight in a riot of colour was an ancient one, now less indulged since the ascendancy of Calvinism. 'They delight in variegated garments, especially stripes, and their favourite colours are purple and blue. Their ancestors wore plaids of many colours, and numbers still retain this custom but the majority now in their dress prefer a dark brown.' In speaking of their ancestors, Buchanan might have been describing the Celtic passion for display at any time during the previous two thousand years.

The trews for which James V ordered material from the High-lands evolved in their modern form at the same time as the kilt and according to Robert Gordon of Straloch who wrote in 1594, the weather had as much to do with the choice between them as fashion did. 'In the sharp winter,' he observed, 'the Highland men wear close trowzes which cover the thighs, legs and feet.' The summer saw the emergence of Highland dress in the form that ultimately won general acceptance. 'Their upper-most garment is a loose cloak of several ells, striped and parti-coloured, which they gird breadth-wise with a leather belt, so as it scarce covers the knees.' Or the thighs either, as so many others remarked.

Striped and parti-coloured: while flamboyance and love of display have been characteristics of the Celtic peoples since the remotest times, this particular manifestation has been given a significance today that is altogether modern. Particular setts, or patterns of tartan, now belong to each clan and serve to identify its members in much the same was as medieval knights could be identified on a field of battle by their heraldic emblems. A clan tartan had no such significance in earlier times. Had it done so, a MacMhuirich bard would have extolled it at the Battle of Harlaw in 1411, and it would have become the subject of such songs of praise as *Cabarfeidh*, the Stag-Antlers of the Mackenzies. If MacDonalds had fought Campbells at Inverlochy in today's clan tartans, Iain Lom would hardly have omitted such a spectacular feature from his description of the battle.

The comments on Highland dress that have been quoted are all the remarks of outsiders, except for those of Buchanan. Con-sequently they could not have revealed what were the feelings of a Gael towards the pattern of his tartan. But the silence of the bards on the subject is sufficient proof that a particular sett was not an emblem of clan pride in their day, and this is confirmed by other evidence. The Redshank of the north of Scotland who commented so proudly on his national dress in 1542 did not make the slightest reference to different patterns of tartan, such as are worn today by the clans which surrounded him, Mackays and Gunns, Sinclairs and Gordons.

In 1594 the Irishman Lughaidh O'Clery wrote in Gaelic that Hebrideans could be distinguished from his countrymen by their dress, despite the fact that in many cases they were both MacDonalds. 'They were recognised among the Irish soldiers by the distinction of their arms and clothing, their habits and language, for their exterior dress was mottled cloaks of many colours.'

About a century later Martin Martin, a native of Skye writing in English, described how the arrangements of these colours evolved. 'The plaid worn only by the men is made of fine wool, the thread as fine as can be made of that kind. It consists of diverse colours, and there is a great deal of ingenuity required in sorting the colours so as to be agreeable to the nicest fancy. For this reason the women are at great pains, first to give an exact pattern of the plaid upon a piece of wood, having the number of every thread of the stripe on it.' Today it is the pre-rogative of a chief to ordain the pattern of a sett for his clan: until very recent times they were the creations of a woman's fancy.

But those pieces of wood on which the different patterns were registered might be passed from mother to daughter over a period of generations, until particular setts became recognisable as belonging to certain districts that were inhabited by particular clans. So a tartan might serve to identify the domicile and even the name of its wearer in some cases, just as a local dialect was capable of doing. Martin suggested as much when he wrote, 'every isle differs from each other in their fancy of making plaids, as to the stripes in breadth and colours. This humour is as dif-ferent through the mainland of the Highlands in so far that they who have seen those places are able at the first view of a man's plaid to guess the place of his residence.' But not, apparently, his clan name, which might or might not be obvious from the place of his residence.

Since pagan times the Celtic peoples had displayed the originality of their craftsmanship in metalwork, stone sculpture and the illumination of Gospel books. By the sixteenth century the patronage that might have supported all these skills had moved far outside Gaeldom, and the craft that had blossomed in the hiatus was an activity of the women in a thousand little thatched cottages during the long dark winters. Wool had become more readily available to them, and they searched out roots and the lichen on rocks from which to make the dyes for their threads, and worked out the patterns that could be woven on their narrow hand-looms. So they found the means of decking out their menfolk in a way that enabled them to make as spec-tacular an impression as their forbears had done in the days of the Gaesatae.

Little could they have dreamed that their fabric would become

the most universally recognised among all the peasant crafts of
the world, that it would be adopted as the emblem of the clans,
that even the Lowlanders — even a Hanoverian king — would
take it to their hearts.

Before the proscription of Highland dress there had been one
Highland chief who attempted to anticipate the modern practice,
established by the convention that clan tartans should be
ordained by chiefs of the name. He was the head of Clan Grant
in Strathspey, which rose to prominence after the eclipse of the
Gordons in that area as a result of the revolution of 1688.

The name Grant is the French equivalent of the Gaelic *Mór*
or More, meaning Big. In 1246 the Anglo-Norman William le
Grand possessed property in Stratherrick through marriage with
a local heiress, and twelve years later Sir Laurence le Grand was
Sheriff of Inverness. By the time Sir Iain (or John) Grant became
Sheriff of Inverness in 1434, a clan of that name had spread from
Stratherrick into Glenmoriston and Glenurquhart north-west of
Loch Ness. Sir Iain himself married a Celtic heiress of the ancient
royal house of Strathearn, and it was through this alliance that
the Grant Chiefs moved into Strathspey where the 32nd Grant of
Grant, Lord Strathspey, still lives.

Before the Jacobite uprising of 1715 (which the Grants opposed,
thus earning their place in the Mackenzie rant of *Cabarfeidh*),
Sir Ludovick Grant of Grant ordered all his dependants to wear a
particular pattern of tartan described as consisting of 'red and
green dyce.' Yet nearly a dozen family portraits of the time of
Sir Ludovick's son prove that his attempt to introduce a standard
sett for his clan was ignored even by his closest relatives. They
simply picked the patterns they fancied. But this ruling was
respected in a later century when the present Grant tartan was
composed.

It is curious that nobody considered the military potential of
standardised clan setts. There were the clan badge and battle-
cry, resembling the heraldic emblem that was used as an identification in battle, and the motto that became integrated in every
armorial achievement. Throughout Europe heraldry was
systematised so that there should be no errors of identification,
and the Lord Lyon King-of-Arms continues to exercise this
authority in Scotland today. In England there was one fatal battle
during the Wars of the Roses, in which the heraldic star of
the Veres was mistaken for another emblem on the opposing side
with results that turned victory into defeat. It might be supposed
that similar muddles during clan conflicts would have alerted

somebody to the desirability of identifying the contestants by their setts. But apparently this never occurred.

The earliest representation of a clan dressed as a military unit is the set of engravings that were made in Germany in 1631, when the Chief of Mackay took his regiment of 3,000 clansmen to fight on the Protestant side in the Thirty Years War. They are depicted wearing the belted plaid almost to the knees, and although the sett is not minutely drawn, it can be seen to be identical in every costume, as though Mackay had provided a standard material for the regimental dress.

Although this cannot be identified as the original of the Mackay tartan, other clan setts definitely evolved from the regimental costumes of a later date. Between the 1715 and 1745 uprisings, a military police-force or Watch, formed of six independent companies, was planted in the Highlands. Three of these were commanded by Fraser of Lovat, Grant of Ballindalloch and Munro of Culcairn — none of them the chief of his clan. The other three were commanded by Campbells, and all wore their different tartans. But despite this variety they were known collectively as *Am Freiceiceadan Dubh*, the Black Watch, because their appearance contrasted with the red-coated regular army. In 1739 their numbers were increased to ten companies and a thousand men, and this was the nucleus from which the 42nd Regiment or Black Watch evolved during the following decade. Its tartan was standardised, and by 1815 this was being identified as the sett of the Hanoverian clans, Sutherland, Campbell, Munro and Grant, as well as being called the Government tartan. Today it is both the Sutherland and the Campbell of Argyll tartan, though in colours so much paler than that of the Black Watch that at first glance it looks different. The Munros, Grants and Frasers finally opted for more colourful setts in which red and green predominate.

On the other hand, when the Duke of Gordon raised a Fencible Regiment in 1793, he clothed his men in the Government tartan, merely substituting a yellow stripe for one of the black ones in the original sett. So he created the Clan Gordon tartan as it is worn to this day. In this he followed the example set by the Earl of Seaforth when he raised the first of the regiments in 1778 that became known as the Seaforth Highlanders, and enlivened the Government tartan by placing red and white stripes in it, thus establishing a Mackenzie tartan. But when Sir Alan Cameron of Erracht raised his *Reismeid an Errachd* in 1793, the 79th Regiment, he invited his mother to design its tartan. She deserves to be commemorated as the only woman who can be identified as the author of one of today's clan tartans, out of all the thousands of women to whom Scotland owes this achievement. Her maiden name was Marsali Maclean, and she was the daughter of Charles of Drimmin, who died on the field of Culloden leading the Macleans in the Jacobite cause. Her son's regiment became officially known as the Cameron Highlanders from the year 1804, and to this day her tartan is worn by the sept of Erracht, though it is altogether different from those belonging to the Camerons of Lochiel.

The great Jacobite bard Alexander MacDonald (Alasdair Mac Mhaighstir Alasdair) had composed his eulogy of the *Breacan Uallach*, the Gallant Tartan, at the time of the Forty-Five, meaning the dress itself. After this was outlawed in the aftermath of Culloden, it became a symbol of what had been lost in the Highlands. But men could still wear their traditional dress in the regiments, and so the martial spirit of the Gael focussed with pride enhanced by past misfortune and present deprivation on the military achievements associated with the forbidden dress, the badge of their race. So at last the sett of the tartan, in addition to the dress, began to be invested with something resembling the mystique of the Regimental Colour.

After the lifting of the proscription there was a mounting surge of enthusiasm for the recovery of the old setts that had been worn before it, in which many people assumed that these had been identified with particular clans rather than with different districts. A succession of enthusiasts explored the Highlands in search of evidence to support this and were disappointed. But they found the remedy in choosing appropriate patterns that should serve as clan tartans in future. For instance, the records show that Islay, former seat of the Lords of the Isles, had contributed an annual rent to the crown from the year 1587, consisting of sixty ells of black, white and green cloth. The lands from which this tribute was raised were occupied during almost the entire period in which it was paid by the Macleans, and the Hunting Maclean tartan is of precisely those colours. So this sett commemorates the disastrous conflict between Macleans and MacDonalds over that district of Islay, which the Campbells were able to exploit so profitably.

A deep desire underlay the growing tartan cult, a wish to preserve a Celtic identity on the part of people whose traditional society was in process of disintegration. Prominent amongst those who sought to consolidate it was that gallant soldier and loyal Highlander, General David Stewart of Garth. It was he who helped to influence the Highland Society of London to make a collection of tartans and banners of the clans, authenticated once and for all by their chiefs, and he enlisted the support of many of these chiefs himself. So the Society built up its unique collection of samples, attested by the signature and seal of each clan head, that was made available for consultation to George IV when he planned his state visit to Edinburgh. It was not King George who created the tartan mania, but the arbiter of fashion who rode the tide at its flood.

However, the junketing in Edinburgh did nothing to diminish this surge of enthusiasm, and while it led to many absurdities, it fired others to follow the example set by David Stewart of Garth. Among these was James Logan, who took the trouble to tour the Highlands on foot, collecting the patterns of the fifty-five tartans that he published in 1831, together with a great deal of other useful information.

Logan was the son of an Aberdeen merchant who had pursued his business there at a time when other Highlanders such as the learned Gregorys graced that city, while many Highlanders found more humble occupations in the towns during the whole-sale exodus from their glens. If the merchant's forbears came from the north, then they probably belonged to the tribe of Lobans, Lobhans or Logans of Easter Ross, in the neighbourhood of Clan Munro territory. They possessed a legendary hero named Gilligorm, slain by the Frasers in no particular century. His widow gave birth to a deformed son who was called *Crotair Mac Gilligorm* and entered the Celtic Church in which priests were permitted to marry. He was educated by the monks of Beauly Priory, founded the churches of Kilmuir in Skye and Kilchrinin in Glenelg, and fathered a son whom he called *Gille Fhinnein*, the Devotee of Saint Finnan. The children of the Devotee became the *Clann Mac Gill'innein*, Clan Maclennan, and thus oral tradition coupled the Logans and Maclennans, although there is no historical evidence to connect them. Like the legends of the Brahan seer, that of Gilligorm contains a serious flaw in sup-posing that there were Frasers in the neighbourhood at the time when he was said to have been killed by them.

But as in the case of several other clan names, that of Logan could have reached Aberdeen from an entirely different, southern source. For there were the Logans of Restelrig, whose worthy knights Sir Robert and Sir Walter accompanied the Good Sir James Douglas to the Holy Land with the heart of King Robert Bruce, and died with Douglas in Spain in the year 1329. Another

Sir Robert married a daughter of the first Stewart sovereign and became Admiral of Scotland, but the dynasty of Restalrig was later outlawed and extinguished. Nevertheless, Logans have lived in Lothian from that day to this. If James of Aberdeen belonged to this stock, his name still deserves to be commemorated among those of the clans whose tartans he was instrumental in establishing.

What neither James Logan nor anyone else ever recovered was a single one of those sett sticks with notches cut into them, which would have provided the imperishable evidence of ancient weaving patterns. They were useless when the dress was proscribed — they might even have been considered incriminating evidence — and they could be used as kindling. Even so, it is astonishing that not one has survived. For want of them, odd pieces of tartan that happened to have been preserved since before the proscription sometimes provided the basis for a clan sett. The waistcoat that Alexander and Flora MacDonald of Kingsburgh gave to Prince Charles when he was a fugitive in Skye became a treasured relic, and has provided the sett of the MacDonald of Kingsburgh tartan.

The oddest source of clan tartans was the pair of brothers who believed that they were the heirs of the Jacobite royal house and called themselves the Sobieski Stolberg Stuarts, although their actual surname was Allan, a sept name of Clanranald. Since they never attempted to profit by their pretensions (in the manner of His Serene Highness Prince Gregor of Poyais), nobody sought to unmask them. Fraser of Lovat accommodated them in a property at Aigeis by the Beauly River where they could enjoy their strange, medieval life-style. Here they were able to build up their impressive knowledge of Highland history, which lent credence to their production of seventy-five clan tartans in the *Vestiarium Scoticum*, supposedly based on a sixteenth-century manuscript. However spurious, their tartans were not less 'authentic' than most of the others, the principal difference being that theirs had not been chosen by a chief. But they were based on a profound knowledge of the craft form, and many of them have been officially accepted since. In Inveraray Castle can be seen their Campbell of Argyll tartan, woven to their specification on the orders of Mac Cailein Mór.

A few years later there appeared McIain's illustrations to James Logan's *The Clans of the Scottish Highlands*. These ever-popular pictures represented the Gael with legs like Rob Roy's (but with their thighs covered by the kilt as Victorian propriety required) and expressions at once stern and spiritual. There were also fanciful portraits of demure ladies, wearing all sorts of discreet fashions that adapted the use of the tartan to contemporary taste.

The conventional rule that David Stewart of Garth appears to have done most to establish, giving a chief the responsibility for ordaining the tartan of his clan, is still observed. In the present decade Sir Iain Moncreiffe of that Ilk has ordained a sett that did not exist before for his name, while the 14th Earl of Dundonald has determined which is the proper Cochrane tartan. Now that the dress of the Gael has been adopted as Scotland's national costume, the recognised head of a Lowland name may evidently bestow a particular tartan on folk whose forbears never wore it. In the southern Border country such clans as Armstrongs, Elliots and Scotts possess their own tartan, though not the Turnbulls because no chief of that name can be found. It was not so in earlier times. Had the Border folk worn this costume, their wives would have exercised their own fancy in designing setts just as Highland women did.

As for the form of the dress, the chiefs and other leaders of Gaelic society have naturally been its arbiters ever since these copied Roman fashions in unconquered Ireland. More recently, some have exercised a posthumous influence through their portraits, and those that were painted before the proscription have naturally been studied with the greatest interest. Richard Waitt's portraits, executed around the time of the 1715 rebellion, are particularly valuable for their delineation of costume, although he was an indifferent artist. The most famous of them are those commissioned by the Grant Chief, especially as they include his ferocious-looking champion and his piper. A few decades later the more distinguished artist Allan Ramsay was assembling his gallery: the Chief of Clan Duff wearing trews and plaid, the 4th Earl of Loudoun wearing the red tartan of the regiment he raised in 1745, Flora MacDonald in a tartan costume. His English contemporary Joshua Reynolds painted Archibald Montgomerie, who belonged to Ayrshire but was the brother-in-law of Sir Alexander MacDonald of Sleat, and raised the 78th Highlanders. While these court painters delineated their fashionable subjects, civilian and military, David Allan was depicting the more homely scenes of Highland life, in which he preserved the everyday dress of ordinary people.

Henry Raeburn was born after Highland dress had been proscribed, and lived until the year after its triumph at the royal visit to Edinburgh in 1822. So it was his brush that expressed the flamboyance of the tartan craze at its full flood. He did not live to paint George IV as the Chief of Chiefs, as he was ordered to do — that was left to David Wilkie — but Raeburn executed the most famous portrait of a chief of this era, the arrogant, theatrical Alasdair MacDonell of Glengarry.

At least as illuminating as all these portraits are the illustrations of the Gael in military uniform. About a hundred years after the men of Mackay's Regiment had been depicted in Germany, where their appearance created such a sensation during the Thirty Years War, the British War Office published its manual in 1742, showing how Highland dress should be worn by soldiers of the 42nd Regiment. One was depicted from the rear, showing how the belted plaid was held in position by a belt round the waist, its upper half drawn over the shoulders as any civilian Highlander would have worn it. Another figure was drawn from the side, with the upper half of the plaid hanging down so as to demonstrate that this was longer than the amount of kilted material below the belt, and fell half-way down the calf. A year later, when Highland troops were posted to Europe, foreigners took to depicting them once more in a most graphic frieze that captures their appearance on the march.

The kilt below the waist was still the same single rug as the plaid above it. But by the time these illustrations were made, an Englishman named Thomas Rawlinson had come to Glengarry to conduct iron smelting, and there he had adopted Highland dress. The climate there is an exceedingly wet one, and he discovered that when he became drenched with rain he could not remove his upper garment without being deprived of its lower half also. He hit upon the solution of dividing it in two where it had been held in place by the belt. This had the added advantage that the kilt could be sewn permanently into pleats, instead of having to be folded every time it was put on: which seemed so sensible to Iain Macdonall of Glengarry that he adopted Rawlinson's modification, and so helped to popularise the kilt as it is worn today.

Such is the origin of the claim that an Englishman invented the kilt. The part he played is not in doubt, and he deserves credit for it. He did not invent the kilt, but he introduced an improvement in its design, such as a foreigner is apt to contribute in any society.

The conventional rule that tartans can only be ordained by chiefs has had its disadvantages. In the fields of literature and music the Scottish clans have produced possibly the longest dynasties of hereditary practitioners on record, in the MacMhuirichs and MacCrimmons, but they possess no chiefs to invest these resounding Gaelic names with a tartan of their own. It has been objected that they were merely the dependents of other clan chiefs, but this could be said of a great many other clans which possess their own setts. The Chief of Chiefs might have remedied the matter, but while Queen Victoria did not neglect to ordain a Johore tartan and to decorate Balmoral as though she were another of the Sobieski Stolberg Stuarts, neither the MacMhuirichs nor the MacCrimmons have been favoured either by her notice, or by that of her successors.

The descendants of the thirteenth-century Murach Albanach were represented in 1800 by Lachlann MacMhuirich, who proved to be the last of his line. Since the muniments of the Lords of the Isles had vanished and the library of the Beatons been lost, it is a tragedy that the Celtic enthusiasts were too busy tartan-hunting to save the MacMhuirich Gaelic manuscript collection before it was cut up for tailor's strips. By this time the very name of Scotland's learned clan was being bowdlerised to Currie, still a common one in South Uist where the MacMhuirich bards once lived under the patronage of MacDonald of Clanranald. Many crossed the Atlantic during the nineteenth-century clearances, and a large proportion of these settled in Nova Scotia. Here Chief Justice Lauchlan Currie died in 1969, after adding lustre to the long record of his clan in the field of Gaelic learning.

Scotland's musical clan, the MacCrimmons, have not as certain origins as the MacMhuirichs. They can only be supposed to have arrived in Skye from Harris in the Outer Hebrides early enough to be already numerous there by 1580, when they became involved in a feud between the MacLeods and the Mathesons. This was when the bagpipe was supplanting that gentle instrument of peace, the clarsach.

The bagpipe was indeed a weapon of war, not only because its music could be such a stirring incitement to battle, but inasmuch as its piercing notes could communicate specific messages over long distances. It was not unknown for a piper to have his fingers cut off by the enemy as a precaution like the spiking of guns or the dismantling of walls. After Culloden a piper lost more than his fingers, as an indirect tribute to the efficacy of his instrument. His name was James Reid, and he was amongst those captured and tried at York for his part in the Jacobite uprising. He pleaded that as a piper he was a non-combatant, since he went into battle unarmed. The court ruled that the bagpipe was a military weapon, and so James Reid was condemned to death and hanged. It was one of the many enormities in the aftermath of Culloden that he and his companions were taken over the Border to be tried in an English court. But it is doubtful whether the judgment concerning the bagpipe was unsound.

Scotland's national instrument is to be found in many other parts of the world, based as it is on the reed, which has been adapted for musical purposes in all river civilisations; while the retention of air in a bladder has been developed by a number of mountain peoples. Other countries of Europe possess the bagpipe, and Italy and Germany are among those that have evolved a richer musical tradition than Scotland, so that it is the more extraordinary that Scots should have exploited this instrument as no other peoples in the world have done. And the clan that played the most influential part in this development was that of the MacCrimmons. Earlier compositions than theirs survive (such as the fifteenth-century Munro tune called *Blar Bealach nam Brog*), but it was Donald Mór MacCrimmon who pioneered the form of theme and variations which is now called pibroch. The original Gaelic term *piobaireachd* means no more than piping, and it dervies from the same Latin root *pipa* as the English word does. It is the Gaelic word for the chanter of the bagpipe that is of ancient Celtic derivation, for *feadan* means also a reed or a water channel.

A date and a spectacular occasion are given to Donald Mór's first celebrated pibroch. The Chief of Dunvegan was Ruaridh Mór MacLeod, fortunately a most astute ruler at a time when the Mackenzies were closing in for the kill in Lewis, the Gordons were cheerfully implementing the anti-Gaelic policies of James VI, and Archibald the Grim was seizing every available pretext to plant his Campbells in other people's property. Mac Cailein Mór was far the greatest danger to MacLeod, since his house had acquired the feudal superiority of Skye. But perhaps Ruaridh Mór thought that he could quarrel with his neighbour MacDonald of Sleat without provoking his superior, since any assault on a MacDonald was in Campbell interests.

If so, he found himself mistaken when an order arrived from Edinburgh that Ruaridh Mór of Dunvegan and MacDonald of Sleat should hand themselves over to the King's two Lieutenants, Argyll and Huntly. The rivals had the good sense to sink their differences at once, and celebrated their reconciliation in 1603 in three weeks of festivity at Dunvegan. Such extravagant gestures were not uncommon amongst people who rarely did anything by halves, but on this occasion there was a feature never to be forgotten. Donald Mór MacCrimmon, piper to Ruaridh Mór, composed his *Failte nan Leodach*, MacLeod's Welcome, which proved to be the foundation of the art of pibroch as the MacCrimmons were henceforth to compose, perform and teach it.

It proved auspicious also in another way. While the MacLeods of Lewis fell victims to the Mackenzies, those of Skye live still in Dunvegan today, Chiefs of the whole Clan Leod. After Islay had fallen to the Campbells, the MacDonalds of Sleat became the Chiefs of Clan Donald and remain so today.

Another of MacCrimmon's compositions commemorates a very different sort of episode. To avenge the murder of his brother he crossed from Skye to Kintail, and took part in the punitive raid in which a number of people were burned in their homes. He is said to have composed his exultant pibroch *A Flame of Wrath* to celebrate this act of revenge. Whether or not Donald Mór was compelled to flee from Skye and seek asylum in Strathnaver as a result, he was certainly piper to the Chief of Mackay by the year 1612. It is typical of the misfortunes of a society whose crime record alone held any interest to the distant administration, that this pioneer among European composers was noticed only in connection with a brush with the law, in which he became involved with Mackay during that year. Edinburgh, which resounded to the strains of the bagpipe during George IV's visit, and is now the seat of the military school of piping, knew nothing of the manner in which Donald Mór MacCrimmon planted his art in Strathnaver.

He had been taught piping by his father and passed his skill to his son Patrick Mór, who composed the famous elegy for Ruaridh Mór, the revered MacLeod Chief. He is believed to have been the author not only of the pibroch, but also of the words and air, adapted for a sung lament. This was to become another Highland art, the composition of words and tune adapted to the musical idiom of pibroch, and Patrick Mór's lament for Ruaridh Mór of Dunvegan was to be an inspiration to every poet and musician of the future, none of whom were ever able to excel it.

Sir Roderick, 15th MacLeod of MacLeod, as Ruaridh was known in English, well deserved such a tribute since he succeeded in bringing his lands and dependants safely through all the dangers of James VI's reign, and so provided the MacCrimmons with a stable base for the development of their art. In 1614 he visited

James VI in London and received a knighthood from him, bringing home the communion cup with its London silver mark of 1613 that remains in the local parish church. In his castle he kept a rather different kind of drinking vessel, as Boswell was to remark when he visited it in Dr Johnson's company. 'We looked at Rorie More's horn, which is a large cow's horn with the mouth of it ornamented with silver. It holds rather more than a bottle and a half. Every Laird of MacLeod, it is said, must as a proof of his manhood drink it off full of claret without taking it from his right arm. He holds the small end of it backwards, and so keeps it at his mouth.' Doubtless MacDonald of Sleat was invited to perform the same feat in the course of *MacLeod's Welcome*.

Ruaridh Mór died in 1626 and was buried at Fortrose, where the Brahan Seer prophesied that the graveyard might one day overflow. The Gaelic chronicler saluted him as 'the best Gael in Scottish Gaeldom in his time.' Before the century was out, his successor would receive very different Gaelic comment, that he was impoverishing his clansmen by raising their rents to pay for his extravagances abroad.

But this change, which represented the fulfilment of Stewart policy in turning Highland chiefs into anglicised absentees, did not immediately affect the MacCrimmons. Patrick Mór and his son Patrick Òg consolidated their family's reputation as teachers, exponents and composers of pibroch. Patrick Mór's most cele-brated composition is his *Lament for the Children*, a reminder of the epidemics that could decimate a family in those days, for one of them carried off six of his seven sons. But Patrick Òg survived, whose most admired lament commemorates Iain Garbh, John MacLeod of Raasay.

His death occurred in about 1672 in circumstances that were long remembered and richly embellished by the story-teller. From his isle of Raasay, which lies between Skye and the main-land, Iain Garbh had sailed in his *birlinn* or war galley with sixteen of his kinsmen to attend a christening in Lewis. After a merry bout of drinking he and his companions set off to make their return journey across the hazardous Minch in a northerly gale, and were all drowned when their boat capsized within sight of their destination. It was said that one of them had heard an unearthly voice the previous night, warning them three times that those who sailed to Raasay would be drowned. But the report which reached James Fraser, Minister of Kirkhill near Inverness, led him to record that 'drunkenness did the mischief.'

Patrick Òg, who immortalised this tragedy, was particularly

celebrated as a teacher. Among his students was Charles MacArthur, of a clan of hereditary pipers who had their school either in Islay or in the isle of Ulva, and who were to rival the MacCrimmons themselves in their position as hereditary pipers to the MacDonalds of Sleat. Patrick Òg also taught Mackay pipers, whose clan had received their inspiration from his grandfather, and who subsequently provided the hereditary pipers to the Mackenzies of Gairloch. The most famous of these was John Mackay, known as *Am Piobaire Dall*, the blind piper, who also studied under Patrick Òg. No doubt the blind piper learned the skill of Patrick Òg's father in composing both a pibroch and a song to a related tune, for he practised the same art, notably in his *Lament for Choire an Easain*.

The blind piper lived to a great age, from 1666 until 1754, and consequently heard the lament by Malcolm MacCrimmon, Patrick Òg's most gifted son, for his brother Donald Bàn who was killed in the Forty-Five. Donald Bàn himself is said to have composed that most haunting of laments, *Cha till MacCruimein*, MacCrimmon will not Return, to which his fiancée contributed the words. But since Donald Bàn left a widow, the latter attribution appears fanciful.

By this time the MacCrimmon college of piping was established at Borreraig, where six generations of this musical clan taught before it closed. They did not write down their music, but preserved the immemorially old Celtic art of memory training, transmitting pibroch in an intricate system of mouth-sounds called *cainntearachd*, which means chanting. They were incurring the risk inherent in oral tradition, which must perish in the end unless it is written down in time, and the danger was increased by the fact that there were three different systems of *cainntearachd* in use, that of the MacCrimmons, of the MacArthurs, and of Campbells who established a separate school and had written down their pibroch notation by 1816. Once again, the Campbells triumphed by accommodating themselves to the amenities of the modern world: their collection, containing sixty-four pibroch unknown elsewhere, remains available for study.

The entire MacCrimmon corpus of music, by contrast, was placed in jeopardy when the MacLeod Chief withdrew part of his endowment from the MacCrimmons in a time of financial stringency. Malcolm's son Iain Dubh was then running the college at Borreraig, and he left Skye in disgust and only returned, years later, to die in Glendale. Boswell and Johnson heard no MacCrimmon music at Dunvegan during their visit in 1773.

But the piper's art was placed in jeopardy by something more serious than the withdrawal of MacLeod patronage. The penal statutes that followed the defeat of the last Jacobite uprising at Culloden proscribed the bagpipe with arms and Highland dress, as an instrument of war and incitement to sedition. The question arises, whether the embargo was strictly enforced in the lands of the Hanoverian clans whose own leaders were generally left to administer justice with little outside interference. Evasion of the law is not generally advertised as often as it is practised, but it is suggestive that after Culloden the Hanoverian Campbells and Mackays emerged as prominant practitioners of pibroch, and there is stray evidence to account for this.

In the Mackay country Rob Donn, the bard, made several references to his friend 'the piper to the Chief' during the period of the proscription. There was no one in the remote province of Strathnaver to enforce the law over the head of the 4th Lord Reay, Chief of Mackay. Near to his home in Durness stood the manse of the Minister, whose young son, Joseph MacDonald, must have been composing his celebrated analysis of pibroch sometime before 1760. Durness appears to have been a nest of seditious musical activity. In his autobiography John MacDonald, who became a Pipe-Major in the Army, inadvertently disclosed another in mid-Argyll when he recorded that he had learned piping there in the 1760s.

But above all, John MacDonald's art was succoured by the institution in which he was to practise it himself. Iain Dubh MacCrimmon's younger brother Donald Ruadh emigrated to America in 1772, where he became a Lieutenant in the Caledonia Volunteers six years later. Then occurred the dramatic episode when MacCrimmon did return, to welcome General Norman MacLeod of MacLeod back to Dunvegan from India in 1799. In honour of the occasion he performed *MacLeod's Welcome*, which his great-great-grandfather had composed for the reconciliation between Ruaridh Mór and MacDonald of Sleat nearly two centuries earlier.

Walter Scott saw Donald Ruadh when he visited Dunvegan in 1815 and commented: 'he is an old man, a Lieutenant in the Army and a most capital piper, possessing about two hundred tunes, most of which will probably die with him, as he declines to have any of his sons instructed in the art.' A few years later Scott was arranging the pantomime of George IV's visit to Edinburgh, and urged the Chief of MacLeod to attend with some of his clansmen. That was when a citizen complained that 'Sir Walter Scott has ridiculously made us appear to be a nation of Highlanders, and the bagpipe and the tartan are the order of the day.' It would have been less ridiculous if MacLeod could have brought with him the living ornament of the longest musical dynasty in Europe.

Of Donald Ruadh's sons, Patrick became a Captain in the Caledonia Volunteers and subsequently a Lieutenant in the Cameron Highlanders. After distinguishing himself in the Peninsular War under Wellington he was appointed barrack-master in Sierra Leone where he perished within the year. His brother Donald emigrated to Canada and became the progenitor of the MacCrimmon sect that multiplied in Ontario. Such is the clan that possesses no tartan for want of a chief to ordain one while the MacArthurs have their own tartan, and even the province of Ontario has its own sett.

One of the strangest elements in this story is the inferior status that has been accorded in the past to musicians whose art is now treated with such reverence. How recently attitudes have changed can be illustrated by an incident involving a MacGillivray.

The MacGillivrays were already one of the principal clans in the west when Somerled drove out the Norsemen, and then died fighting against the King of Scots in 1164. When Alexander II subdued Argyll in 1222 the *Clan Mhic Gillebhrath* became scattered, and while some remained in the Isles, others moved east into the Grampians. Tradition relates that Gillivray was one of these, whose clan sought the protection of the Mackintosh Chief by joining the confederation of Clan Chattan. When the Jacobite uprising of 1745 occurred, Mackintosh held a Hanoverian commission which he refused to dishonour, so Alexander the MacGillivray Chief died in his stead, leading the men of Clan Chattan at Culloden. Thereafter the MacGillivray Chiefs became impoverished, until one died in 1852 leaving all the farms on his estate to his tenants, and his last known successor disappeared in New Guinea.

But during the present century a sept of this clan have built up a world-famous herd of cattle at Calrossie north of Inverness, while Donald MacGillivray the younger of Calrossie has also earned distinction as an exponent of pibroch. His name was already associated with the bagpipe, for a set of pipes was found on the field of Culloden after the battle and given to the MacGillivrays who were pipers in the isle of Barra. These presented the instrument to the Highland Museum at Fort William after its establishment there, and it has been played subsequently on numerous occasions, including the Empire Exhibition which was held in Glasgow in 1938.

During the reign of the late Dame Flora MacLeod of MacLeod, Donald MacGillivray was invited to perform at Dunvegan. Evidently none of her family recognised him on his arrival, and asked him who he was. He replied in his Highland speech that he was a piper, and was instantly directed to the servants' premises, where he was able to enjoy the society of others as Gaelic as himself. Meanwhile, in the rooms of the castle in which a clan gathering was assembled, Dame Flora looked in vain for Young Calrossie, and finally asked her daughter whether he had been seen. He was to perform on the pipes, she explained. The dreadful error was exposed, in consternation they sent to the kitchen to retrieve the piper who was also the son of a Laird, and so MacGillivray exchanged its society for the social world of which Boswell had been able to remark to Johnson when he came to Dunvegan, 'our entertainment here was in so elegant a style, and reminded my fellow-traveller so much of England, that he became quite joyous.'

CHAPTER ELEVEN

Ashes and the Phoenix

By their very nature, the clans depended on their chiefs, the children on their tribal father. The intimacy of this relationship was illustrated by Martin the Hebridean, writing a little before 1700, by many examples such as this one. 'When a tenant's wife in this or the adjacent islands dies, he then addresses himself to MacNeil of Barra representing his loss, and at the same time desires that he would be pleased to recommend a wife to him, without which he cannot manage his affairs, nor beget followers to MacNeil, which would prove a public loss to him. Upon this representation, MacNeil finds out a suitable match for him.'

Women could solicit the chief's help equally. 'When a tenant dies, the widow addresseth herself to MacNeil in the same manner, who likewise provides her with a husband, and they are married without any further courtship.' Such day-to-day responsibilities required that the chief should reside amongst his clansmen, combining in himself the offices of magistrate and welfare officer, estate manager and taxation official.

His capacity to fulfil these duties depended on his concern and on his resources, since most of his clansmen had no contractual relationship with him, only the fragile claim of 'kindliness.' The title to property of the majority of Gaels flowed solely from their chief's, and each of these belonged to the feudal system of landownership that had been imposed on Gaeldom, with its structure of subinfeudation. There were the regalities, the feudal superiorities that made one chief the vassal of another. There were chiefs such as the fortunate Munros who held their titles directly from the crown, and unfortunate ones like the Mackays who held theirs from the Gordons. Instead of rationalising the system of ownership to the tribal lands on an equitable basis, successive Stewart sovereigns had made an appalling mess of it.

By the eighteenth century the status of the Highland peasant contrasted dismally with that of similar societies in Scandinavia. Here, in a comparable environment, the farmer generally owned the land he tilled. In Sweden, indeed, Parliament had actually possessed an Estate of peasants since the Middle Ages. In

Scotland the Shetland and Orkney Islands, which had remained under Scandinavian rule until the fifteenth century, originally enjoyed the same blessing of peasant proprietorship. But after they had passed to the Scottish crown, the Stewarts made the same mess here as elsewhere, bestowing the islands on illegitimate relatives who destroyed the titles of their free farmers and reduced them to servitude and poverty.

Only the office of chief, modified over the centuries, served to protect the Gael against the rigours of the feudal system, and this required that the chief should place his undefined patriarchal obligations before his absolute feudal rights. It was a great deal to expect of a man who might be generally believed to hold his property in trust for his clan, but who actually owned it without any such restrictive covenant. It proved a great deal too much to expect from the majority of chiefs. The destruction of the old clan society was to be as much their doing as the result of any external influence.

Even the MacLeods of Harris and Skye felt the wind, despite the skill with which their 15th Chief Ruaridh Mór steered them through the dangers of James VI's reign. The 17th Chief moved to Edinburgh just before the restoration of Charles II, and the bill for his clothes alone in the year in which he attended the court of King Charles would have supplied the salaries of a dozen ministers. So Clan Leod began to taste the ills of insolvency and absenteeism on the part of their chiefs. There was a respite when this one died prematurely and his brother the 18th Chief proved long-lived and prudent. He kept his clan clear of the dangers of the revolution of 1688, and succeeded in sinking three-quarters of the debt that had all but wrecked the estate. But his son the 19th Chief doubled it again in a brief reign of six years. Once again it was a brother who succeeded as the 20th Chief. He chose to live economically in Perth, but although this helped to avoid plunging his clan into deeper ruin, they were paying their rents to support an absentee when the eighteenth century opened.

There is an eloquent comment on this situation in the Gaelic elegy which Roderick Morrison composed for the 18th Chief who had laboured to rescue the clan estate, comparing him to his spendthrift son. Morrison was known as Ruaridh Dall, because he was blind, and also as the Clarsair Dall, since he was the last of the distinguished bards who composed and sang for the clarsach or little harp. He belonged to the family of the brieves of Lewis, though it is uncertain whether he himself belonged to the branch of Lewis or Harris. Morrison described the extravagant ornaments of dress, the decorated belt and gold buckles of the 19th Chief, for which he declared that he would be compelled to pay a higher rent. His strictures contain a curious echo of the classical writers in their comments on the love of display of the Celtic male.

Pure chance gave the MacLeods a respite when Norman succeeded as the 22nd Chief in 1706, a mere baby, and continued in that office until his death in 1772. During his minority the estate was so well managed that much of its debt was liquidated, and although a few MacLeods did join the Jacobites in 1715, the safety of the clan as a whole was not jeopardised. Norman MacLeod himself resisted the attempt to lure him into supporting the uprising of 1745, and so saved his people from the consequences of its defeat.

The most bizarre incident in which the 22nd Chief became involved during the decades between the two rebellions concerned the abduction of a woman. Small Hebridean islands had been found convenient dumping grounds for unwanted women over a long period, and MacLeod possessed a particularly remote one in St Kilda. In 1715 the Jacobite Chief of Clan Donnchaidh, Robertson of Struan, kidnapped his sister Margaret, to whom their father had left a sum of money that he needed for himself. Fraternal affection made him unwilling to murder her, so he bribed the MacLeod steward of St Kilda to take Margaret there, after he had brought her as far as Uist himself. But she managed to escape back to Perthshire, and although her brother caught her again he never succeeded in planting her on St Kilda.

It can be seen that the pastime of marooning ladies on rocky islands like so many Lorelei was not simply a practice of the beastly Hebrideans. Even an Edinburgh judge adopted the same solution when he felt that he had suffered enough from a drunken, violent and mentally unbalanced wife. His name was Lord Grange, and he was a brother of the Earl of Mar who led the Jacobite uprising of 1715; he also possessed a character that was not esteemed much more highly than that of his spouse.

In 1732 he arranged for Lady Grange to be carried off to the home of a mainland MacLeod, whose clansmen accommodated her first in a little isle called Heiskir. It did not belong to their Chief, but to his neighbour and rival MacDonald of Sleat, evidence that there were certain matters over which the two clans could agree harmoniously. But the family who already lived on Heiskir appealed to MacDonald after two years that the eccentricities of Lady Grange had almost driven them insane, and so MacDonald appealed to MacLeod who generously offered that ultimate lodging, St Kilda. He ordered two of his clansmen to conduct her there, and there she remained for eight years, attempting to devise a means of escape.

Finally she hid a letter in a ball of wool that she had spun, and sent it for sale in Inverness. Its message was read and a ship was despatched to St Kilda to rescue her. But the jungle telegraph was not less efficient then than it is today in the Highlands, and before the ship arrived, Lady Grange had been whisked away. MacLeod was now heavily compromised, as so many chiefs had been before him, by roguery in the seat of justice in Edinburgh. Lord Grange was able to use his influence on the bench to bar any proceedings after the fate of his wife had become public knowledge there, but MacLeod was exposed to blackmail over his part in the affair, at the same time as remaining lumbered with the person of Lady Grange. The treatment she had received had not proved beneficial to her mental condition, though she did live on in Skye until 1745 and became in her latter years a perfectly harmless lunatic.

Just before the death of Norman the 22nd Chief there occurred the dispute over the terms of the MacCrimmon tenure of Borreraig which led to the closing of their college of piping there. A few years later, Johnson and Boswell witnessed the emigration fever that was infecting Skye. But up to this time the experience of the MacLeods in their islands was rather different from that of many clans on the mainland opposite.

Among these were the Camerons of Lochiel in Lochaber, whose tenure of their clan lands had been so precarious in the past. Mary, Queen of Scots had appointed the Mackintosh chiefs hereditary stewards of Lochaber. Archibald the Grim of Argyll had established a feudal superiority of Lochaber in about 1608. The Gordons of Huntly possessed ancient claims to territory within the province. That long-lived Chief Sir Ewen Cameron of Lochiel was lucky as well as skilful to die unscathed in 1719, after narrowly escaping disaster for his Jacobite sympathies. His son had already joined Mackintoshes and Gordons, MacDonalds and Mackenzies in the uprising of 1715, and fled to France after its failure to enjoy the hollow grandeur of a Jacobite peerage. Compared to the MacLeods, the Camerons entered the eighteenth century in a climate of insecurity.

Nor were they the only Lochaber clan to do so. A sept of the Macmillans of Knapdale to the south had been settled here since the fifteenth century, where they became dependants of the Clan Chattan and bound themselves as 'hereditary servants' of the Mackintosh Chief. Consequently they provided a hostile element when Lochiel sought the protection of his Campbell superior against the pressure of Gordon and Mackintosh, to the extent that Lochiel borrowed money from Argyll with the object of attempting to buy them out of their properties. However, Macmillans are believed to have fought alongside Camerons in the Jacobite cause at Killiecrankie, and again in 1715.

The most significant outcome of their intervention in these conflicts is that they induced one of the contestants, William Macmillan, to abandon the clan lands and seek his fortune at Dumfries near the southern border. In the same neighbourhood his descendant Kirkpatrick Macmillan, a blacksmith, invented the bicycle and confounded the pessimistic predictions of his neighbours by riding it to Glasgow.

There were other splinter groups of clans in the Cameron country, refugee MacGregors, and MacPhees from the clan of Colonsay which had once provided the keepers of the records of the Lords of the Isles. A sept of the MacLachlans from Strath-lachan in Argyll were settled here long before they joined the Jacobites at Killiecrankie and in 1715. All shared the same uncertain future when Sir Ewen of Lochiel died in 1719, and his grandson became leader of his clan while Donald's father spent the remainder of his life in a comfortable and ennobled exile.

Donald became known as the Gentle Lochiel, and has been invested with a reputation as the paragon of Highland chiefs, though this has not gone unchallenged. The Pretender invested him with plenary powers in Scotland to negotiate with the clans to support his restoration, but when Prince Charles arrived in 1745, lacking any military provision for an uprising, Donald sent his brother Dr Archibald Cameron to advise him to return to France. Prince Charles invited Donald to his presence and persuaded him to change his mind. When the Jacobite standard was raised in Glenfinnan, the Gentle Lochiel appeared with between seven and eight hundred men, and his support was believed to have influenced others and tipped the balance in favour of the fatal undertaking.

But the romantic picture of a devoted clan, uniting enthusiastically behind a beloved chief in support of the Catholic faith and the legitimate Stewart sovereign has been debunked. There is evidence that Lochiel used the threat of imprisonment, death and burning of homes to compel his dependants to take up arms, many of whom were extremely reluctant. This was no more than what other chiefs were doing, in this as in the 1715 uprising. Nor were Lochiel's men by any means all Camerons: he was able to use his threats to compel those who owed him no loyalty as their Chief. The MacLachlans were capable of providing a company, the Macmillans three hundred men. A certain Donald MacPherson deposed after the rebellion had been crushed that he had been told, 'if he did not join the Prince, Lochiel would hang him.'

But the gallantry of those who fought their last fight at Culloden is beyond denigration. Lochiel was totally disabled when both his ankles were shattered by grape-shot, and it is believed to have been John Macmillan of Murlaggan and his brother Ewen who carried him from the field, mounted him on a horse before the enemy dragoons could seize him, and led him down the Great Glen to his home. This was a wooden house that stood above the Bay of Achnacarry at the southern end of Loch Lochy. Here his clansmen had managed to bury his silver and jewellery before the Hanoverian troops arrived. Lochiel watched from a hiding-place as they looted everything that they could load on the wagons they had brought for the purpose, then burned the house to the ground. The Gentle Lochiel fled to France, where he received the command of a French regiment and died in 1748.

He was more fortunate than others. His brother Alexander was a Catholic priest whom he had forbidden to minister to the people on his estates. Although a non-combatant, he was executed after Culloden. So was his brother Dr Archibald, who had contributed his medical services. It is one of the most disgraceful episodes of the Forty-Five that although Dr Archibald Cameron was not apprehended until eight years afterwards, he was nevertheless hanged, drawn and quartered, the last victim in Britain of that cruel and degrading form of execution.

The fate of ordinary people was correspondingly savage. From Culloden the army of the Butcher Duke of Cumberland moved to a place in the middle of the Great Glen that still bears his obscene name — Fort Augustus. Detachments were sent in all directions from here to drive in the livestock from the surrounding hills. Since people subsisted almost entirely on animal husbandry, to take from them their cattle and oxen, their horses, sheep and goats, was to condemn them to ruin and starvation. All over the green plain beside Fort Augustus the herds were gathered for the largest cattle fair in Highland history. News of the bonanza had sped south to the Scottish Lowlands and to England, and dealers rushed to the place to divide the spoils.

The hungry natives crept out of the hills to watch, and some tried to trade the few possessions they had left for food from the stores that had been brought to Fort Augustus to feed the army. But Cumberland ordered a flogging for any soldier caught selling food to the inhabitants. Yet he did reject a proposal that a bounty of £5 should be paid for the head of any rebel brought back by his men. Plenty of people were killed who were not rebels at all, but simply unable to explain this fact in English, and wearing the Highland dress in which they could be mistaken for rebels. But to offer a prize for a head that could not speak at all in its own defence seemed, even to Butcher Cumberland, to be going too far. He compensated his troops for any disappointment they may have felt by allowing one woman to every tent of six men.

The Gentle Lochiel had a third brother who was more fortunate than the others. He was arrested after Culloden and imprisoned in Fort William. Despite the advocacy of Alexander Campbell, the Lieutenant Governor there, he was convicted, 'on very slender evidence and after very arbitrary proceedings,' and sentenced to banishment from Scotland for ten years. He became a West Indian merchant and a burgess of Glasgow, and it was perhaps his marriage to an influential Campbell's daughter that helped him to avoid a worse fate. He returned to found the sept of Fassiefern and to beget thirteen children. But his property passed to the Campbells in 1844, in intriguing circumstances.

Sir Duncan, the last Cameron of Fassiefern, possessed no legitimate heir, only a daughter born to Mary Cameron, a hen-wife who became a kitchen-maid in his house. This child was sent away to be educated, and was not told on her return who her mother was. So it came as a shock to her when she scolded a servant, who slapped her face and told her not to speak to her mother in that manner. She complained to her father who advised her to ignore feminine gossip, and reprimanded Mary Cameron. But Mary had the last laugh when Sir Duncan was persuaded to marry her in order to prevent his property from passing to collateral relatives. This he did secretly, and Mary never came to live in his home as his wife.

At his death the expectant mourners assembled there to hear his will read, and were shocked when the minister entered with the former hen-wife, to introduce her as Lady Cameron. Her daughter was already married to Alexander Campbell of Inverawe, but not before the date of her parents' marriage.

It is not hard to guess whether he was a party to the secret.

Other Campbells had enjoyed a bite of the cherry far earlier, when the lands of Lochiel were included among the forfeited estates of the rebellious Jacobites. In the year of Culloden the Chief of Mackay had sent a memorial to the government on this subject. 'As I have the right settlement of the Highlands much at heart, I beg leave to hint to you whether it would not be for the interests of the Government, and a means to establish these wild people in peace, that His Majesty should not give any of the forfeited estates in property to any subject. But all to depend on the sovereign, right factors employed with power to grant long leases, to use the people well, promote the industry and ever to plant colonies of old soldiers among them, and thereby make them taste the sweet of being free of tyrannical masters.'

There was much sound sense in this advice, and if the Mackay country also had been handed out in crown leases to the cultivators of the soil, a future Chief of Mackay would not have been able to sell the clan lands to one who would evict them from their homes in the notorious Sutherland clearances. But the present Chief was a loyal Hanoverian, safe from any danger of confiscation.

Among those who were appointed to administer the forfeited estates of Lochaber was Alexander Campbell, who held the post of Baron Baillie. But far more celebrated is Colin Campbell of Glenure, whose murder was commemorated by Duncan Macintyre in a Gaelic elegy, and by Robert Louis Stevenson in his novel *Kidnapped*. The Red Fox, as he was called, was the brother of Campbell of Barcaldine whose castle in Lorne is still inhabited, though not by his descendants. As factor of the forfeited estates, Glenure broke the regulation that no property in them should be let to anyone related to a person attainted for treason. His doing so appears to have been an act of kindness, though it led to a complaint to higher authority.

In 1752 Colin of Glenure was murdered near the Ballachulish ferry at Onich, in circumstances and for motives that have remained a mystery ever since. What is most generally agreed is that the man who was hailed before a Campbell jury at Inveraray and hanged for the crime was innocent. It was a time for settling private scores, and the two deaths may have been equally unrelated to one another and to the administrative affairs of the forfeited estates. The Red Fox was succeeded as factor by his nephew Mungo Campbell, who continued to collect evidence with Alexander the Baron Baillie about local losses suffered at the hands of Cumberland's soldiers, and the terms on which the lesser folk of Lochiel's lands had held their property. They were also kept busy proceeding against thieves, since people who have been dispossessed must take to marauding, until it becomes a way of life. Stealing was a capital offence, though some were sentenced instead to banishment to the plantations.

The penal statutes had also to be enforced, which disarmed the clans and deprived them of their national dress. These were imposed on loyal and disloyal clans alike, together with the abolition of the old feudal jurisdictions of the chiefs, and their affect was not only humiliating to Highland pride, but also served fatally to loosen the last, fragile ties that still bound clans and chiefs in mutual loyalty.

The effects rapidly became apparent everywhere, and not least on the Lochiel estates when these were restored in 1784 to the Cameron Chiefs, two years after the Chief of the Grahams, the Duke of Montrose, piloted a Bill through Parliament which restored the outlawed kilt and tartan to Scotland. Donald Cameron of Lochiel was a minor at the time, and did not visit his patrimony until he had come of age in 1790. He arrived, a foreigner, to act the part of a brutal landlord. The rents of his tenancies had more than doubled since the forfeiture of Lochiel, and Macmillans were among the first to arrange systematic emigration to Canada for whole communities. Archibald Macmillan chartered three ships in 1802 which carried over a thousand men with their families down the Firth of Lorne to begin a new life in Canada.

It might have been possible to suppose that these folk were influenced solely by such considerations as the rise of population, pressing on the limited economic resources of the region, and that their recently restored Chief had nothing to do with their decision to emigrate. But a letter that Archibald Macmillan wrote in 1805 proves otherwise. 'We cannot help looking to our native spot with sympathy and feelings which cannot be described, yet I have no hesitation in saying that considering the arrangements that daily take place, and the total extinction of the ties twixt Chief and clan, we are surely better off to be out of the reach of such unnatural tyranny.'

This was no isolated comment. At home in Lochaber, Allan Cameron observed the building of a grand new castle for the Chief, on the spot where the old wooden home of his ancestors had been destroyed after Culloden. To meet its expenses he was adopting the method that many Highland chiefs were resorting to at this time, selling the clan lands to foreign sheep-farmers who could only begin their enterprises after the native inhabitants had been cleared from them. In 1803 Allan Cameron reported, 'Lochiel's lands are in the papers to be let at Whitsuntide first, nothing but spurring and hauling, and I'm afraid the tenantry have no chance . . . The grand castle at Achnacarry is going on with great speed. The estimate, I am told, is from eight to nine thousand pounds sterling.'

The eviction of their clansmen by the Cameron Chiefs culminated in a dramatic episode, in the notice of ejection which Donald of Lochiel served on Samuel Cameron in 1884. It led to violence for which he was taken to court and sentenced to a fine, with the alternative of imprisonment. Lochiel had perhaps forgotten the episode by the time he was inspecting the 79th Queen's Own Cameron Highlanders in Edinburgh. This was the regiment founded by Sir Alan of Erracht, for which his wife Marsali Maclean had designed the tartan.

Lochiel asked the Colonel to present to him any member of his clan in the ranks, and the Colonel innocently ordered the son of Samuel Cameron to meet his Chief. So great was the young man's anger, and so forcefully did he express it, that he was placed under arrest, and sentenced to imprisonment for insulting and insubordinate behaviour. But when the full story became known to the officers of the regiment, they sent a piper to pipe Samuel Cameron's son out of his gaol, while it is said that Lochiel swore after this incident that there would be no more evictions on his lands. Since the Crofters' Act was passed at this time, giving the Gaelic peasantry security of tenure at last, the Chief's good intentions were by now superfluous.

His descendants are among those who have preserved the clan lands to this day despite all the hazards of the past. Colonel Sir Donald Cameron of Lochiel, a Balliol scholar with a distinguished record of public service both in war and in peace, lives among the mountainous acres that his forbears managed to hold against Campbell, Gordon and Mackintosh, and to recover from a Hanoverian sovereign. As for the descendants of his clansmen, these formed a Clan Cameron Association only a few years after the outburst of Samuel Cameron's son in Edinburgh, though in Lochaber itself they are represented chiefly by the stones of Achnacarry Castle.

'The total extinction of the ties 'twixt chief and clan' was a widespread phenomenon throughout the Highlands and islands in the aftermath of Culloden, and the Chiefs of Lochiel were so far from being among the worst offenders that they are rarely mentioned in accounts of the *Fuadach nan Gaidheal*, the dispersal of the Gaelic peoples from their homeland. The Macnab story, for instance, is a good deal more horrific.

The Macnabs had survived as many crises as any clan, particularly within the Campbell sphere of influence. They had been dispossessed completely after fighting on the wrong side in the war that King Robert Bruce won, though his son David II restored some of their former lands in Glendochart as a reward for their support. They came perilously near to suffering the fate of their kinsmen and neighbours the MacGregors during the reign of Archibald the Grim of Argyll, and were listed among the 'broken clans' by the year 1594. A few years later they were involved in an incident typical of those times.

There was a sept of the MacGregors called MacNeish who suffered severely in the persecution of their kinsfolk, and maintained themselves by raiding from remote hide-outs. Some of them fortified themselves on an island in Loch Earn, from where they waylaid a consignment of whiskey on its way to the Macnab Chief. As soon as the loss was discovered, four of Macnab's sons carried a boat for eight miles through the hills, from Loch Tay to Loch Earn, and rowed to the island to surprise the MacNeishes in the dark. The next day they brought the heads of their victims home in a sack, as well as the residue of the whiskey.

At this time the seat of the Chief was a castle on an island in the River Lochy, but it was destroyed by the troops of Oliver Cromwell after Macnab, a loyal supporter of Montrose, had died at Worcester, fighting for Charles II. Dispossessed by the Campbells, the Macnabs were restored to their lands as soon as Charles II recovered his throne.

They avoided the pitfalls of King William's usurpation in 1688 and the Jacobite risings that followed, which might have ensured them a prosperous future, especially when Francis their Chief added an inheritance from his mother to the clan resources. But by the time Francis Macnab died in 1816 he had squandered most of his assets, spread venereal disease amongst the womenfolk of the area, littered the country with over thirty of his bastards, and failed to provide a legitimate heir. None of Sir Henry Raeburn's portraits of Highland chiefs is more expressive than his delineation of this debauched turkey cock, ridiculous in all his finery as Lieutenant-Colonel of the Royal Breadalbane Volunteers.

At least he had been a resident chief, living in the house of Kinnell to which his forbears had moved after the destruction of their castle in the river, able to speak to his troops and dependants in Gaelic. He was succeeded by his nephew Archibald, who had prepared himself for the responsibilities of a Highland chiefship by a life of dissipation in London and Paris. Arriving as a foreigner to exploit the amenities of Kinnell, he increased the burdens on the encumbered estate until it would bear no more, then bolted to evade his creditors in 1820, leaving his wife and eight children behind.

The Macnab lands were sold to the Chief's principal creditor, the 4th Earl of Breadalbane, who evicted their inhabitants in order to secure richer tenants. Archibald attempted to return to the fleshpots of London but his creditors pursued him there. By the assistance of his Macnab factor he escaped to Canada, and here, to his astonished delight, he discovered that the traditional Gaelic respect for a Highland chief was not yet dead, that it might even yield fresh dividends. Several hundred of his clansmen had already emigrated to Canada and there were many other Gaels also to whom a real chief was an entertaining novelty, as he found when he was welcomed at a public dinner in Montreal.

But Macnab's interest in his clansmen abroad was not of the kind they expected. He used his rank as a chief and the social airs he had acquired in London and Paris to insinuate himself with the scions of the British aristocracy who then enjoyed the perquisites of colonial rule, almost entirely irrespective of personal merit. Through their help he obtained a grant of land in 1824 which enabled him to operate the feudal system for the last time in any part of the British Empire. He could never have attempted this unless he had found evidence of incurable gullibility on the part of Gaels still believing in the traditional bond between the tribal father and his children. Archibald Macmillan might have given them timely warning, but Canada is a large country, and he and his settlers from Lochaber lived in a different part of it.

Having left his clansmen at home to the tender mercies of Campbell of Breadalbane, he now invited them to his new settlement in Canada, sending bonds for them to sign which did indeed commit them to bondage services. But these documents would have afforded them at least some legal protection if they had not surrendered them on demand when they arrived in Canada. By 1830 Macnab had over sixty captive families in a state of vassalage to him, and was operating a tyranny as cruel as any the

Highlands had seen in the past. The final ignominy was the sight of the Chief consorting with his sluttish housekeeper, who bore him a son in addition to those he had abandoned in Scotland.

The methods by which Macnab succeeded in exploiting his clansmen for so long were finally exposed by two Buchanan brothers. The small Buchanan Clan, offspring of *Buth Chanain*, the Canon's House, occupied lands in the Lennox neighbouring Loch Lomond. In the sixteenth century they had produced George Buchanan, one of the outstanding Latinists of Europe and author of the libels that demolished the reputation of Mary, Queen of Scots, to whose son he was appointed tutor. After the Reformation, Buchanan Chiefs filled the office of parish clerks. In the eighteenth century Dugald Buchanan, schoolmaster at Kinloch Rannoch, composed the most inspired religious poetry in the Gaelic tongue. Although the Buchanans were not involved in the Jacobite risings, they too lost their ancestral lands, and many of them had crossed the Atlantic by the time Macnab arrived there.

In 1843 the Buchanan brothers in Canada secured his conviction on criminal charges which totally discredited him in the eyes of those who had wept with gratitude at the arrival of a chief twenty years earlier. The newspapers explored his unsavoury career in malicious detail, and when he brought a libel action against them, the jury assessed the damages for demolishing the character of Macnab of Macnab at £5. The Chief slunk home, to face the wife and children he had deserted so long before. Out of her personal means, his wife presented a house in Orkney to him, where he lived until his death in 1860, amongst people who could congratulate themselves that the clan system had never operated in their islands.

The disgraced Macnab lived to see James Buchanan become President of the United States, after the emancipation of his people from their clan shackles in the New World, while his kinsman Sir Allan Macnab became Prime Minister of Canada. Long afterwards, when the house of Breadalbane had dissolved in ashes, a Macnab Chief was able to purchase Kinnell House and its surrounding lands from the dismembered Campbell estates, and here another Chief still lives where his clan has vanished.

In the United States the clan spirit that survived the Atlantic crossing had been subjected to a different kind of ordeal, well illustrated by the fate of Flora MacDonald and her kinsfolk. Flora owes her immortality among the folk-heroines of the world to the events of a mere ten days of her life, in which she rescued the fugitive Prince Charles during his flight after Culloden. After she had taken him to Skye from the Outer Hebrides, he slept a night in the home of Allan MacDonald of Kingsburgh, whom Flora subsequently married. Twenty-five years later, Johnson and Boswell visited Skye, where Johnson slept in the very bed at Kingsburgh that the Prince had used, and Boswell described his saviour. 'She was a little woman of a mild and genteel appearance, mighty soft and well bred. To see Mr Samuel Johnson salute Miss Flora MacDonald was a wonderful romantic scene to me.' The sequel was less romantic.

In the following year Allan and Flora MacDonald sailed from the Clyde to settle in the Carolinas, arriving in Cumberland County when about ten thousand Highlanders were already established there. Her old stepfather came too, and her daughter Anne, married to a MacLeod. In 1775, the year after their arrival, the American War of Independence broke out.

One might suppose that Jacobites of thirty years before would have felt little sympathy for the Hanoverian cause in this conflict, or that people who had found freedom in the New World would have had no inclination to defend a distant tyranny from the old one. But the MacDonalds displayed their innate capacity for choosing the wrong side once again, and justice should at least be done to the integrity which drove them on their fatal course.

These Highlanders had all been compelled to take an oath of allegiance to the Hanoverian King as a condition for being allowed to emigrate at all. Many of them, in addition, were officers retired on half pay, and inasmuch as the army had always been a favourite profession for the younger sons of chiefs and for tacksmen such as Allan MacDonald and Flora's stepfather, it was natural for such men to obey a call to the colours without question. The clan network also operated here. Allan possessed a cousin Alexander MacDonald in New York who was a half-pay officer. He not only raised a company of Highlanders in the north, but wrote to Allan in North Carolina, inciting him to do the same. At a time when the Governor had so little authority ashore that he had to live in a ship, Allan MacDonald offered to raise the Gaels for the King.

So Flora said good-bye to her husband and her two sons when they marched away to the coast, joined by her son-in-law. The Highland force had to cross a river, and they made for a low bridge of planks in an area of wooded, swampy ground. But the patriots had already arrived there, removed the planks from the centre of the bridge and greased the timbers. They lay in hiding

beyond it, and when the Highlanders tried to rush the bridge
they were mown down in a matter of minutes. The massacre
of Moore's Creek was the first decisive victory in the American
War of Independence. Flora's husband and one of her sons were
taken prisoner, and all her family possessions were seized. She
was nearly sixty years old when she returned home penniless,
a cripple, her husband also a cripple, her son from Moore's Creek
dead from his wounds, another lost at sea. 'The cast in both my
arms are living monuments of my sufferings and distress,' she
wrote, 'and the long jail confinement which my husband under-
went has brought on such disorders that he has totally lost the
use of his legs.' Four months later she died, to become young
again in the world's memory.

Paradoxically, the MacDonalds did not suffer more severely
at the end of the day by espousing lost causes than a clan which
invariably chose the winning one. The loyalty of the Mackays to
Charles I protected them from the Gordons of Sutherland after
the restoration of Charles II. In the revolution of 1688 they
provided King William with his Commander-in-Chief in Scotland,
Hugh Mackay of Scourie, and Mackays constituted almost the
only clan levy to fight under him at Killiecrankie.

Most beneficial of all, an infant Chief succeeded in 1680 as
the 3rd Lord Reay, whose estate was managed competently
during his minority. Since one of the hazards of the clan system
was the size of a chief's family, the number of daughters to be
endowed and of sons to be provided with land, such a respite
could be enormously beneficial. As an adult, the 3rd Lord Reay
gave active support to the Hanoverian cause in 1745, and submitted that advice concerning the disposition of the forfeited
estates.

The Mackays, like the Munros (and largely through their
influence), were deeply committed to the religious settlement
which the revolution of 1688 achieved. In 1750 an observer went
so far as to assert: 'the common people of the Mackays are the
most religious of all the tribes that dwell among the mountains,
south or north.'

They were also esteemed as the most disciplined soldiers, and
if this was true, there was a good reason for it. Since the 1st Lord
Reay had taken his clan regiment to fight in the Thirty Years
War in Germany in 1628, the Mackays had maintained a per-
manent connection with the Scots Brigade in Holland. Clansmen
from Strathnaver went abroad for periods of limited service and
were replaced on their return. General Hugh Mackay commanded

the Scots Brigade in Holland when he sailed with King William in 1688, and his grandson Hugh Mackay died in Holland in 1775, a Lieutenant-General. Another of the same family became a Baron of the Netherlands in 1822, and his son was Dutch Prime Minister before succeeding to the Chiefship of Mackay.

The effect of this long and unique source of military training was remarked upon in 1750: 'the Mackays are said to be a better militia than any of the neighbouring clans, for which this is assigned as a reason.' Ten years later they gave the same impression when a body of them arrived in Inveraray. 'After a fatiguing march, they made as fine an appearance as any troops I ever beheld, and though they are but a young corps, there is scarce a regiment in His Majesty's service better disciplined.' Here was another source of security to Clan Mackay, whose young men could find lucrative employment both at home and abroad if the pressure of a rising population on local resources became too great. Some of them carried their military skills across the Atlantic, where they played a leading part in defending the colony that General Oglethorpe established in Georgia in 1732.

In the remote province of Strathnaver, if anywhere in the Highlands, it should have been possible for the ancient tribal way of life to remain viable, and for much of the eighteenth century it did so. Fortunately the details of that archaic social world have been preserved in the ample poetry of Rob Donn, the most eloquent voice ever heard in the Mackay country. Rob Donn's testimony is unique in depicting both men and women whose lives were as free, as happy, as culturally rich and as economically secure as those of any community have ever been. Here is no outsider's picture, such as Dr Johnson or the Scottish historians have provided, but the genuine worm's eye view of a sub-tenant's son, an illiterate Gaelic monoglot, expressed with the utmost insight and candour.

The essential role of the chief as the linchpin of a clan society is made abundantly clear in Rob Donn's poetry, and of the four Lord Reays who were chiefs during his lifetime, he singled out the one who most worthily fulfilled his duties as the tribal father. The 4th Lord Reay had lived in the house at Balnakil near Durness while his father ruled from Tongue, and he remained there during his own chiefship from 1748 until his death in 1761. 'The apex of society and of entertainment,' he was present when the rents were being collected, and quick to cancel the arrears of those he knew to be in financial difficulties. He supervised the appointment of the schoolteacher, provided drink for his clansmen on the sands of Balnakil below his mansion, where they gathered on holidays to play shinty, was an accessible adviser and judge. 'Your forgiveness was ready for the man who deceived you the day before.'

His wife came from Pronsy in Sutherland, but was equally well integrated in the tribal family. A few years after Culloden, when refugee Camerons were still being hunted in the hills of Lochaber, an army deserter fled to Durness, pursued by a detachment of soldiers. He darted into the Chief's house at Balnakil, and up the narrow stairs that lead to the main reception room. At the top of those stairs there is a small closet, into which Lady Reay thrust the deserter before turning to meet his pursuers and invite them to take refreshment in the impressive panelled room beyond. She summoned the women about the place and improvised a dance. 'There were alert, eager young men there, dancing to a tune they didn't know.'

While all this was going on, the deserter was slipped beneath the ample skirts of one of Lady Reay's attendants, who made her way down the stairs to where the fugitive could run for safety. 'I don't know the *pass* he went out by, on my life,' Rob Donn protested. 'But between the woman's legs, without bonnet or weapons, very near the pass where he was born, there he made his escape.' Rob Donn has used the English term for a military pass in the first instance, then the Gaelic one which also means something else.

The bard's praise of this Chief and his wife was not that of a sycophant. When Mackay's younger brother, whom he esteemed less, appeared before him in an extravagant coat, he observed, 'there isn't a button or a button-hole in it that hasn't taken money off a poor man.' He was even more outspoken about the young widow of a subsequent chief, for whom he expressed detestation on more than one occasion. She pined from a mysterious illness until a young doctor came to Strathnaver who instantly diagnosed her complaint, Rob Donn tells us, prescribed a poultice and himself acted as the plaster.

One of the essential freedoms that Rob Donn's poetry reveals is total freedom of expression. Roderick Morrison the blind harper had exercised it in his comments on the MacLeod Chief, but a member of the Hebridean family of brieves enjoyed an altogether higher status than that of Rob Donn. Anyway, he did not utter treason, as Rob Donn did in his comments on the disarming Acts after Culloden. 'The English have taken the opportunity to leave you weakened, so that you will not be reckoned warriors any longer. But when you are without your weapons and equipment you will receive a thorough frisking, and your punishment will be all the more immediate. I see your misery as something unprecedented — the best part of your hawks chained to a kite. But if you are lions, retaliate in good time, and have your teeth ready before your mouths are muzzled.'

For this astonishing outburst in the heart of Hanoverian country, Rob Donn was hailed before a court in Tongue in which sat Donald Forbes the Magistrate, Hugh Mackay the Chief's son, and an English officer. He was lucky to be discharged with a caution, but even this did not silence him. 'The court we had in Tongue — long will we remember its proceedings. A judge and a clerk were there, without reason or justice in them. Forbes was there with his wiles, and Hugh, and the Englishman. How evil that trio is wherever it assembles.'

What is apparent is that traditional clan society, which was essentially aristocratic in character, gave to its poorest members the privileges of a supposed kinship with the chief. They might be obliged to perform unlimited servile labours as the price for holding their precarious tenancies. They could even be drafted into the army as a punishment for displeasing their superiors. What distinguished them from Russian serfs of the same period was their relationship with the chief, for so long as they were treated by him as his clan, or children. When he ceased to do this, there was scarcely any difference whatever.

The Achilles heel of the Mackay country was its most fertile valley, down which the Naver river ran from Loch Naver to the north coast. In addition to obtaining the feudal superiority of the whole province of Strathnaver during the sixteenth century, the Gordons of Sutherland had acquired the ownership of this entire valley in the seventeenth. It was inhabited by the most ancient and numerous sept of the Mackays, known as Abrach after their original ancestress who came from Lochaber. The Abrach Mackays were exposed to the immediate danger of eviction, to make room either for Gordons or for sheep, though it might be possible for them to find asylum in the Mackay territories that lay either side of the Naver valley.

By the time of Rob Donn, the earls who appointed its ministers and collected its rents had changed their name to Sutherland, thus qualifying to be called Chiefs of Clan Sutherland, but at the same time endangering their title to the earldom, which was not supposed to pass from the surname of Gordon. It was the accident of succession to this chiefship and earldom that provided the first, ominous writing on the wall for Clan Mackay. In 1766 the last Gordon (or Sutherland) Earl died, leaving a baby daughter as his heir. There was an expensive lawsuit before the House of Lords affirmed her title in 1771. Meanwhile she was brought up in Edinburgh and never visited her clan lands until she was an adult.

The factors of an absentee chief descended on her estates to extract what they could for her and for themselves, and the evidence of their depredations is devastating. 'The evil is the greater that the estate being parcelled out to different factors and tacksmen, these must oppress the subtenants in order to raise a profit to themselves, particularly on the article of cattle, which they never fail to take at their own prices.' So an inhabitant of the Naver valley testified in 1773. At about the same time the English naturalist Thomas Pennant visited the lands of the little absentee Chieftainess, and remarked on the apathy of the local people, 'perhaps on the motive of Turkish vassals who are oppressed in proportion to their improvements. Dispirited and driven to despair by bad management, crowds are now passing, emaciated with hunger, to the eastern coast, on the report of a ship being loaded with meal.'

Defenders of the Sutherland estate management have frequently suggested that the population had outrun local means of subsistence, and that bad weather and crop failures could be blamed for such scenes as Pennant described. But it so happens that the Revd Alexander Pope, Minister of Reay, left evidence on this very subject in a letter he wrote in May 1774, of which such apologists were ignorant. 'The crop in the Highlands was last year so plentiful that very little will be bought by the Highland Lairds, besides Edderachillis has been so stuffed with herrings that they are full of money, and cheap to get their victual from Ross, which is far better grain than our Caithness small corn.' It is perfectly obvious that the diagnosis of the observant Englishman and of the local tenant who was one of the victims of the system is the correct one.

The remedy for those who could afford it was to emigrate across the Atlantic. In 1773 a Lowlander called James Hogg who had been farming in Caithness decided to settle in North Carolina, like Allan and Flora MacDonald of Kingsburgh. He chartered a ship from Thurso, in which people from the harrassed Sutherland estates were particularly eager to find a berth. Hogg observed, 'I rejoice in being an instrument, in the hands of Providence, to punish oppression, which is by far too general; and I am glad to understand that already some of these haughty landlords now find it necessary to court and caress these same poor people, whom they lately despised and treated as beasts of burden.' Hogg's strictures were aimed at more than one landlord, but the majority of his passengers were escaping from the lands of the Countess, whose agents caressed nobody.

On the contrary, their response to the exodus displayed nothing except anger, for the policy of clearing away the inhabitants to make room for sheep farms had not yet been conceived. These were still required as a source of rent, to fulfil unlimited services when ordered to do so, and to enlist in the family regiment on demand. How rigorous this last requirement was stands revealed in a threat that the Countess made in 1799, when she was old enough to show her claws. Her vassals had responded with growing resentment and apathy to a recruiting campaign conducted by her cousin General Wemyss, so that he threatened to discontinue it. 'I would have him do it,' she wrote to her factor, 'or at least threaten to do it if they do not come in in a certain time, as they are really unworthy of attention, and need no longer be considered as a credit to Sutherland or any advantage *over sheep* or any other useful animal.'

This appears to be her first mention of the dreadful weapon she was to use against the people of the northern Highlands. Her clansmen did come forward after all to enlist in the 93rd Regiment of Sutherland Highlanders, but it did not save the survivors or their families from eviction when they return home at the end of the Napoleonic War. As for those who disobliged their dictatorial Chieftainess by joining other regiments, a blacklist was made of them, and their families were rendered homeless at the next term. They were described as 'tenants in Kildonan who thought proper in the course of the recruitment to show a preference of other Regiments to the two which the Marquess and Marchioness recommended.' By this time the Countess of Sutherland had married the fabulously wealthy English Marquess of Stafford, whose town residence opposite Buckingham Palace is now known as Lancaster House.

The eviction of the inhabitants of Kildonan and the Mackay lands in the Naver valley began before the discharge of Highland soldiers after the Battle of Waterloo and continued for years after it, making the Sutherland clearances one of the most notorious horror stories in Scottish history. It only remained for the Chief of Mackay to sell the pass to the remainder of Strathnaver.

In 1797 the 7th Lord Reay succeeded to the title, a spendthrift absentee of whom the local bard commented that when he ought to have been attending to his responsibilities he was away in London, frequenting the most disreputable streets. As his estate became increasingly burdened by debt, the Staffords relieved his difficulties with loans. Finally they bought his entire patrimony for a sum that would amount in today's currency to several million pounds, and yet he died bankrupt, leaving only an illegitimate daughter. The chiefship then passed, an empty title, to the more worthy line of the Dutch Mackays. At last the house of Sutherland was able to complete the policy that Sir Robert Gordon of Gordonstoun had enunciated two centuries earlier, when he was Tutor, to 'purge the country piece by piece of the Irish barbarity.'

The head factor of the Countess-Marchioness, James Loch, expressed succinctly the change of attitude which caused other Highland chiefs besides his mistress to oppose emigration before the Napoleonic War, and then to evict their clansmen after it. 'The Earls of Sutherland continued to find that the principal means by which they had to maintain that station in the country which their rank and descent entitled them to hold was by raising, for the service of government, one of those corps well known by the designation of a family regiment.' Hence the punitive anger of the Chief when some of her clansmen opted for another regiment.

The market in cannon fodder had slumped by the time Loch wrote in 1820. 'As the country advanced in civilisation, other objects of ambition arose which money alone could procure, and the population of the Highlands remained no longer an object to be encouraged beyond that point which was required for the necessary demands of labour on the estate, or to realise a money rent.' The children of the tribal father, for whom he was believed to be holding the clan territories in trust, are described as though they were another of its fauna like grouse, cattle or sheep, to be bred or culled according to the whim or needs of the chief.

The extent to which the Highland chiefs adopted this attitude varied very greatly. There was a MacLeod Chief who impoverished himself in trying to succour his clansmen during the nineteenth century. The Chiefs of Clan Diarmaid played a leading part in rescuing what remained of Gaelic oral tradition and literature at a time when the Sutherland factor was still enunciating the old Gordon hostility to 'that barrier which the prevalence of the Celtic tongue presents to the improvement and civilisation of the district.' This may help to explain why Gaels today have been glad to hold ceilidhs in the Campbell castle of Inveraray; but when the present Countess of Sutherland invited them to hold their annual festival of Gaelic poetry and music in Dunrobin Castle, her conciliatory gesture was rejected.

But no betrayal of a clan by its chief appears more reprehensible in retrospect than that of the Mackays, or perhaps that of the MacDonalds of Clanranald. Here were two tribal societies, one in the remote islands, the other in a distant corner of the mainland; one still Roman Catholic, the other Calvinist; but both still deeply Celtic, preserving a rich culture of extreme antiquity behind the fragile redoubt of their chief's good faith. In each case something rare and irreplaceable, that had been sustained by the devotion of centuries, was frittered away by degenerate men who simply deserted their clansmen to squander all in a gigantic spending spree. Between 1828 and 1837 the islands of Clanranald were being sold off to foreign buyers at the very time when the remaining Mackay estates were passing under the heels of Sutherland factors and entrepreneurs.

The Mackays took collective action of a most remarkable kind in the face of the threat to their future. It was the year 1806 in which their lands in the Sutherland estate were let to English sheep farmers at three times the rent they had previously been paying, while they were cleared from a large area at the southern end of the Naver valley. It might still have been difficult for them to foresee the enormities to come, and even harder to conceive that their own chief would sell to the house of Sutherland the remaining territories in his possession. Yet in that year 1806 a body of clansmen founded Mackay's Society in Glasgow, the pioneer enterprise of its kind. It was organised as a clan without a chief, run by Mackays who had already taken to city trades, grocers, vintners, a cloth glazier, weaver, smith and plasterer. These men declared that their aims were to help their clansmen 'in the time of afflictive dispensations' wherever they might be. The phoenix had not waited to rise until the ashes were cold. It had done so before the fire had even taken a hold.

Mackay's Society, reconstituted as the Clan Mackay Society in 1888, was not the earliest to bear a clan name, though it was the pioneer in the scope of its objectives. There had been a Buchanan Society founded as early as 1725 in Glasgow, which was comparatively near to the Buchanan lands, to assist the poor of the clan and to educate its children. But the Mackays anticipated even the MacGregors, who founded their Society in 1822, the year of George IV's visit to Edinburgh. It was another fifty years before all the other clans followed the same example, at a time when the Clan Mackay Society was once again leading the way, in publishing books that were designed to preserve the history and literature of their people.

To the south of the Mackay country lies the district of Assynt, home of a sept of the MacLeods, many of whom chose an inspired course in the time of afflictive dispensations. Their chieftain was designated *Mac Nèill*, and signed himself Neilson in English documents. He lived in the castle of Ardvreck, whose ruins still stand on a peninsula in Loch Assynt, beneath the contours of Ben Quineag. Here Montrose sought asylum after his final defeat, and Neilson earned Iain Lom's savage denunciation by handing him over to his enemies. 'Neilson from dreary Assynt, if I caught you in my net I would give evidence to compass your condemnation, and I would not save you from the gallows.' Poor Neilson was already caught in another net, bedevilled by debt, and likely to have been condemned whatever he had done. Anyway, it was his wife who was instrumental in handing over Montrose, a Munro of the clan most devoutly loyal to the Covenant that Montrose was thought to have betrayed in taking up arms for Charles I.

In the following century the unfortunate MacLeods of Assynt were assaulted in the rival take-over bids of Mackenzies and Gordons, and even found themselves compelled to pay their rents twice, when they were raided by officials of these competing owners. Such were the circumstances in which Norman MacLeod was born there in 1780. He studied divinity, returned to preach to his clansmen, and when he fell foul of the minister there, he sailed away with his flock to seek a better life in the New World.

Those who accompanied him present a dramatic contrast to the Macnabs whom their Chief lured to Canada, and show how Old Testament tribalism could easily be grafted on the clan system. For MacLeod's flock probably looked upon themselves as something resembling a thirteenth tribe of God's chosen people, making their timely escape from Pharaoh. Certainly a Gaelic bard in nearby Kildonan had already used this analogy in a poem they were bound to know. 'I am seeing the shadow of things that happened long ago when the children of Israel were in distress in Egypt. God took them with a strong hand away from Pharaoh himself, and He divided the sea for them.'

The MacLeod Druid settled with his clansmen at Pictou in Nova Scotia, where they remained for several years before they decided to make another move, this time to Australia. Norman

MacLeod's son David had gone on ahead, and wrote enthusiastic letters, extolling the great continent. What is most remarkable in this story is that the seventy-one-year-old patriarch did not coerce his flock to accompany him, although he ruled them with a rod of iron of which they might have wearied by now. Yet those who elected to remain found after his departure that they could not live without their spiritual chief, and a second ship hurried after him with 747 people on board.

It was in 1851 that they sailed for Australia, but they did not remain there long. Tempted by reports that New Zealand bore a stronger resemblance to their native homeland, they accompanied MacLeod to Waipu in 1854, where he was still riding to every corner of his scattered parish when he was over eighty years old, supervising the life of his kinsfolk as MacNeil of Barra had done in the description of Martin Martin in an earlier century.

It is among the descendants of such people in New Zealand and Australia, Canada and the United States, that a sense of their clan heritage could not be snuffed out, either by distance, the passage of time, or the evil memories they carried with them. Like the Gaels who live still in the ancestral lands they remain aware that theirs has been, for good and ill, a unique historical experience. So distinctive is it that Lowland Scots have latterly shown a deep desire to share in it, either by seeking out a Gaelic grandmother (and most Lowlanders have some Highland descent), or by organising themselves into Lowland clans, not all of which are as fictitious as others.

Thus the defeated race has won the final victory in Scotland, in capturing the national consciousness of the country, and those who scoff that this is all very unhistorical are scarcely given a hearing. Sir Walter Scott with his artist's eye was thinking historically on a deeper level when he laid on his tartan pantomime in Edinburgh in 1822. As though he were another Brahan Seer, he was anticipating the impulse that would drive Macnabs into the arms of their terrible Chief in Canada, send the flock of MacLeods from Assynt scurrying to Australia in the wake of their Druid, gather the descendants of defeated MacDonalds at the Highland games of North Carolina, and finally transform Edinburgh itself into the seat of pibroch, a centre of Gaelic learning, the tartan-bedecked stage for the annual military tattoo of the Highland regiments.

Index

When searching for a name in the index, please note that Iain (or Ian) is Gaelic for John. Kenneth is an English equivalent of Coinneach, Alexander of Alasdair, and Norman or Tormod or Tormad. Torcuil is derived from the Norse Thorkil, and was at one time rendered as Tarquin. The Gaelic Ruaridh or Ruari is often spelt Rory in English.

Picture Credits